WITHD

D0867549

PUBLIC LIBRA

101 Places in Italy

101 Places in Italy
A Private Grand Tour

FRANCIS RUSSELL

WILMINGTON SQUARE BOOKS
an imprint of Bitter Lemon Press

WILMINGTON SQUARE BOOKS
An imprint of Bitter Lemon Press

First published in 2014 by
Wilmington Square Books
47 Wilmington Square
London WC1X 0ET

www.bitterlemonpress.com

Copyright © 2014 Francis Russell

All rights reserved. No part of this publication may be
reproduced in any form or by any means without
written permission of the publisher

The moral rights of the author have been asserted in accordance
with the Copyright, Designs and Patents Act 1988

Some portions of this book were previously published in
52 Italian Places (Allemandi, 2007)

A CIP record for this book is available from the British Library

ISBN 978-1-908524-324

Designed and typeset by Jane Havell Associates
Index by Marianne Ryan
Printed in China

In memory of
Contessa Ester Bonacossa (1903–92),
who introduced me to so many
places and people in Italy

CONTENTS

9

INTRODUCTION

THIS is an expanded, and I hope improved, edition of a book written in 2005 at the suggestion of Umberto Allemandi. The patterns of civilization lie more thickly upon the Italian peninsula than on any commensurate area of the earth. Successive civilizations have left their trace: Greek and Etruscan, Roman and Byzantine. Invaders have come and gone. But the peoples of Italy have shown an irrepressible artistic resilience un matched elsewhere. England was in the van at certain moments. So, arguably more often, was France. Holland had its great century. But only of Italy can it be said that for three millennia no century or indeed generation has failed to leave its contribution, and that, with a consistency that can only humble the foreigner, so many strata of this creative achieve ment have determined the course of civilization throughout Europe.

Like anyone who revisits a country he loves, I am irresistibly drawn back to the places and works of art that aroused and have sustained that love. But I always try also to see sights that are new to me. In this respect Italy has proved – and will always prove – to be inexhaustible. Umberto asked for a selection of the fifty places that matter most to me; self-indulgence led me to raise the number to fifty-two. A hundred (and one) are included in this book. As will be obvious to the reader, my deepest interest lies in painting of the Italian Renaissance. The pursuit of this determined the course of

my early sightseeing. But pictures – and sculptures – only make proper sense in the context of the buildings for which they were commissioned. They reflect the political and religious complexion of their cities and towns, which in turn must be seen in the context of their land-scapes, the territory from which they drew their livelihood and upon which their strategic or economic importance depended.

Umberto charged me to be personal in the expression of my views. No sightseer is unprejudiced. I selected the places I myself would most have liked to revisit, and which, perhaps selfishly, I thus believed would give most pleasure to others. Where great towns are con-cerned, I outlined what I would choose to see again, the walks or perambulations I would take, the churches or museums in which I would linger. Buildings, how-ever wonderful, that are not readily accessible to the public are omitted. It is not within the scope of this book to record opening hours of museums. But in Italy, churches open early and the trav-eller is advised to take advantage of this.

The selection was mine and involved many sacrifices. As I write I hear the advice of Ester Bonacossa, Etta to her English friends, when I was planning tours: 'don't forget Cividale'; 'don't neglect Cefalu'. In this expanded edition Cividale is one of four dozen additional places, many of obvious importance but others equally eloquent of the past, that ought to be better known. I have been more self-indulgent in my selection. Some of the omissions for which I was fairly taxed – and indeed regretted myself – have been made good. A number of smaller towns have been chosen, mostly because they can readily be visited in conjunction with more major centres, particularly in areas that offer most to the sightseer. Montesanto is here as a warning not to neglect opportunity.

But much, too much, more inevitably is still omitted: Aosta, Saluzzo and Ivrea in Piedmont; Vigevano, Lodi and Cremona in Lombardy; magical Torcello and unselfconcious Chioggia, Bassano, Fanzolo and Treviso in the Veneto; San Daniele del Friuli and Spilimbergo in Friuli; Modena, Faenza and Forlì in Emilia-Romagna; and in Tuscany, long-prosperous Prato, Collodi, palace-lined Montepulciano and Massa Marittima. I have had to be equally ruthless in Umbria, forfeiting Spello, Todi, Amelia, Narni and Norcia, as well as Senigallia, Ancona and Recanati, Fabriano and Tolentino in the Marche, not to mention numerous remote early churches both there and in the Abruzzi. Nearer Rome, many interesting places, including Cerveteri and Subiaco, are passed by. So further south are Sulmona, which I have not seen since the recent earthquake, Capua, Sant'Angelo in Formis and Herculaneum, as well as, in Basilicata, Altomonte, where the exquisite Simone Martini might not recompense every traveller for a long diversion. In Sicily Cefalù is still an absentee, as are Catania, Agrigento – both ancient and modern – and Marsala.

Some sites are briefly touched upon in the entries for neighbouring places, and in a few instances, particularly in Sardinia, churches and other places that can be conveniently seen on brief journeys are linked. A few places, including Frascati and Ninfa, are absent because I have not visited these; while others, notably Taormina, are passed over for the irrational reason that these failed to come up to personal expectation. Those who want to explore are admirably served by the red guidebooks of the Italian Touring Club and that pocket-sized volume so indispensable to my early Italian sight-seeing, the 1932 Oxford edition of Berenson's *Italian Pictures of the Renaissance*.

Italy has changed since I came to know it in 1966, and continues to change. White oxen are no longer used to plough in Tuscany. Peasant farmers have left for the towns. Tracts of country have been suburbanized, whether by Italians or foreigners, their former farmhouses severed from the landscape by intrusive fencing. New building in many areas has been uncontrolled. So has the motor car. But prosperity has meant much that seemed in danger has been safeguarded; and just as the Italian authorities have long sought to restrain the export of works of art, so they have taken heroic steps to preserve a prodigious architectural inheritance. Despite valiant efforts to prove the contrary, many of the artistic achievements of twentieth-century Italy do not represent a natural or organic process of evolution. And I am certainly not qualified to write about these. While I would love to see again that enchanted room muraled by Severini for the Sitwells at Montegufoni, I cannot claim a strenuous appetite for Modigliani or Morandi. I have been more impressed by architecture of the Fascist period in Libya and Ethiopia than in Italy and do not intend to revisit Carlo Scarpa's celebrated mausoleum at Riese, although I do admire Giancarlo dei Carli's cascading additions to the University of Urbino and his housing scheme near Terni. But it is not for such things that most tourists go to Italy. Works of art cannot be taken by storm. Buildings and towns take time to explore. I shall always be grateful to those – recorded in the same geographical order as the text – whose unstinted hospitality has enabled me to take that time: the late Contessa Ester Bonacossa in Milan and at San Remigio; Signora Francesco Sella and the Mazzotta family in Milan; Mrs Henry J. Heinz, Jr, at the Casa Ecco; the late Contessa Marina Luling Buschetti and subsequently Diamante and Vittorio dalle Ore at Maser; the late Contessa Anna Maria Cicogna, Elisabetta Foscari, Luciana Moretti and François Borne in Venice; the late Marchese Franco Bianci di Castelbianco at San Domenico di Fiesole, the late Sir John Pope-Hennessy, the late Mrs Elizabeth Marangoni, the late Sir Harold Acton, Fausto Calderai and Neri Torrigiani in Florence; the late Mrs Vincent Astor at Montevettolini; the late Principessa Letizia Boncompagni, the late Mrs Earl Magrath, Contessa Viviana Pecci-Blunt and the late comte Henri de Beaumont at Marlia; the Francesco Pesenti in the Lucchese; the late Conte Giovanni Tadini at Agnano; the Cavendishes at the Casa al Bosco; Max and Joy Ulfane at Fighine; the late Miss Ursula Corning, as whose guest at Civitella Ranieri – and in 1984 at San Fabiano – over thirty-three summers I must have spent a total of some twenty months; the late Marchese Uguccione Ranieri di Sorbello, Marchesa Marilena Ranieri di Sorbello and their son Ruggero, almost every year since 1968 at the Casa Sorbello, Perugia, and, once, at Pischiello; the Bizzari at Todi; Alessandra Montani della Fargna at Poreta; the late Duca Roberto and Duchessa Franceschiella Ferretti di Castelferreto at Castelfidardo; the late Tomaso Buzzi at La Scarzuola and in Rome; Alice Goldet in Rome; Sir Mark and Lady Lennox-Boyd at Oliveto; Barone Maurizio Barracco at the Villa Emma; the Carlo Knights in Naples and Capri; and Adrian and Jessica White in Sardinia. As I only learnt to drive at the age of thirty-six, I will always be indebted to those who motored me in the past: to Ester Bonacossa; to Ursula Corning and so many of her guests, including the late Mrs Cyril Egerton and her niece, the late Mrs Simon Ricketts; to Hugh Roberts; and, not least, to my mother.

The original edition of this book owed much to the editing of Anna Somers Cocks and her associates, who must have been sorely tried by my dyslexia: I am grateful for constructive suggestions to Alessio Altichieri, Jamie Macdonagh, Antonio Mazzotta, Marco Riccomini and James Sassoon. Mistakes are mine. The illustrations used in the previous volume were not available: I am indebted to Antonio Mazzotta for the use of eight of his images; most of the rest are mine. Above all, I am grateful to John Nicoll and all those who have assisted him in the production of this revised edition.

FR

Piedmont

• Varallo 2

3 Vercelli •

• Turin 1

1

TURIN

OF THE GREAT Italian cities, it is Turin of which the visitor has fewest expectations. I had cumulatively spent over a year in Italy before my first visit in 1973; Hugh Roberts, with whom I was travelling across northern Italy, wanted to spend four days, rather to my surprise. How right he was.

Until the age of the railway, Turin was the first Italian city most English or French tourists saw. Although some crossed the high passes to the Val d'Aosta with its bristling castles, most would have taken the Mont Cenis and thus descended to Susa, pausing perhaps to see the well-preserved Arch of Augustus, and then continued on the successor of the Roman road, passing beneath the spectacularly sited abbey of San Michele della Chiusa.

The natural capital of Piedmont, Turin is set on the flank of a productive plain above a bend of the river Po as it circles the north-western edge of the Monferrat range. Turin had been a major Roman city, as the gaunt Porta Palatina still attests. In 1280 it passed to the house of Savoy; and the city's enduring fascination is inextricably linked with the course of that dynasty, counts and, from the fifteenth century, dukes of Savoy. Exiled in 1536, the Savoys returned in 1559.

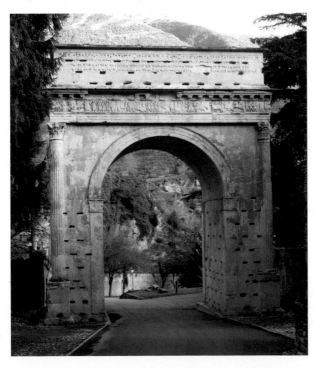

Susa, the Arch of Augustus, 9–8 BC

Their political acuity in dealing with both France and neighbouring Italian states consolidated their power. Vittorio Amadeo II inherited in 1675. His role in the War of the Spanish Succession, in which his kinsman Prince Eugène distinguished himself as the Austrian commander while Turin itself almost miraculously defied the French siege of 1706, led to his elevation as the King of Sicily in 1713 and, after the loss of that island to the Bourbons, King of Sardinia in 1720. He died in 1730, by when he had transformed his capital.

The Palazzo Reale with its ponderous façade, begun in 1646 and completed in 1660 by Vittorio Amadeo's father, is the central monument of Turin. The sequence of staterooms on the piano nobile expressed a determined taste for power. From the piazza in front of the palace one sees equally clearly how the ambitions of the Savoys found architectural expression. A decisive victory of 1557 prompted a vow to build a church dedicated to Saint Lawrence, but it took over a hundred years for work to begin on the west side of the piazza. In 1666 Guarino Guarini was called in, and building proceeded over two decades. Guarini's dome at San Lorenzo, so ruthless in the logic of its internal structure and ingenious in the use of light and shadow, is a *tour de force*.

A short walk from the corner of the palace leads to the chaste late Quattrocento cathedral, Roman in type, to which Guarini appended his stupendous chapel to house the most celebrated treasure of the house of Savoy, the Holy Shroud. The shrine was, and after its restoration will doubtless be again, the most unsettling of baroque statements, a vertiginous orchestration of black marble. Guarini was also enlisted in the urban development of Turin, a cherished project of suc-

cessive rulers. The curving brick cliff of the main elevation of his Palazzo Carignano has no equal.

Opposite San Lorenzo is another major royal monument, the Palazzo Madama, with a wonderfully articulated façade of 1718–21 applied to the much reconstructed medieval castle by that most protean of architectural draftsmen, the Sicilian Filippo Juvarra. Within is a prodigious staircase, regal yet oddly free of pomp. The civic museum on the first floor, recently rearranged, documents the history of the area and used in an old-fashioned way to be the perfect setting for a key collection of pictures and sculptures by the masters of Renaissance Piedmont.

The prosperity of modern Turin means that the complexion of the old town has changed dramatically. Blackened façades are now clean. Crumbling palaces have been rehabilitated, sometimes ruthlessly, as banks and offices. The visitor should wander. Strike across from the Palazzo Madama and follow the Via Dora Grossa (now named after Garibaldi), turning to see how Juvarra's frontispiece of the former dominates the axis, and return by the parallel Via Corte d'Appello to follow the Via Roma to the Piazza San Carlo, with the façade of Santa Cristina by Juvarra and the later copy of this at San Carlo. Linger on the arcaded Via Po, inaugurated in 1673, with its complement of churches and the Royal University – hence the number of bookstalls. To the south are more straight streets and many of the finer palazzi. Among the many churches of the area, none is more satisfying than San Filippo, where Juvarra worked from 1715 onwards; major altarpieces by the most celebrated painters of contemporary Rome and Naples, Maratta, Solimena and Trevisani, testify to the ambition of the new kingdom. Turin had become a major capital; foreigners on the Grand Tour might settle there, and in the early 1760s the English Minister, James Stuart Mackenzie, reported on young British visitors to his brother, the Prime Minister, while making arrangements to buy Consul Smith's collection from Venice for the young King George III.

Like other Italian dynasties, the Savoys were driven away in the wake of Napoleonic victories. They returned in 1814. The neoclassical susceptibilities of King Carlo Felice were satisfied in the great piazza at the end of Via Po and the Chiese Madre on the opposite bank of the river, Bonsignore's solemn reworking of the Pantheon. The king's cousin and successor, Carlo Alberto, commissioned

Filippo Juvarra, Stupinigi, Hunting Lodge, designed in 1729–30.

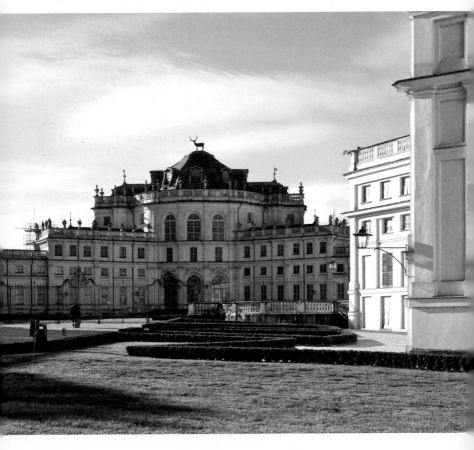

the dramatic equestrian monument of 1838 to their heroic ancestor Emanuele Filiberto in the Piazza San Carlo from Baron Carlo Marochetti; for the anonymous Glaswegian author of Travelling Notes (1864) this was the outstanding artistic sight of Turin. With the Risorgimento and the transfer of the capital of Carlo Alberto's heir, Vittorio Emanuele II, as King of Italy, first to Florence and subsequently to Rome, the Savoys ceased to reside in Turin. It became a political backwater, elegant and aristocratic.

The increasing economic importance of Piedmont was reflected by the development of the museums of Turin, notably the Galleria Sabauda, whose holdings of works by regional painters of the Renaissance were supplemented by much of the dynastic collection of the Savoys, and the Museo Egiziano, which houses the most comprehensive collection of Egyptian antiquities in Italy and is rivalled in Europe only by Berlin, Paris and London. Both institutions are housed in the former Collegio dei Nobili.

The considerable twentieth-century expansion of the city was due in part to Fiat and the Agnelli, who, after the exile of King Umberto in 1945, became its substitute dynasty. The city has now lost its visual relationship with the hinterland. There is no longer any game to pursue in the vicinity of the great hunting lodge that Juvarra designed in 1729 for the ageing King Vittorio Amadeo, reached by an impressive avenue some

five kilometres to the south of Turin. Vast though it is, Stupinigi, the stag-crested domed central block of which seems to thrust upwards through the flanking wings, is neither pompous nor monotonous — as are so many contemporary palaces of similar scale. In winter the white stucco seems to echo the snow-capped mountrains beyond. And despite recent thefts, the royal apartments, with furniture by Pietro Piffetti, pastoral landscapes by Cignaroli and pastel portraits by Liotard, still breathe with something of the spirit of Settecento court life.

The Savoys had other palaces outside Turin, including Rivoli and Raconigi — the latter partly decorated by the Torinese Giovanni Battista Borra, who had travelled as draftsman with Robert Wood and James Dawkins to Palmyra and Baalbec and made his mark in England before returning to serve his monarch. Even grander was the never finished Venaria Reale with a spectacular gallery and the Cappella di Sant'Uberto by Juvarra; the complex and garden have recently been restored. Yet another palace was begun behind the most dramatically placed of Turin's monuments, Juvarra's Basilica di Superga, the Valhalla of the Savoys, on the hill to the east, begun in 1715 and completed in 1731. The huge domed church flanked by massive towers hangs above the city; its platform is the vantage point from which Turin's urban development can best be understood.

2

VARALLO

❧

THE RIVER Sesia carves a circuitous course to the south-east from the flank of the Monte Rosa. Varallo has long been the principal town of the Valsesia. It is best approached by the old road from the south, which passes the still isolated porticoed Cappella della Madonna di Loreto, with a beautiful external frescoed lunette of the Adoration by Gaudenzio Ferrari. High above the main piazza, from which it is approached by a picturesque ramp, is the Collegiata di San Gaudenzio, with a notable polyptych of about 1516–20 by Gaudenzio. Below are the narrow curving streets of the ancient town, whose charm has not been reduced by recent prosperity. A short, but by no means direct, walk leads to the Pinacoteca with half a dozen pictures, including two of David with the head of Goliath, by the most forceful artist of Counter-Reformation Piedmont, Tanzio da Varallo. The impact of these masterpieces is diminished by an irritatingly theatrical display, from which the museum's exemplary collection of maiolica is happily spared.

A few dozen metres beyond the Pinacoteca, you reach the limits of the original conurbation. To the left is the house identified as that of Gaudenzio, who is the subject of a nearby statue of 1874 by another local artist, Pietro della Vedova. This is eloquent of the high place that the greatest master of the High Renaissance in Piedmont held for the generation of Giovanni Morelli and Sir Charles Eastlake. Behind the statue is the great Renaissance conventual church of Santa Maria delle Grazie. The nave is dominated by the arcaded west wall with Gaudenzio's prodigious frescoes of the life and Passion of Christ. Executed in 1513, the series evinces that narrative instinct and sense of objective realism for which Gaudenzio was so remarkable: he leaves us in no doubt that the Bad Thief was bad and the Good Thief repentant. The frescoes, which are enriched by sections of stucco, demand patience and field glasses, and are best seen without artificial light on a clear morning when Gaudenzio's disciplined use of colour tells to particular effect.

Santa Maria delle Grazie was founded by Bernardino Caimi, as was the Sacro Monte for which most visitors come to Varallo. Caimi returned from the Holy Land in 1481 and determined to replicate the pilgrimage route of Jerusalem. After his death in 1499 impetus was lost, but in 1517 the project was revived. Gaudenzio understood exactly what was required of him, but once again momentum faltered. After another long pause, the Sacro Monte found in 1565 a determined advocate in the Archbishop of Milan, Carlo Borromeo; and a series of additional chapels were designed by one of the most consistently rewarding Italian architects of the period, Galeazzo Alessi, who had been brought up in Perugia in the shadow of Perugino and Raphael but is perhaps best known for his Genoese palazzi. Momentum was maintained, and major Lombard and Piedmontese painters and sculptors were called in. The high bluff of the Sacro Monte hangs over the town. Although you can drive and there is a funicular, it is best to walk up the steep path above Santa Maria delle Grazie. The last two bends are marked by chapels and the pilgrim then reaches the Sacro Monte.

Sacro Monte, Chapel V: Gaudenzio Ferrari, Adoration of the Magi (detail).

The first chapel – of 1565–6 – looms beyond the gateway: Alessi at his most simply classical. The Fall of Man is represented. The statues in painted terracotta are by local masters, while Alessi enlisted his Perugian near contemporary, Orazio Alfani, for the murals; he did not repeat the mistake. The pilgrim to this New Jerusalem follows a fixed labyrinthine route, turning and circling up the wooded hillside. The cycle continues with the *Annunciation*. Gaudenzio is first encountered in Chapel V, with the story of the Magi, his statues perfectly complemented by his frescoes. In Chapel VI, Gaudenzio's *Nativity* is particularly inventive: the Virgin rests the Child on an ostensibly real manger. Prodigious in a wholly different way, although far less moving, is the high drama of Chapel XI, the *Massacre of the Innocents*, with no fewer than ninety-five statues, including the slaughtered children's toys, and fluent frescoes by Giovanni Battista and Giovanni Mauro della Rovere.

The chapels are as ingenious architecturally as in their decoration; Chapels XXXIII–V are gathered round what is in effect a piazza, with astounding views up the narrow valley of the Sesia as it carves its course downwards from the west. Many of the finest sculptures in the higher chapels are by Tanzio's brother, Giovanni d'Enrico, who shared his sense of realism and worked particularly happily in conjunction with one of the greatest Milanese masters of the late sixteenth century, Morazzone. Most extraordinary of all is Chapel XXXVII, dedicated to the Crucifixion, for which Gaudenzio took an earlier wooden statue of Christ as the centrepiece of a seamless combination of sculptures and murals that must have seemed startlingly original when it was created and has not lost its capacity to move. In the presence of such a masterpiece, one understands why San Carlo Borromeo saw the Sacro Monte as a powerful instrument of the Counter-Reformation. For the life of Christ is told in a language that must have been instantly comprehensible to the pilgrim. One hopes that most of those who make the pilgrimage today are oblivious to the spurious classicism of the late nineteenth-century façade of the basilica where their circuit ends.

The Sacro Monte set the precedent for those at Varese and Orta. With its sequence of classical chapels, this surely was also among the ancestors of the great gardens of eighteenth-century England and elsewhere, with their defined circuits of temples and other buildings. And in the nineteenth century it struck a strong chord with such visitors as the Revd S.W. King, whose description in *The Italian Valleys of the Pennine Alps* of 1858 could hardly be surpassed, and Samuel Butler, whose *Ex Voto* of 1888 is understandably still in print.

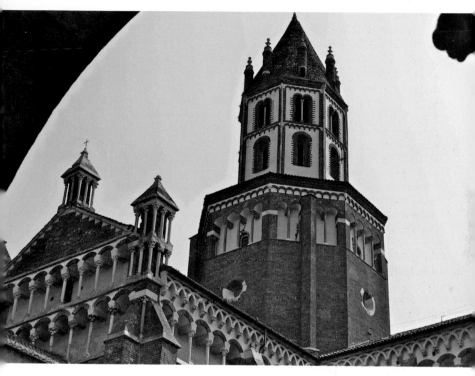

Sant'Andrea, the tower from the cloister.

3

VERCELLI

VERCELLI advertises itself as a 'città d'arte' with some reason. It boasts one of the great Gothic churches of northern Italy, and gave birth to a significant school of Renaissance painters. And although the town has grown considerably, there are still places from which the towers of Sant'Andrea can be seen across fields of waving maize.

It is at Sant'Andrea that a circuit should begin. Although much restored, this remains the quintessential Italian statement of Cistercian austerity. The deep rust of the brick contrasts with the warm stone of the windows and other elements, and the towers are striking. The church, more impressive than lovable, is perhaps seen to best advantage from the adjoining cloister. Much of the fabric of ancient Vercelli survives: a medieval core round the arcaded Piazza Cavour; the massive brick castle of the Savoys, now the Palazzo del Giustizia; palaces that are less numerous and ambitious than those at neighbouring Casale Monferrat – so loved by my old friend Giovanni Tadini, who had the advantage of knowing about their inhabitants, past and present;

a scattering of good neoclassical buildings; an appropriately eclectic synagogue of 1878; and the industrial Gothic of the Mercato Pubblico of 1884. But the sightseer has come for other things.

Some way east of the Piazza Cavour is the Museo Borgogna, housing the collection left to the city by Antonio Borgogna (1822–1906) and the municipal holdings. The most distinguished of Borgogna's early Italian pictures was a tondo of his Sienese period by Sodoma, who was born at Vercelli. The collection of pictures by painters who, unlike Sodoma, remained at Vercelli is comprehensive, with an unrivalled group of altarpieces and smaller works by Defendente Ferrari, a touching artist who learnt much from northern pictures, as well as the vacuous productions of his follower Girolamo Giovenone and panels by the grand protagonist of the Piedmontese school, Gaudenzio Ferrari, and by his able successor Lanino. The upper floors house more of Borgogna's pictures. The star is Hans Baldung Grien's Charity, which with the Dürer Adoration in the Uffizi is one of the finest German Renaissance pictures in Italy; Borgogna bought it from the Manfrin collection at Venice, where once it kept incongruous company with Giorgione's Tempesta. Borgogna was also interested in some aspects of contemporary painting. He bought pictures of historical and Arab subjects; he owned Gaetano Chierici's La buona matrignana, showing a hen protecting her chicks from rats, and, less expectedly, a triptych

of 1885 by the Bruges painter Edmond van Hove which reinterprets the art of Quentin Massys with an almost pornographic intensity.

Leave till last the noblest achievements of the Renaissance in Vercelli, Gaudenzio's frescoes in the church of San Cristoforo. In 1529–30 he painted the Madonna del Melarancio for the high altar; the enlargement of the choir means that this is now placed much higher than the artist intended. Commissions followed for the frescoes in the chapels on either side of the presbytery. Work began in that on the right, dedicated to the Magdalen. On the east, altar, wall, is the prodigious upright Crucifixion, the lower part of which is unfortunately covered by a later altar, so that, for example, we cannot see the hands of the dice-playing soldiers. The drama is concentrated. The Virgin swoons; the Magdalen is seen from behind in profil perdu; a white horse returns our gaze. This and the equally original compositions on the right wall were delivered in 1530–32.

The balancing frescoes of the Chapel of the Assumption are of 1532–4. The iconography of the Assumption of the Virgin allowed less scope for diversion than the Crucifixion. On the lower tier of the side wall are the Birth of the Virgin and the Adoration of the Magi, between which are introduced portraits of kneeling donors in fixed profile who seem oddly less palpable than the kings and their attendant dwarf and pages.

• Genoa 4

Liguria

4

GENOA

❖

SO LONG the maritime rival of Venice, Genoa, which cleaves to hills that descend abruptly to the Ligurian coast, remains a major port. It also remains a place of contrasts, as anyone who strays from the Strada Nuova with its astonishing procession of palaces will find if he takes the narrow salita downwards to the appropriately dedicated church of the Magdalen: even on a Sunday morning whores stand in wait. But that should not deter the sightseer, for there is much to be found within the tight confines of the medieval town. Genoa rewards the patient walker who disregards fixed itineraries.

Genoa had become a significant Mediterranean power by the eleventh century, contributing to the success of the Crusades yet eventually helping to undermine the Frankish kingdom of Jerusalem. The wealth of the Genoese republic is implied by the great Romanesque cathedral of San Lorenzo; the campanile is the most splendid among several in the city, while the treasury still boasts such prized relics as the cup which Christ used at the Last Supper and a chalcedony platter thought to be that on which the head of the Baptist was delivered to Herod, with a beautiful fifteenth-century enamel head of the saint. Equally remarkable is the large silver-gilt reliquary of the saint made in 1438–45 by Teramo Danieli in collaboration with Simone Caldera. Near the site of the original castle is a secular counterpart to the campanile, the tower of the Embriachi,

Cathedral, west door (detail).

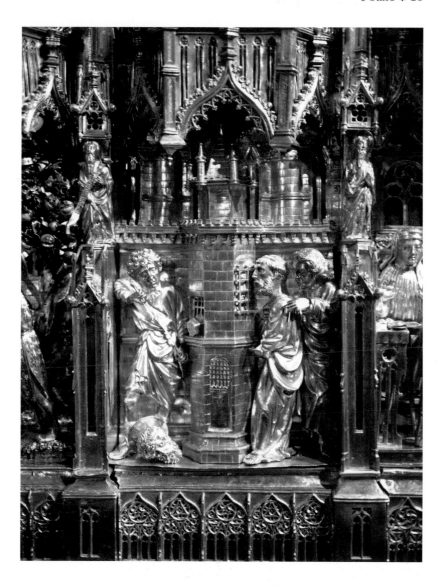

Cathedral, Museum: Teramo Danieli, Reliquary of Saint John the Baptist, 1438–45 (detail)

whose most ambitious fortification was the castle of Jebail in what is now the Lebanon. The significance of Genoa as intermediary with the East is expressed also in artistic terms, most notably in the *Last Judgement* at the west end of the cathedral, which is by a major master of towards 1300 from Constantinople. Parallel ties with the north are expressed in the exquisite fragments of Giovanni Pisano's tomb of the wife of the Holy Roman Emperor Henry VII, Margaret of Brabant, who died at Genoa in 1313; these are now divided rather perversely between the new museum of Sant' Agostino and the Palazzo Spinola.

Medieval Genoa faced the sea, and despite later building one can still sense something of its waterfront – now Via Gramsci – by the old port. The city gradually expanded landwards, and one small area, round the Piazza San Matteo, gives an idea of its late medieval character, with the striped Gothic façades of the houses of the Doria. The elaborate portal of one of these is surmounted by a relief of Saint George, whose popularity is attested by several others in the city, notably that of the Palazzo Valdettaro-Fieschi by the productive Ticinese Quattrocento sculptor Giovanni Gagini.

The patrons of Genoa would continue to look for outside talent. Her merchants commissioned at least two works from Jan van Eyck, whose world is echoed in the frescoed *Annunciation* by Justus van Ravensburg (1451) in the upper cloister of Santa Maria di Castello; this is charged with the realistic detail of the north. In 1506 Gerard David supplied a major altarpiece for the Sauli family, for San Girolamo della Cervara rather than Genoa itself; four elements of this are now in the Palazzo Rosso, including the *Crucifixion* in which Christ is majestically

silhouetted against a bank of dark cloud. Joos van Cleve's Raggi triptych remains in the church of San Donato, while Giulio Romano's *Martyrdom of Saint Stephen*, a masterly homage to Raphael, is still in the church of that saint.

Andrea Doria, 'padre della patria', was favoured by Emperor Charles V. His Villa Imperiali (Palazzo del Principe), to the west of the town, has now been sensitively restored by his successors. This is remarkable not least for the elaborate decorative scheme devised by Raphael's former pupil Perino del Vaga, whose heroic *Fall of the Giants* is one of the less familiar masterpieces of Renaissance decorative painting. Portraits by Sebastiano del Piombo and Francesco Salviati and an exceptional group of Flemish tapestries suggest the artistic horizons of the family. The Doria also employed the Tuscan Montorsoli, in the church of San Matteo, and the Perugian Galeazzo Alessi.

Alessi, an architect of genius, was responsible for another Sauli commission, the vast domed church of Santa Maria Assunta in Carignano (1549–1602), which recalls Sangallo's scheme for St Peter's in Rome. Alessi may also have been consulted about the scheme for the Strada Nuova. Conceived in 1550, this is a canyon of palazzi built for members of the closely interrelated Genoese patriciate, Pallavicino and Spinola, Lomellino and Grimaldi, among others, bankers whose wealth was vastly augmented by their control of the silver of the Spanish empire. Garibaldi, after whom the street is now named, would not have sympathized with them.

Although Genoa had already produced a significant painter of her own, Luca Cambiaso, numerous commissions continued to be awarded to artists from elsewhere. The *Crucifixion* by Federico Barocci from Urbino in the cathedral is a deeply felt statement of Counter-Reformation piety, wonderfully rich in colour, while Francesco Vanni's *Last Communion of the Magdalen* (Santa Maria Assunta in Carignano) is a visionary restatement of Sienese sensibility. Rubens's youthful reaction to his experience of Italy fires his *Circumcision* of 1605 in the church of the Gesù, where his more mature *Saint Ignatius* is complemented by major altarpieces by Guido Reni and François Vouet.

Such were the painters preferred by the patricians who rushed to be painted by the young Anthony van Dyck in the early 1620s. Van Dyck set the standard of Genoese portraiture for a century, and no Genoese master of the period was immune to his influence. Yet, by the mid-seventeenth century, Genoa was both less rich and less dependent on outside talent. Castiglione's *Nativity* of 1645 at San Luca, in the commercial heart of the city, is an indigenous masterpiece of enchanting originality, and would, half a century later, be balanced by a comprehensive scheme of decorative frescoes by another local master, Domenico Piola, whose numerous altarpieces in Genoese churches are consistently effective. Nonetheless, outsiders continued to find employment: the French Pierre Puget supplied two prodigious sculptures at Santa Maria Assunta in Carignano and the equally extraordinary gilt-bronze high altar at San Siro, while the Bolognese Marcantonio Franceschini had in 1714 a key role in the beautifully coordinated decoration of the church of San Filippo Neri, which represents the later baroque of Genoa at its most appealing.

Damage in the Second World War and the ruthless restoration programmes of Franco Albini at both the Palazzo Bianco and the Palazzo Rosso of the Strada Nuova mean that, despite their splendid collections, one must look elsewhere to understand secular taste in baroque Genoa. The visitor should abandon the Strada Nuova and cut down through the maze of the old city for the Palazzo Spinola, which was decorated in two phases (1614–24 and 1730–37), the latter for Maddalena Spinola di San Luca. Her suite of rooms on the second floor remains substantially intact. Then make for the Via Balbi, the second of the new roads of the city constructed between 1602 and 1620, passing the all but inaccessible Palazzo Durazzo Pallavicini, to visit the Palazzo Reale, so named since its acquisition by the King of Piedmont in 1824. With twenty-five bays – as opposed to its neighbour's fifteen – this was remodelled by Carlo Fontana for Eugenio Durazzo from 1705 onwards. Of the interiors created for the Durazzo, three are particularly memorable: the Sala del Veronese (so named for a picture which the Savoys sent to Turin) with restrained rococo decoration; the splendidly orchestrated Galleria degli Specchi, whose frames are invaded by gilded ivy; and the Anteroom beyond, with an enchanting ceiling that is the undisputable masterpiece of Valerio Castello, most appealing of the later Genoese baroque painters. The Savoys would later lay a heavy neoclassical hand on the palace, their resourceful designer Palagio Palagi unexpectedly employing an English craftsman, Henry Thomas Peters, on parquetry floors and the furniture of a bathroom. Look out from the terrace across the restored gardens towards the sopraelevata – the road which does such visual violence to the city – and the port beyond.

Lombardy

9 Isola Bella •

• Como 10

Castiglione Olona 8
•

• Bergamo 13

• Saronno 7

Treviglio 11
•

• Milan 6

14 Brescia •

• Crema 12

• Pavia 5

15 Mantua •

5

PAVIA

❖

PAVIA'S RISE was due to her position near the confluence of the Ticino with the Po and at the junction of major Roman roads. Conquered in 572 by the Lungobards, or Lombards, she became the capital of their kings. The Visconti established their signoria in 1359 and founded the university two years later. Already overtaken economically by Milan, Pavia was nevertheless of continuing strategic importance, and it was outside the walls that King Francis I of France was captured in 1525 by the forces of Emperor Charles V. Spanish rule was followed by that of Austria, and it is to Empress Maria Theresa and her son Joseph II that the neoclassical university buildings are due.

Pavia is visibly prosperous. Public buildings and private palaces abound. Of the churches two, both Lungobard foundations, are of particular interest. San Michele, facing a small piazza 200 metres north of the Ticino, was reconstructed after 1117. The sandstone façade is a masterpiece of controlled decoration. Across the town, near the angle of the city walls, is San Pietro in Ciel d'Oro, which was reconstructed in 1132. The west front follows that of San Michele, but was more ruthlessly restored in the nineteenth century. Behind the high altar is the Arca di Sant'Agostino, in which the relics of Saint Augustine of Hippo were placed; the sculpture blends Pisan and local influence. To the east of the church, also restored, is the enormous brick castle begun by Galeazzo II Visconti in 1360–65. The north side of the quadran-

gular structure was destroyed in 1527, but the vast porticoed courtyard still testifies to the resources of the dynasty.

Interesting as the city is, Pavia's outstanding monument is the Certosa, some nine kilometres to the north. From a distance its pinnacles strike a defiant note across the level plain. The foundation stone was laid by Gian Galeazzo Visconti in 1396, but his death in 1402 interrupted work. This was resumed and given further impetus by Francesco I Sforza, ruler of Milan from 1450. Successive architects, Venetian and Milanese, were called in. The façade was designed by the sculptor Giovanni Antonio Amadeo, but its upper half was only completed in the sixteenth century. The reliefs, so typical of Milanese Renaissance taste, are by Amadeo and his associates, while the portal of 1501–6 is largely by Benedetto Briosco. The interior is of equal magnificence. Some pictures have gone – including the main tier of Perugino's altarpiece, which is now in London – but nowhere can Milanese sculpture of the Renaissance be studied more comprehensively, and much glass of the period survives. So do the fine choir stalls designed by Ambrogio da Fossano, il Bergognone, the one major Milanese painter of his generation who did not allow himself to be unduly swayed by the example of Leonardo. His frescoed Ecce Homo in the north transept, framed by trompe l'oeil architecture, shows how moving an artist he could be.

Leave from the south transept, pausing to examine the delicate door-case by Amadeo, to the small cloister (1462–72). The arcades are decorated with terracotta. The luxuriant green of the enclosed garden contrasts with the varying hues of the brick of the walls and the vertiginous pinnacles of the southern

Certosa: Ambrogio Bergognone, Carthusian at a Window, *fresco.*

flank of the church. A passage leads to the enormous Chiostro Grande, its outer wall with the twenty-four cells of the monks. The eye, lifted upwards in both church and the small cloister, is here drawn horizontally. The decoration is less sumptuous, for we are now in a world of silence and devotion.

The Carthusians were suppressed by the Emperor Joseph II, who redeployed their riches or such projects as the university. But it says much for the intelligence of the Italian state that, as recently as 1968, the Certosa was made over to the Cistercian Order.

6

MILAN

✿

OF THE GREAT Italian cities only Milan has been comprehensively cut off from its hinterland by modern building. So it is reassuring to ascend the campanile of the cathedral on a clear winter's day and see the Monte Rosa gleaming on the horizon. Milan has a complex past – Roman, Byzantine and Lungobard – and has long been the dominant city of Lombardy. Power passed in the twelfth century from the archbishops to the commune, and in 1277 the Visconti established their signoria. Their duchy was taken over in 1450 by Francesco I Sforza, whose younger son Ludovico il Moro is celebrated not least as the patron of Leonardo. The French endeavoured to secure Milan, but on the extinction of the Sforza line in 1535, this passed to Spain and, in the early eighteenth century, to Austria. The French invasion of 1796 led to the creation of the Cisalpine republic, of which Milan was the inevitable capital, and its successor, Bonaparte's kingdom of Italy. The Austrians recovered Milan in 1814, retaining it until 1859, when it was absorbed in the new kingdom of Italy, of which it was to become the financial powerhouse.

The Stazione Centrale – as good a place to arrive as any – is a gargantuan statement of Italian ambition. Designed in 1906, this took a quarter of a century to build. And later you may wish to linger in an earlier and more engaging statement of national confidence, the cruciform Galleria, with its patriotic dedication: 'A Vittorio Emanuele II dai Milanesi' (To Vittorio Emanuele II from the Milanese).

This most spectacular of shopping arcades, off the Piazza del Duomo, was begun in 1865, and like the station remains close to the pulse of Milanese life.

Even a brief study of a map shows how Milan grew: the clearly marked line of the later walls, the names of whose gates survive, and the roughly oval circuit of streets that marks the earlier walls with which the massive brick Castello Sforzesco was associated. The Piazza del Duomo lies at the geographical centre, presided over by the unhappy façade of the Duomo itself. It is within that the great building asserts its magic, the tall columns soaring to the vaults. By day the Renaissance stained glass deserves study; at night, as candles glitter, one is lost in a primordial forest of stone. The decoration is rich, and there are two exceptional masterpieces. The Trivulzio candelabrum in the north transept, with its monsters and humans emerging from trailing fronds, is a prodigy of Norman medieval metalwork, so it is disgraceful that the tourist is now denied access to it; while the tomb of Gian Giacomo de' Medici of 1560–63 in the south transept is arguably the masterpiece of Leone Leoni.

Milan is famous for its churches. The Basilica di Sant'Ambrogio, dedicated to the patron of the city, was the seminal building of the Lombard Romanesque; while in Santa Maria delle Grazie to the north-west, the domed crossing and choir added by Bramante to the late Gothic nave represent the consummation of late fifteenth-century Milanese classical architecture. The church and its cloister are visually more compelling than the abused ghost of Leonardo's Last Supper in the refectory nearby.

If you want to escape from fellow

tourists there is a particularly satisfying walk from the Piazza del Duomo. Take the Via Torino and pause at the first church, set back on the left, San Satiro, where Bramante's ingenious trompe l'oeil treatment of the choir disguises the constraints of the site. Further on, to the right, is San Giorgio al Palazzo, with a chapel decorated in 1516 by the most consistent Milanese painter of the period, Bernardino Luini, whose altarpiece of the *Deposition* is beautifully complemented by his frescoes. Head on for the Porta Ticinese, but stop at San Lorenzo, set behind a row of sixteen Roman columns that were pillaged from earlier buildings and re-erected as part of the portico of the basilica. Much of the original structure, datable about ad 400, survives. The scale of the building is impressive, but inevitably it is overlaid with much later work. Further south, just before the gate, is Sant'Eustorgio, another early foundation, rebuilt in the late eleventh century, but with an elegant campanile of 1297–1309. The church itself is fine. But it is for the Cappella Portinari, to the east of the choir, that one returns. Pigello Portinari ran the Milanese branch of the Medici bank and called in a fellow Florentine, Michelozzo, to design his chapel. The frescoes of 1466–8 are, however, by the outstanding Lombard master of the time, Vincenzo Foppa. Nowhere is the sobriety of the man more eloquently expressed. In the chapel is the fourteenth-century arca of the *Dominican Saint Peter Martyr* by the Pisan Giovanni di Balduccio and his assistants, which demonstrates that Portinari followed in a long tradition when he employed Tuscans in Milan.

To return by an alternative route make east for the Corso Italia. On the opposite side of this is Santa Maria presso San

Santa Maria presso San Celso, façade by Galeazzo Alessi, 1565 and later.

Celso. Work started in 1490 under the direction of a sequence of architects: Galeazzo Alessi's front was begun in 1560. There are outstanding altarpieces by Bergognone and the Venetian Paris Bordon, among others. Returning northwards you pass San Paolo Converso with a vigorous façade designed by the painter Giovanni Battista Crespi, il Cerano. Turning right immediately after the church, you emerge on the Corso di Piazza Romana opposite San Nazzaro Maggiore, which is entered through the remarkable funerary chapel of the Trivulzio, designed by an earlier painter, Bartolommeo Suardi, il Bramantino. Not far to the north of this is Sant'Antonio Abbate with pictures by many leading Lombard painters of the post-Renaissance period, including – flanking an altar on the left – Giulio Cesare Procaccini's poignant *Visitation*. Between this and the Duomo,

San Paolo Converso, façade by Giovanni Battista Crespi, 1611 and later.

behind the Palazzo Reale, is San Gottardo al Corte, a Visconti foundation of 1330–6, with a splendid campanile and Cerano's visionary *San Carlo Borromeo.*

The museums of Milan are justly celebrated. It makes sense to visit them in chronological sequence. The earliest, the Ambrosiana, was founded by Cardinal Federico Borromeo and still contains much of the remarkable collection he presented to it in 1618, including the celebrated profile portrait of a lady long given to Leonardo, a distinguished group of panels by Luini, Caravaggio's only pure still life, a key series of works on copper by Jan Breughel the Elder and a most remarkable survival, Raphael's majestic cartoon for the *School of Athens.*

Other early acquisitions include Leonardo's wonderful *Portrait of a Musician.*

Housed in the former seat of the Jesuits, the Pinacoteca di Brera was founded in 1803. Milan, as the capital of the Cisalpine republic, received a not ungenerous proportion of the spoils looted by the French from elsewhere in Italy – and because the city reverted to Habsburg rule in 1814 there was no question of restitution. The religious houses of Lombardy were despoiled – the Brera's holding of Lombard masters is unrivalled – as were those of Venice. The Papal States in particular suffered grievous losses: from the Marche come Gentile da Fabriano's Valleromita polyptych, Piero della Francesca's incomparable Montefeltro altarpiece and a group of Crivellis only outshone in the National Gallery at London; and from Città di Castello in Umbria, Raphael's peerless early *Marriage of the Virgin*. Beauharnais, Bonaparte's viceroy, himself presented what is perhaps the most moving picture in the collection, Bellini's poignant *Pietà*. Among the later pictures are Caravaggio's *Supper at Emmaus* and Bellotto's breathtakingly fresh views of Gazzada.

More recent pictures, by such artists as Francesco Hayez and Gioanni Segantini, are shown in the Galleria d'Arte Moderna, housed in the neoclassical Villa Reale, built in 1790 for the Belgioioso family. Very different in character is the Museo Poldi Pezzoli. Gian Giacomo Poldi Pezzoli, who died in 1879, left his collection to the public. Although this core donation has been vastly expanded, the museum still just retains something of the atmosphere of a private house. Works of art complement the pictures, the most memorable of which, Pollaiuolo's familiar profile *Portrait of a Woman*, two distinguished Botticellis and the Mantegna *Madonna*, formed part of the original bequest. The collection makes an interesting contrast with its somewhat later counterpart in the Palazzo Bagatti Valsecchi. This was built in the Lombard Renaissance style by Giuseppe and Fausto Bagatti Valsecchi, whose pioneering taste for cycling was matched by their connoisseurship. Bellini's majestic Saint Giustina has pride of place in the most atmospheric neo-Renaissance private house in Italy.

The Castello Sforzesco is for the determined sightseer. The vast quadrangular fortress of the Visconti and their Sforza successors was subjected to a 'radical' restoration from 1893 onwards. Nowhere else can Lombard Renaissance

sculpture be studied so comprehensively. Bambaia's recumbent effigy of Gaston de Foix represents its high point, but now suffers from the proximity of Michelangelo's visionary, if unfinished, late *Rondanini Pietà*. Both are abominably displayed. In the substantial Sala della Balla on the first floor are the tapestries of the Months designed for Leonardo's patron Marshal Trivulzio by Bramantino and woven at Vigevano. Wonderfully imaginative in detail, these are arguably the most accomplished tapestries ever executed in Italy and certainly stand comparison with the finest Flemish productions of their time. Rather oddly they are hung in reverse order.

Castello Sforzesco: after Bramantino, December from the Trivulzio Months, tapestry (detail).

7

SARONNO

BECAUSE OF the activity of the Arundel Society Saronno was less unfamiliar to a Victorian audience than it is today. Too close to Milan for comfort, the town itself has no claims on the tourist. But on its northern fringe is one of the most beautiful sanctuaries of northern Italy, the Madonna dei Miracoli. A miracle of 1447 led to the construction of the church, begun in 1498 to the design of the versatile Giovanni Antonio Amadeo, whose scheme for the sanctuary itself was realized. Work on the church followed, and the subtle classical west façade projected by Pellegrino Tibaldi at the behest of San Carlo Borromeo was only completed in 1612.

But satisfying as the building is, it is for the frescoes by Bernardino Luini and Gaudenzio Ferrari that this is most remarkable. Pass through the church to reach the sanctuary. On the cupola Gaudenzio painted a *Concert of Angels* in 1534–6, a swirling interwoven composition, the unceasing movement of which seems almost deliberately to challenge the more static mode of Luini, who had died in 1532. On the left is the Cappella del Cenacolo, for which Andrea da Milano supplied an effective and characteristically Lombard polychrome group of the *Last Supper*.

Beyond, at the entrance to the Anticappella, are frescoes of four saints by Luini, finished in the year of his death. More remarkable is Luini's work in the Anticappella, with large compositions of the *Marriage of the Virgin* and *Christ among the Doctors*. Luini was aware that these would be seen laterally by pilgrims bound for the Cappella della Madonna beyond. Here the painter pulls out every stop. The lateral murals, the *Circumcision* of 1525 – in the background of which the Holy Family sets out for Egypt passing an accurate representation of the sanctuary and campanile from the east – and the *Adoration of the Magi*, whose train winds down through the landscape, are projected though arches which are shown from a position just within the chapel; there are Sibyls in the spandrels of the arches and in the lunettes above, and on those of the other walls the Evangelists are paired with the Doctors of the Church. Wind may ruffle the palm tree in the *Circumcision* yet Luini's dignified classicism is immutable. This and his discursive narrative taste help to explain why the Arundel Society went to the not inconsiderable expense of reproducing the Saronno frescoes. The very sobriety of Luini's types reminds us that he was an early exponent of the 'Lombard realism' that some seventy years later would be the springboard for the artistic revolution wrought by Caravaggio. Luini responded to the challenge of the commission, but may have found it more congenial to paint the less orchestrated lunette of the *Nativity* in the cloister. In the words of a wise fellow guest to whom I once showed these, the murals at Saronno are indeed 'perfectly marvellous'.

*Above: Madonna dei Miracoli: Bernardino
Luini, Christ among the Doctors, fresco
(detail), 1525.

*Right: Madonna dei Miracoli: Bernardino
Luini, Adoration of the Magi, fresco, a
Page (detail), 1525.

8

CASTIGLIONE OLONA

❖

THE ROAD from Saronno to Varese leads through a distressing sequence of overgrown settlements. These do nothing to prepare us for the charm of the old town of Castiglione Olona, scarcely half a mile off to the left, on a spur above the wooded valley of the Olona. Castiglione was held from early medieval times by the Castiglioni family. Branda Castiglioni (1350–1443) had a successful career as Bishop of Piacenza, as Legate to Hungary and, from 1412, as Bishop of Vespré. Like other churchmen the cardinal, as he became in 1411, knew he had to build within his lifetime, but as he died in his nineties he had more time than could rationally have been anticipated to make his mark at Castiglione.

The road descends to the triangular central Piazza Garibaldi. On the east, set back, is the cardinal's palace, Casa Castiglioni. On the ground floor is the small chapel, with rather worn murals by the Sienese master Vecchietta. The main stair mounts to a loggia with views out over the town and vestigial decorative frescoes, including a relatively unusual compartment with covered jars. Off this is the large hall, from which a door opens to the bedchamber, with contemporary murals of putti among trees by a local artist. Beyond is a further chamber with a remarkable panorama by the Tuscan master Masolino da Panicale, whom (with Masaccio) the cardinal had previously employed at San Clemente in Rome, showing his see in Hungary, a sizeable town in a valley between steep bare hills, some of which are crested with castles.

Across the piazza a road rises, passing the church of the Santissimo Corpo di Cristo completed between 1441 and 1444, which has been attributed to Vecchietta. The chaste classicism of the pilastered walls affirms the cardinal's

Palazzo Castiglioni, staircase: Lombard School, Vessels, fresco (detail), c. 1430.

interest in contemporary Tuscan taste. The road climbs up to the gate of his most ambitious foundation, the Collegiata. Castiglioni himself is seen kneeling before the Madonnna and Child in the lunette of 1428 above the main door. The imposing brick church represents the moment when the late Gothic melts into the early Renaissance; and to experience the processional subtlety of the building (which is now entered by a side door), you should walk to the west entrance before approaching the apse. The decoration is a further affirmation of the cardinal's leanings. The outer arch was frescoed by a lesser Florentine, Paolo Schiavo, while the vault and the upper and part of the lower register of murals are by Masolino, from whom Schiavo took over in the *Stoning of Saint Stephen*. The rest of the altar wall and the fictive architecture and marbling below are by Vecchietta, as is the trompe l'oeil portrait. Masolino is at his most lyrical in the narrow triangular compartments of the vault, notably the *Annunciation* and the centrally placed *Coronation of the Virgin*, with their sinuous elongated figures. The cardinal's tomb is on the left of the choir.

The Baptistery is to the north of the church. This is an intimate space, with an outer rectangle opening to a narrower area, in which Masolino's murals tell to marvellous effect. Above the door there is a surprisingly accurate view of Rome, in which the Pantheon and other monuments can be seen. The frescoes represent the life of Saint John the Baptist, the *Baptism* itself dominating the end wall, the

Baptistery, sixteenth-century graffiti.

Jordan set in a hilly landscape which flows into that of the adjacent *Preaching in the Wilderness*. On the right wall of the outer section, again linked in space, are the celebrated scenes of *Herod's Feast* and *Salome receiving the Baptist's Head*; the loggia in which she is placed is too deep to convince. Graffiti remind us that even in the sixteenth century monuments were not invariably treated with respect.

The Baptistery murals reveal the workings of a painter of ineffable charm at a moment of artistic rediscovery. The reverse might be said of the extraordinary seventh-century murals in Santa Maria Foris Portas near the atmospheric ruins of the Roman town of Castelseprio four kilometres to the south. Here we see a beautiful last gasp of the art of the ancient world, the Virgin in her fluttering robe resting after giving birth to her tremulous Child, the Magi described in bold swathes of reddish brown with a sense of movement that would be lost for many centuries.

9

ISOLA BELLA

❧

ISOLA BELLA seems to float upon the waters of Lake Maggiore. From Stresa the ordered terraces defy the drama of the hills beyond. The brief crossing conveys us to the landing stage near the palace conjured into existence for Count Carlo III Borromeo from 1631 onwards, but only completed in 1958. The palatial interior houses part of the remarkable collections of the Borromeo, rich in Lombard works both of the Renaissance and later periods; it is not difficult to understand why Mussolini arranged for the Stresa Treaty between Italy, England and France to be signed here in 1935. The grand baroque and neoclassical rooms on the piano nobile are perhaps less memorable than the sequence of rooms on the ground floor, grottoed chambers decorated with stucco and marbles and pebbles that catch light reflected from the water. Among the objects that have come to rest in these rooms are such rare survivals as horse trappings from the time of Cardinal Federico Borromeo.

To the south of the palace is the gar-

den, also begun in 1631. The count and his architect, Angelo Crivelli, exploited a natural hill, which was partly cut away and then built up with substructures supporting ten superimposed terraces. The resulting rectangular ziggurat dominates the island. On the upper terrace, some thirty-three metres above the lake, is the theatre, presided over by the heraldic unicorn of the family. Carlo III's third son, Vitaliano VI Borromeo, who succeeded in 1652, continued the project, calling in Carlo Fontana and Francesco Castelli; he died in 1690, the year in which the Dutch painter Gaspar van Wittel, known in Italy as Vanvitelli, prepared the studies on which his views of the island were based. The terraces were originally planted with cypresses, citrus trees, box and vegetables. Later generations have enriched the planting, but the design of what is in effect a baroque answer to the Hanging Gardens of Babylon is unimpaired. Wandering up and down the terraces, not all of which are accessible, we are almost uncomfortably aware that we are in a garden like no other, a statement of patrician control over a once untamed landscape.

The Borromeo have held the islands that bear their name since 1501. In the mid-sixteenth century they built a villa on the larger Isola Madre, the lost terraced garden which can be seen in some of Vanvitelli's views. The island is now celebrated for its botanical garden. This is most easily reached from Pallanza, which itself is best known for the Giardini Botanici of the Villa Taranto, but more memorable for a romantic neo-baroque terraced garden, San Remigio, created from the 1890s by the half Anglo-Irish Marchese and Marchesa Silvio della Valle di Casanova, which has until recently languished under state control.

Below: Isola Bella.
Opposite: the lower terraces.

10
COMO

❧

COMO, at the southern end of the eponymous lake, is the successor of a significant Roman town and indeed retains much of its plan. After a ferocious struggle with Milan in 1118–27, Como remained independent until 1335 when it was taken by the Visconti. Thereafter the city was under Milanese control. The Piazza del Duomo, far from the port, lay at the centre of both civic and religious life. The Broletto was built in 1215, while the cathedral beside it was only begun in 1396. Como had a remarkable tradition of masons, supplying craftsmen to work throughout Italy, but the cathedral is their most impressive achievement. The early Renaissance façade with its profu-

Cathedral, the Porta della Rana from the Broletto.

sion of sculpture repays close attention, but it is easier to access the key figure, Tommaso Rodari, in the Porta della Rana on the north front. The space within is unexpectedly dark, and it takes some time to adjust the eye to survey the tapestries suspended between the columns of the nave, many of which were devised by Giuseppe Arcimboldi. The altarpiece of the fourth chapel on the right is by Luini. He also painted the inside shutters of the Sant'Abbondio altarpiece, representing the two *Adorations*, which with Gaudenzio's later *Flight into Egypt* and *Marriage of the Virgin* of the outer sides now flank the third altars on both sides of the church. As at Saronno, Gaudenzio emerges as the more inventive artist.

There are two other notable churches, the late twelfth-century San Fedele of particularly ingenious plan, and, in a now rather run-down area outside the walls, the Benedictine Sant'Abbondio, which was consecrated by Pope Urban II in 1095. Thoroughly but not unsympathetically restored in successive campaigns, this is an austere masterpiece of Romanesque architecture. The deep polygonal apse is decorated with a major fresco cycle of about 1350.

Como is understandably famous for the villas beside the lake. The most accessible, some forty kilometres up the west side of the lake, is the Villa Carlotta at Tremezzo. Built in the early eighteenth century, this was acquired in 1801 by Count Sommariva, whose success in the service of Bonaparte was matched by his energy as a patron of neoclassical sculptors. A number of his acquisitions remained in the villa when it passed to the Saxe-Meiningens, notably Canova's *Palamedes* and a version of his *Magdalen* in Penitence, now most unworthily displayed. The planting of the garden is

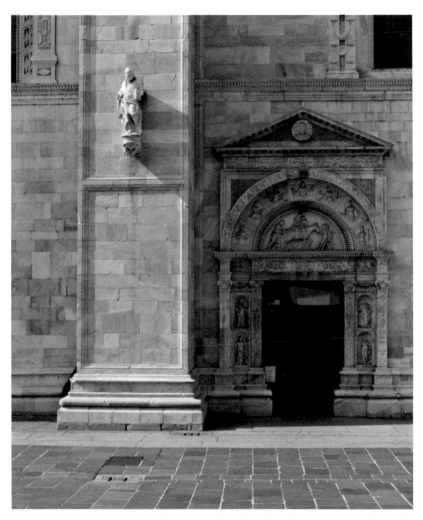

Cathedral, the north door by Tommaso Rodari.

equally abysmal, but this does not seem to diminish its popularity. Across the arm of the lake, but in easy reach by ferry from Cadenabbia, is the architecturally more distinguished Villa Melzi, built in 1808–10 in the most elegant neoclassical taste for another adherent of the French, Francesco Melzi d'Eril, and set in a lakeside jardin anglais. Numerous lesser villas can be seen from the road to Tremezzo, which passes a number of modest Romanesque churches.

11

TREVIGLIO

❧

THE LAND to the east of Milan was for many centuries a frontier territory where patterns of artistic patronage were often determined by political allegiance. Only thirty-three kilometres away, beyond the Adda that flows from Lake Como towards the Po, is Treviglio, with its great campanile to which the road from the west is aligned. Treviglio was twice controlled by Venice (in 1445–54 and 1499–1509), but her traditional fealty was to Milan. The town drew on the agricultural riches of the plain, and it is fitting that there is now a tractor depot on the outskirts.

Treviglio preserves her ancient core. This centres on the Collegiata of San Martino, the late Settecento front of which is rather put out of countenance by the massive Romanesque campanile of brick at its northern angle. The church retains its Quattrocento plan, but the interior has been much altered. The choir is flanked by intelligent canvasses, the *Last Supper* and the *Fall of Manna*, by Giovanni Battista Moroni's most plausible follower, Giovanni Paolo Cavagna. But it is not for these that we have come. On the right wall is the former high altarpiece, the polyptych by Bernardino Butinone and Bernardino Zenale, which, as Berenson wrote, 'still lights up with splendour the sordid market town of Treviglio, where

both were born'. This is in some ways the most characteristic achievement of Milanese painting of the time it was ordered, 26 May 1485, just before the impact of Leonardo's arrival was felt.

The altarpiece is in three tiers above a predella: *Saint Martin and the Beggar* are flanked by panels with three saints below; above are the *Madonna and Child* with angels between further trios of saints; and at the apex, seen in perspective in a roundel in the pediment, is the *Risen Christ*. The gilding of the frame is echoed by that of the fictive arcade within which the figures are set. The painters knew when to be extravagant in colour, yet also understood the power of restraint. This is beautifully demonstrated in the main panel: Saint Martin's charger is white, as are his armour and the beggar's drawers, their pallor only emphasized by the orange of the horse furniture and the sharp green of the festoon. In the background is a walled town with a great gateway, presumably Tours, while the campanile of Treviglio itself is seen, beside Saint Peter, in the adjacent panel. The artists knew of the achievement of Mantegna, of the Ferrarese, and above all of Foppa, but had digested these in their own manner.

Treviglio, although not sordid, is, as it were, a one-polyptych town. But before leaving take the road from the northwest angle of the piazza to the sanctuary of the Beata Vergine delle Lacrime. On the left of the presbytery is a predella by an associate of Butinone with a view of the Collegiata in its Quattrocento state.

Opposite: Duomo, the Campanile.

12

CREMA

❧

TREVIGLIO is Lombard; its neighbour Crema, previously like her larger namesake Cremona a fief of the Visconti of Milan, was held from 1449 until 1797 by Venice, and a Venetian orientation can still be sensed in this most charming of cities in the Lombard plain. 'Few people visit Crema,' John Addington Symonds observed in *Sketches in Italy* of 1879. This is still the case.

Crema should be approached from the west through Faustino Rodi's elegant Arco di Porta Ombriano put up in place of the original gate in 1805. The great

Andrea Nono, Santissima Trinità, 1737–9.

campanile of the Duomo is already in sight. The street, now the Via XX Settembre, has an air of unassertive well-being. Soon on the left you pass the chromatic rendered façade of the church of the Trinità by a local architect, Andrea Nono, which was completed in 1740. Further on a road on the right leads to the ambitious Palazzo Virmercati Sanseverino (1592–1602) and a group of other mansions that testify to the long prosperity of Venetian rule. Return to the main road and continue towards the Torazzo – a clock tower above an arch with the lion of Saint Mark in place – of the Palazzo del Comune, behind which the Duomo can already be seen. This is a characteristic Lombard brick construction, begun in 1284 and finished in 1341, and for Symonds no other building of the type was more beautiful. The façade is much higher than the body of the church, while the wonderful campanile, which rises to an octagon, is at the east end; as Symonds wrote, this is of 'the gracefullest, most airily capricious fancy'.

Continue eastwards. From the last turn on the right before Piazza Garibaldi can be seen the grandiloquent but unfinished baroque Palazzo Terni de' Gregori Bondetti, whose Piacentine architect,

Faustino Rodi, Arca di Porta Ombriano, 1805.

Giuseppe Cozzi, knew exactly how to exploit the lateral viewpoint; opposite the palazzo is the Museo Civico. The Piazza Garibaldi is closed with a second arch of 1805 by Rodi, the Arco di Porta Serio. From here a road lined by planes leads after more than a kilometre to the great monument of Renaissance Crema, the sanctuary of Santa Maria della Croce.

The original architect, Giovanni Battagio (1490–3), was strongly influenced by Bramante, and there are few more satisfying brick structures in his style; Symonds understandably admired 'its tranquil dignity and harmony of parts'. Externally circular and rising to a dome, with extensions at the arms of the cross of which that on the south side is the principal entrance, the church is octagonal within. The presbytery is raised above a crypt. That the decoration is later reminds us of the trouble relatively small communities had finding money for such projects. The frame above the high altar is dated 1499, but it was not until some two decades later that the altarpiece was supplied. The lesser Venetian painter Benedetto Diana's *Assumption of the Virgin* is his masterpiece: the aged Virgin, dressed in deep blue, is set against a glowing yellow ground and flanked by angels emerging from clouds touched with butterscotch and bronze, while the apostles stand below, their paler robes, in which pink and reds and greens predominate, contrasting with the slate grey of the classical architecture behind. Diana was no protagonist. He reacts to the achievement of greater men. And at Crema he rose to the occasion.

13
BERGAMO

❖

THE OLD ROAD from Milan runs north-east, past Gorgonzola to cross the river Adda at Vaprio, where a number of prominent Milanese families built villas that have changed relatively little since Bernardo Bellotto recorded these in the 1740s. Beyond, the road turns somewhat northwards for the last fifteen kilometres to Bergamo, which from 1428 until 1797 was the western outpost of Venetian territory.

The upper town, the Città Alta, is as satisfying as any of its size in northern Italy, its plan dictated by the strategic promontory which its defences exploit. The logical place to begin is the central Piazza Vecchia, overlooked by the palazzo of the Podestà Veneto, the local governor. Walk through the portico of the Palazzo della Ragione into the Piazza del Duomo. On the left is the not very appealing cathedral, ahead the flank of the magnificent Santa Maria Maggiore, with the façade of the adjoining Cappella Colleoni. Designed by Giovanni Antonio Amadeo and built in 1472–6, this domed monument to the great condottiero Bartolomeo Colleoni is perhaps the purest achievement of the Lombard Renaissance. In the eighteenth century the interior was enriched with a series of canvasses by Giovanni Battista Tiepolo, Giuseppe Maria Crespi and others. The elaborate classical decoration of the façade contrasts with the Gothic porch of the church. The interior is lavishly decorated with tapestries and an exceptional baroque confessional. The choir stalls have no equal. The intarsia panels, with

Giovanni Antonio Amadeo, the Colleoni Chapel, 1472–6.

scenes from the Old Testament, were designed by no less a genius than Lorenzo Lotto. For Sir John Reresby, writing in 1654, 'they would pass for painted by some extraordinary hand'. And nowhere are the wayward eccentricities of that most individual of Venetian Renaissance masters more evident than in these inventive designs.

Lotto worked in and around Bergamo on a number of occasions between 1516 and 1533. Because his stature was not properly recognized until the appearance of Berenson's monograph in 1894, there was no incentive for the French to appropriate pictures by him. To see two closely related masterpieces of 1521, descend from the Città Alta to the palazzo-lined Via Pignolo. Go first to Santo Spirito. Lotto's altarpiece is on the fourth altar on

the right. The *Madonna and Child* are enthroned between four saints with the infant Baptist below and a wonderfully animated semi-circle of youthful angels above. The glowing eloquence of Lotto's colour is matched by the energy of his characterization. Uphill, in the relatively modest San Bernardino in Pignolo, is the later of the two pictures, again a *sacra conversazione* with the *Madonna and Child* and four saints, but with a recording angel in place of the Baptist and four flying child angels holding a canopy above the throne. Of the two pictures, this is the more concentrated masterpiece.

Higher up the Via Pignolo is the turn on the right for the Accademia Carrara, one of the most distinguished museums of its scale in Italy. Among the components of the collection are the pictures acquired by the pioneer of the art of attribution, Giovanni Morelli, including one of Bellini's most perfect Madonnas. Naturally artists who worked in the city are well represented: Andrea Previtali and Giovanni Cariani; Lotto with his beautiful, if truncated, *Mystic Marriage of Saint Catherine* and the wonderfully animated predella panels of 1516 from his great altarpiece in the church of San Bartolommeo in the lower town; Moroni with a dozen of the portraits that record the patrons of mid-sixteenth century Brescia and Bergamo with such determined objectivity; and his early eighteenth-century successor Fra Galgario with some two dozen canvasses, including the refreshingly unsentimental *Young Painter*. The careers of both Moroni and Fra Galgario demonstrate that, subject to Venice as this was, Bergamo was no artistic backwater.

14

BRESCIA

Brescia was a significant settlement of the Gauls well before it was drawn into the orbit of Rome. Its subsequent fate was determined by patterns of political dominance throughout northern Italy. Brescia emerged as a free commune in the early twelfth century, but later was held in signoria by an almost bewildering succession of families, including the Scaligeri of Verona and the Visconti of Milan; in 1426 it passed to the Venetians, for whom it was to become of vital importance for the production of cannon. Their relatively benign rule was interrupted in 1509–16 but lasted until 1797. The letters of Lady Mary Wortley Montagu give an idea of the civilities of patrician life in the area in the mid-eighteenth century.

The city is rectangular in plan, with the Castello at the north-east angle. More or less in the centre is the small piazza fronting the richly decorated Palazzo del Comune (or Palazzo della Loggia) of 1492–1574. This was begun by Filippo de'Grassi, who was also responsible for the west section of the Monte di Pietà on the south side of the piazza. To the east side is the larger Piazza del Duomo. On the opposite side is the Broletto, with its eleventh-century tower, the powerhouse of civic life in medieval Brescia. South of the Broletto is the Duomo Nuovo, and beyond this the rather more remarkable Duomo Vecchio. This ambitious late eleventh-century rotunda overlay a much earlier church; the presbytery was added in 1488–98. Above the high altar is the Assumption of the Virgin by Alessandro Bonvicino, Il Moretto, the grandest, if not always the most appealing, of the great masters of Renaissance Brescia.

Both Moretto and his older contemporary Girolamo Romanino are splendidly

Loggia, begun in 1492, door to the staircase.

represented in the Pinacoteca Tosio-Martinengo in the south-east corner of the city. Romanino was deeply affected by his experience of Venice and is a seductive artist, while Moretto's late *Ecce Homo with an Angel*, restrained in colour, is one of the most moving north Italian pictures of the mid-sixteenth century. The museum offers a comprehensive view of painting in Brescia and the area from the Trecento onwards, with fine examples of such artists as Foppa and Civerchio. There is also a little known early masterpiece by Raphael, a small panel of Christ blessing.

A remarkably high proportion of the major pictures supplied to Brescian churches in the Renaissance remain in situ: works by Moretto can be seen in nine churches, while Romanino is represented in eight. Few visitors have the time to visit them all, and unfortunately the key churches are widely spaced. Sant'Alessandro, at a corner on the shortest route from the Duomo Vecchio to the Pinacoteca, is a building of little consequence. But on the first altar on the right is a picture of huge interest, the *Annunciation* that is the most substantial extant work by Jacopo Bellini, Giovanni's father. Some little way to the north-east is an architecturally even less appealing church, San Clemente, with a fine altarpiece by Romanino and five by Moretto.

Making to the north-west from the Palazzo della Loggia, it is not difficult to find San Giovanni Evangelista, another much remodelled church, for which both Romanino and Moretto worked extensively. The latter's uncompromising *Massacre of the Innocents* is on the third altar

on the right, while his high altarpiece of 1521–2 is flanked by the shutters he supplied for the organ. The Cappella del Sacramento of the left transept, built in 1509–10, was decorated by both artists, Romanino receiving the left wall, with a lunette of the *Mass at Bolsena* and other scenes, while Moretto was responsible for that opposite and for the *Coronation of the Virgin* with portraits of the donors, Francesco and Giovanni Cesari, above the altar. The two painters worked simultaneously in 1521–4, and their collaboration was constructive rather than competitive; yet even so one senses that Romanino's was the easier narrative flow, while Moretto had a more elevated sense of his role.

The church of Santi Nazzaro e Celso is near the south-west angle of the town on Via Matteotti. Moretto is seen at his most seductive in the *Coronation of the Virgin* of 1534 on the second altar on the left, and at his most austere in the *Blood on the Redeemer* of 1541 on the third altar of the opposite side. Both he and Romanino were deeply aware of the distinction of the *Resurrection with the Annunciation and Saints*, which was ordered for the high altar in 1520 from Titian and delivered two years later. The continuing presence of this relatively early masterpiece by the great Venetian shows how significant a contribution an import of the kind could make in a city like Brescia, and although the patron, Altobello Averoldo, was in the papal service, the commission can perhaps be seen as a subtle statement of Brescian loyalty to Venice, which had only recovered the city from the French four years earlier.

The Duomo Vecchio (right) and the Duomo Nuovo.

15

MANTUA

❖

PROTECTED to the north by a bend of a tributary of the Po, the Mincio, where it forms two lakes, Mantua had the distinction of being mentioned in the Aeneid and has long been one of the major towns of the Po Valley. But it is to the Gonzaga that it owes its outstanding monuments. Luigi Gonzaga secured the signoria in 1328. His descendants were successively marquises from 1433 and dukes from 1530. The direct line died out in 1627. In the resulting war the city was sacked and the ducal picture collection sold to King Charles I of England. Neither under the cadet branch of the family which succeeded, nor under sub-

sequent imperial rule, did Mantua fully recover.

The prodigious ducal palace is at the north-eastern corner of the town, protecting the Ponte San Giorgio, Mantegna's view of which in his *Death of the Virgin* in the Prado is still recognizable. The entrance to the palace is on the unexpectedly large Piazza Sordello. The medieval building was altered as fashion dictated until the eighteenth century. Its plan is complex. And the public tour is exhaustive. The relatively recently discovered fresco by Pisanello marks the emergence of the Gonzaga as sophisticated patrons, and works by Rubens and Feti testify to the enduring artistic leanings of the family. At the heart of the palace is the late fourteenth-century Castello di San Giorgio. The courtyard was designed by Mantegna and executed by the Florentine architect Luca Fancelli, Perugino's father-

Palazzo Ducale: Andrea Mantegna, Camera degli Sposi, fresco (detail).

in-law. Successive remodellings have mercifully spared what must always have been the most thrilling room in the castle, the Camera degli Sposi. Frescoed by Mantegna between 1472 and 1474 for Marchese Ludovico Gonzaga, this is one of the high points of Renaissance art. Inspired by his profound study of antiquity, the painter records his patron and his relations and hangers-on with a heroic objectivity. Long known as the 'camera picta', the painted room, the Camera dei Sposi was unprecedented in the implied unity of its pictorial surfaces and the intelligence – and beauty – of Mantegna's visual conceits.

After such a masterpiece, the Duomo on the other side of the Piazza Sordello may come as an anticlimax. Yet, despite the late façade, this too is a pioneering building, designed by Raphael's artistic co-heir, Giulio Romano, court painter to Francesco II Gonzaga, who succeeded at Mantua in 1519.

At the southern end of the piazza, the Voltone di San Pietro leads to the Piazza delle Erbe. On the opposite side of this, to the right, is the most celebrated of Mantua's churches, Sant'Andrea. This was planned by the high priest of Quattrocento classicism, Leon Battista Alberti, in 1470 and begun two years later by Fancelli; the massive late baroque cupola was designed by Filippo Juvarra. The interior is monumental yet restrained, and in it, most appropriately, is the tomb of Mantegna. Work on the church overlapped with that on San Sebastiano 800 metres south-west on the Largo XXIV Maggio. This was designed by Alberti in 1460. Restoration has not affected the integrity of the elegant interior, perhaps the first of the Renaissance on a Greek cross plan.

Continuing in the same direction for 300 metres, one is confronted on the left by the uncompromising rusticated façade of the Palazzo Te, the extraordinary villa created for Francesco II Gonzaga between 1525 and 1535 by Giulio Romano. A painter by training rather than an architect, Giulio was wonderfully inventive in his deployment of architectural forms. Yet, however original the building must have seemed to contemporaries, it is in the frescoed decoration that Giulio's own restless personality was more freely expressed. He knew how to divert his patron – and succeeded triumphantly. The visitor can still see why. The Sala dei Cavalli, with heroic murals of horses, is followed by the most sophisticated of all Giulio's mythological compositions in the Sala di Psiche. Giulio's imagination was fertile. Almost simultaneously he could design elaborate silver vessels all alas lost – and the overwhelming drama of the Fall of the Giants in the Sala dei Giganti. Giulio was supported by an équipe of painters who worked from his own clearly defined drawings. He was fortunate in the skill of his associates, including the young Francesco Primaticcio, whose work at Fontainebleau was to be a natural sequel to the project.

The strategic importance and long economic prosperity of the Po Valley mean that the area has a rich architectural inheritance. Late medieval brick fortifications abound, and lesser dynasties ensured that their towns echoed those of more powerful counterparts. Cadet branches of the Gonzaga were no exception. At Sabbioneta, thirty-three kilometres south-west, Vespasiano Gonzaga created his own capital on a grid plan. Both the Palazzo Ducale and the Palazzo del Giardino were begun in 1568, to be followed by the octagonal church of the Incoronata and Vincenzo Scamozzi's

Palazzo Te: Sala dei Cavalli, designed by Giulio Romano, fresco (detail).

sophisticated Teatro all'Antica. Another branch of the family held Castiglione delle Stiviere, thirty-eight kilometres north-west of Mantua. Here too there is a former ducal palace; equally imposing is the Collegio delle Nobili Vergini, founded for daughters of families who did not wish to pay dowries by the brother of the then marquis, the future San Luigi dei Gonzaga. Sabbioneta and, less immodestly, Castiglione show how the Gonzaga and their buildings at Mantua influenced their relations.

The Trentino

• Trent 16

16

TRENT

❧

TRENT must always have had the air of a frontier city. On the left bank of the Adige near the confluence of the Férsina, the city controls the key transalpine route to northern Italy from Innsbruck and central Germany across the Brenner Pass. The Roman Tridentum was already a place of some consequence. In the early eleventh century, the Holy Roman Emperors granted control of the Trentino to a succession of prince-bishops, who were to rule Trent more or less continuously until the French invasion of 1796. Restored to Austria after the defeat of Bonaparte, the Trentino and the Alto Adige to the north were Italy's major prizes for her less than glorious intervention in the First World War. A cataclysm of a different kind, the Reformation, had for two decades made Trent the epicentre of the Catholic world: the Council of Trent, which was opened in 1545 and reconvened for the last time in 1562, set the future course of the Roman Church.

At the heart of the city, on the south of the Piazza del Duomo, is the Romanesque cathedral. This was begun to the design drawn up by the Ticinese mason Adamo d'Arogno in 1212 but subsequently modified. The restrained north façade does not prepare one for the rich external decoration of the central apse. The austere interior was the setting for the opening of the Council on 13 December 1545. The piazza itself, with a pretty eighteenth-century fountain, is flanked by a number of fine buildings, including the much-restored Palazzo Pretorio, and, at the corner of the Via

Belenzani, the Casa Bella, the façade of which with frescoes of c. 1530 by Marcello Fogolino is a precious survival.

The Via Belenzani, generously wide, is flanked by a sequence of distinguished palazzi, some of which housed those who attended the Council. Ahead is the baroque church of San Francesco Saverio, on the Via Roma. Turn to the right to reach the vast Palazzo Fugger of 1602. Less ambitious but more appealing is the Palazzo Tabarelli, down the Via Mazzurana to the right, with a richly decorated front of 1512–27.

Palazzo Tabarelli.

Castello del Buonconsiglio: Girolamo Romanino, a Putto, fresco.

Further east, set against the town wall, is the Castello del Buonconsiglio, which was from the thirteenth century the seat of the prince-bishops. The medieval fortress was extended for Bishop Bernardo Clesio in 1528–36 and now houses a number of museums. The frescoes supplied for Clesio in 1531–2 by the Brescian master Girolamo Romanino are among the signal achievements of decorative painting of their time. The sequence begins on the ground floor and continues up a staircase to the piano nobile, culminating in the loggia opening to the Cortile dei Leoni and in the Audience Chamber reached from the latter. Romanino's affinity with the north is exemplified in the realism of his portraits of the labourers who attend the slightly sinister official on the staircase and in the lunettes of groups of musicians juxtaposed with Old Testament and mythological scenes in the loggia. He clearly knew how to divert and edify his patron.

The Veneto

23 Possagno •
• Maser 22
• Castelfranco 21
•Vicenza 18
•Verona 17 19 Padua •
•Venice 20

17

VERONA

❧

VERONA has long haunted the English imagination. The city lies on the banks of the Adige as it cuts in a reversed S downwards to the plain. On the ancient route from Turin to Aquileia and from the Brenner Pass to the south, the Roman city of Claudia Augusta was rich enough to boast a substantial amphitheatre, the Arena. Verona retained her eminence, as residence in turn of the kings of the Ostrogoths and the Lungobards. Later, as a free commune, she was inevitably caught up in the struggles of successive emperors. The signoria of the Scaligeri, which lasted from 1260 until 1387, was a period of immense prosperity. Verona's independence ended in 1405 when she passed to Venice. But political dependence did not inhibit Verona's artistic individuality. The Gothic fantasies created for the Scaligeri were succeeded under Venetian rule by the sinuous line of Stefano da Zevio and the early Renaissance naturalism of Pisanello. In the sixteenth century Verona supported one great architect, Michele Sanmicheli, and boasted a school of painters, the most spirited of whom, Paolo Caliari, il Veronese, became in effect a Venetian. The last two centuries of Venetian rule were less productive, although the buildings of the neoclassicist Luigi Trezza merit more attention than they have received. After the fall of Bonaparte Verona became a stronghold of the Quadrilateral, the series of fortresses that secured Austrian rule until 1866.

The old road from the west keeps to the flank of southern shore of Lake Garda. This reaches the sixteenth-century walls at the Porta San Zeno, one of the simpler of the series of gates and bastions designed by Sanmicheli. A little beyond is the piazza dominated by the monumental Romanesque façade and campanile of the Basilica di San Zeno Maggiore. Below the rose window by Maestro Briolato is the main portal of c.1138 by the sculptor Niccolò, its celebrated bronze doors with panels illustrating biblical scenes and the life of Saint Zeno. These were begun in the twelfth century and, like so much later Veronese art, reveal northern influence. The interior of the basilica is equally impressive, restrained to the point of austerity. On the high altar is Mantegna's majestic triptych of the *Madonna and Child* between groups of four saints, shorn alas by the French of its predella. Painted in 1457–9, this was the most influential north Italian altarpiece of its generation.

The road continues to the river and the spectacular thirteenth-century Castelvecchio which, with the fortified Ponte Scaligero of 1354, commanded the western approach to the medieval town. The castle contains a distinguished picture collection. At the eastern corner of the Castelvecchio is the reconstructed Arch of the Gavi, built late in the first century ad of the local white stone. The wide Corso Cavour that runs north-east to the heart of the city follows its Roman predecessor. This is flanked by a notable series of palaces, including on the right Trezza's Palazzo Balladoro and two buildings by Sanmicheli: the Palazzo Canosa (1530–37) on the left, its back to the river, and the splendid Palazzo Bevilacqua to the right. Ahead is the Roman Porta dei Bursari. A sharp turn to the right, into the Via Oberdan, leads to the great monument of Roman Verona, the spectacular first-century AD Arena, which is exceeded in size only by the Colosseum in Rome and the amphitheatre at Capua.

The medieval city overlies its Roman predecessor. From the Porta dei Borsari, the line of the *decumanus maximus* is followed by the Corso Porta Borsari and the Corsa Sant'Anastasia. The successor of the forum is the Piazza delle Erbe, surrounded by medieval houses. The Arco della Costa on the north-east side leads to the Piazza dei Signori. This is in effect a courtyard surrounded by civic buildings, the most appealing of which is the late fifteenth-century Loggia del Consiglio. Opposite is the Volta della Tortura, through which, by walking round the Palazzo dei Giudici on the left, you come to the most celebrated monuments of medieval Verona, the tombs of the Scaligeri. Cangrande I della Scala, who died in 1329, followed by Mastio and Cansignorio, who died respectively in 1351 and 1370, were buried in prodigiously elaborate free-standing structures that resemble contemporary reliquaries. In these, Veronese Gothic architecture and sculpture reached its apogee.

Not far to the south of the Piazza delle Erbe is San Fermo. The numerous frescoes in the church include, on the left wall, Pisanello's *Annunciation*. In the crypt are some of the best-preserved Romanesque murals in the Veneto, including, on one of the piers, a forceful *Baptism*.

A short walk north-east of the piazza is Sant'Anastasia, perhaps the most impressive of Veronese Gothic churches. Built in brick by the Dominicans, this was begun in 1290. The fine main door is of the following century. Above the arch of the chapel to the right of the presbytery is the celebrated fresco of *Saint George* by Pisanello which, with the San Fermo *Annunciation*, is among the few

San Fermo, crypt: Veronese School, Baptism, *fresco, 13th century.*

extant monumental works by the artist. The Piazza Sant'Anastasia is linked by the Via Duomo to the Duomo, a massive and imposing building, oddly unlovable for all the magnificence of the decoration of the façade by Maestro Niccolò and the scale of the Romanesque apse.

Bellotto's celebrated views of Verona remind us how little much of the city has changed, although both the beautiful partly Roman Ponte Pietra and the Ponte Navi had to be reconstructed after the last world war. While the great monuments of the medieval city are concentrated in the peninsula so effectively defended by the Adige, there is much of interest on the opposite bank. One might begin just within the walls near the earliest of Sanmicheli's gates, the Porta San Giorgio, with the fine Renaissance church of San Giorgio in Braida. The *Martyrdom of Saint George* on the high altar is a dramatic masterpiece by Veronese. There are also excellent altarpieces by Girolamo dai Libri, the most accomplished local painter of the turn of the fifteenth century, and by Moretto. Further down the left bank of

the Adige as it curves to the south is the Roman theatre, built against the hillside. Beyond is Santa Maria in Organo, with an elaborate façade by Sanmicheli and distinguished marquetry choir stalls by Fra Giovanni da Verona. The Via Santa Maria in Organo continues as the Via Giusti, dominated by the Palazzo Giusti del Giardino, known thus for the terraced garden with its celebrated view over the city.

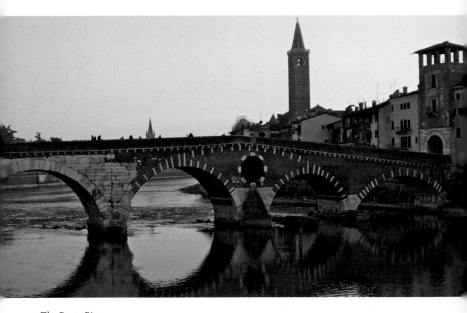

The Ponte Pietra.

18

VICENZA

✿

VICENZA passed to Venetian rule in 1404. Much survives of the medieval town, but it was as a Venetian dependency that Vicenza became a major artistic centre. Of her painters the finest was Bartolomeo Montagna, an accomplished follower of Bellini. It is, however, to her architects, and above all to Andrea Palladio, that the city's fame is due, and nowhere else can their achievement be so fully studied.

The traveller from the west arrives in the Piazza Castello. Ahead is the main street, the Corso Palladio, flanked by Palladio's Palazzo Bonin and the Palazzo Piovini of 1658 by Antonio Pizzocaro, an oddly neglected local architect. After some 300 metres on the right is the former Palazzo Trissino, by Palladio's successor Vincenzo Scamozzi, with a restrained courtyard. The streets on both sides of the palace run into the Piazza dei Signori, across which is the prodigious basilica. This late Gothic successor of the earlier Palazzo Comunale was spectacularly refaced by Palladio, whose project was approved in 1549. Opposite is Palladio's later (1571) Loggia del Capitaniato, which backs onto the Palazzo Trissino. The road to the right of this leads across the Corso Palladio to the Contrada Porti, which is literally lined with palazzi, including Palladio's Palazzo Barbaran da Porto (no. 11) and Palazzo Iseppo da Porto (no. 21). It is fascinating to observe how the architect responded to the challenges such commissions offered.

Return to the Corso Garibaldi, and turn left to reach the finest late Gothic palace of Vicenza, the richly decorated Palazzo Da Schio. Further on, again on the left and set back, is Santa Corona, a major Dominican foundation of 1261. At the end of the left aisle is a magnificent altar of 1501, probably designed by Rocco da Vicenza. This frames a little-known masterpiece by Giovanni Bellini, his late *Baptism*. Age had only quickened Bellini's ability to use landscape for emotional effect.

Continue on the Corso, passing the so-called Casa di Palladio, to reach the lateral façade of the architect's most ambitious and elaborately decorated Vicentine house, the Palazzo Chiericati. This houses the Pinacoteca Civica. The pictures include a significant group by Montagna, an irresistible early altarpiece by the purest of Bellini's pupils, Giovanni Battista Cima, in which a lizard is shown, and Tiepolo's serene *Immaculate Conception*. Diagonally opposite the palace is the best known of all Palladio's buildings in the town, the Teatro Olimpico, designed in 1580 at the very end of his career. Faithful to the precepts of Vitruvius, the theatre has no rival of its date.

The charm of Vicenza is partly owed to its position on a curve of the river Bacchiglione. To the south is the Monte Berico. An old woman experienced visions of the Virgin here in 1426 and 1428, and a shrine was built to commemorate these. From near the Porta Lupia, the processional route, covered by an eighteenth-century portico of 150 arches symbolizing the beads of the rosary, climbs steeply to the Basilica di Monte Berico. The much altered building is not prepossessing. But it boasts two masterpieces, Montagna's noble Pietà of 1500 and, in the refectory, Veronese's sumptuous Feast of Saint Gregory, which

Santa Corona: Giovanni Bellini, Baptism (detail).

was slashed by Austrian troops during the abortive revolution of 1848.

The two most celebrated villas of Vicenza are east of the basilica. The Villa Valmarana dei Nani and its foresteria were decorated by Giovanni Battista Tiepolo and his son Giovanni Domenico in 1757. The programme in the villa was literary, with rooms dedicated to the Iliad, Orlando Furioso, the Aeneid and Gerusaleme Liberata implying parallels between Homer and Virgil, on the one hand, and the great Italian poets, Ariosto and Tasso. The Valmarana wanted to live in a world of poetic enchantment and the Tiepolo obliged. In the foresteria the mood is less sophisticated, with the car-

nival scenes and illustrations of rural life that Domenico was so uniquely qualified to supply.

A quarter of an hour's walk between high walls overhung with trees leads to the last and most perfect of Palladio's villas, the Villa Rotonda. This was begun in 1550, but only finished by Scamozzi over half a century later. The approach is unforgettable, and the villa sits majestically in its landscape, the four porticoed façades at once linked and crowned by the central dome. The logic of the design is inexorably satisfying, and none of the imitations of this in England or elsewhere is so completely successful.

19

PADUA

✿

PADUA is the greatest city of the Venetian terra firma. Between the river Brenta and the Euganean Hills that shimmer so unexpectedly over the plain, and since Roman times the hub of several key roads, Padua began to recover its earlier importance in the ninth century. The university was founded in 1222, and the death of the future Saint Anthony of Padua in 1231 meant that the city became the centre of his cult. The signoria passed in 1337 to the Carrara, who succumbed to the Venetians in 1405. Venetian rule hung lightly on the city, which continued to enjoy considerable wealth. The French arrived in 1797, to leave in the wake of Napoleon's defeat; their Austrian successors withdrew in 1866, when – as was so often the case – after a suspiciously unanimous vote Padua became part of the Italian kingdom.

Every approach to Padua has been marred by new buildings, so the station is the most logical starting point. A brief walk leads to a bridge across the river Bacchiglione and the site of the Roman Arena. Here Enrico Scrovegni built the chapel that bears his name and was consecrated in 1305. The structure is simple. But the frescoed decoration was the most sophisticated, indeed revolutionary, of the period in Italy. Nowhere is the genius of Giotto more cogently expressed. The murals of the lateral walls – scenes from the lives of the Madonna and of Christ – reveal the artist's preoccupation with form and space, as well as his genius for narrative, while the grisaille *Virtues and*

Vices of the dado, trompe l'oeil bas-reliefs, challenge contemporary sculpture. Visitors can no longer linger, so should read their guidebooks before entering the chapel.

Alas, a stray bomb in 1944 caught the great church of the Eremitani behind the Arena, and only fragments survive of the long-celebrated frescoes by Mantegna and his associates. Rather than contend with what is no more than an archaeological reconstruction, I prefer to make for the centre of the town, pausing perhaps in the neoclassical Caffè Pedrocchi of 1830, before trying to lose myself in the arcaded streets of brick buildings. A little to the west of the café, between the Piazza delle Erbe and the Piazza della Frutta, is the substantial Palazzo della Ragione of 1218–19. Inside on the first floor is the immense salone that was intended for the tribunal. Further west is the Piazza dei Signori, with the elegant Renaissance Loggia della Gran Guardia. The street beside this leads to the Piazza del Duomo. The Duomo itself is not of particular distinction. In the annexed Baptistery, however, is the very remarkable cycle of frescoes painted for the wife of Francesco I da Carrara in 1376–8 by Giusto de'Menabuoi. With his contemporary Altichiero Altichieri, Giusto was one of the outstanding painters of his generation in northern Italy. His taste is elegant and discursive.

Return through the Piazza delle Erbe, passing the university, to turn right on the Via del Santo. In the Piazza del Santo is Donatello's wonderful bronze equestrian portrait of the condottiero Gattamelata. Executed in 1453, this more than challenged its classical predecessors and is one of the defining achievements of the early Renaissance. Behind looms the great Basilica di Sant'Antonio, the Santo.

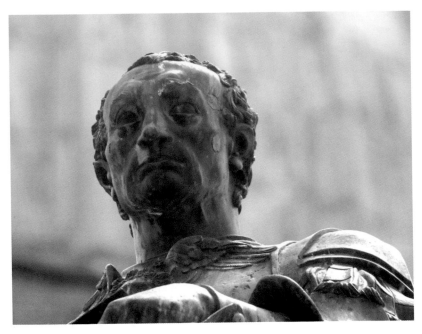

Donatello, *Equestrian statue of Gattamelata*, bronze (detail).

This was begun in 1232, a year after Saint Anthony's death. The interior is prodigious. There are notable frescoes, including those by Altichiero in the right transept, but it is above all for its sculpture that the Santo is remarkable. Although the high altar designed by Donatello has been dismembered, a remarkable series of reliefs from it survive, including a compelling masterpiece, the *Deposition*. To the left is the great candelabrum by the outstanding Paduan High Renaissance bronze worker, Andrea Briosco, il Riccio. He designed the Chapel of the Tomb of the Saint in the left

transept, to which most of the major sculptors active in the area in the early sixteenth century contributed.

To the right of the basilica is the Oratorio di San Giorgio of 1377–84. This is remarkable for the cycle of frescoes by Altichiero and his associate Jacopo Avanzo, perhaps the most successfully monumental murals of their time in the Veneto. Beside the oratory is the Scuola di Sant'Antonio, which was enlarged in 1504–5. The upper salone was decorated with frescoes of miracles of the saint by a number of artists, including the ageing Montagna. The three scenes by the young

Titian still seem startlingly dramatic. How revolutionary these were is perfectly demonstrated by the company they keep. Despite obvious debts to others, Titian had already found a personal language; we see types that will be encountered in much later works and are left in no doubt that the painter had a deep love of landscape.

South-west of the Piazza del Santo is the road to the Prato della Valle. Set in an irregular esplanade, this oval garden is surrounded by a canal lined with seventy-eight statues of illustrious citizens. It was willed into existence in 1775 by the enlightened Venetian podestà, Andrea Memmo, about whom we know so much from Andrea di Robilant's *A Venetian Affair* (2003). At the south-east corner of the Prato is the large Basilica di Santa Giustina reconstructed in the mid-sixteenth century. The interior is, as was intended, dominated by Veronese's enormous and vibrant high altarpiece, the *Martyrdom of Saint Giustina*.

Scuola di Sant' Antonio: Titian, Miracle of the Speaking Infant, *fresco, 1510–77 (detail).*

20
VENICE

❖

NO CITY has quite the magic of Venice. Protected by the lagoon, Venice emerged as a powerful entity in the Dark Ages. By 1000 she controlled the coast of Dalmatia and her destiny as a great colonial and trading empire was set. By the fifteenth century she had gained control of much of northern Italy. A patrician republic, La Serenissima, under an elected Doge, Venice retained her independence until the French invasion of 1797. In the Middle Ages and the Renaissance it was her wealth and power that impressed the world, in the seventeenth century her constitution that was admired, not least in England. With the eighteenth century it was the very fabric of Venice that delighted the outsider – as Canaletto and Guardi learnt to their profit – and the fascination that the city would continue to exercise can be experienced in the pictures of Bonington and Turner, in the impassioned writings of Ruskin, and in the equally eloquent responses of three cosmopolitan Americans, Henry James, Whistler and Sargent.

Despite the development that has disfigured so much of the Veneto, the most memorable approaches to Venice remain the old roads, the villa-lined Terraglio from Treviso or the route beside the Brenta through Dolo and Stra. A causeway now crosses the lagoon towards the city that seems to lie on the waterline. The Grand Canal cuts a reversed S course that divides the city in two unequal sections. This is the main thoroughfare of Venice, designed to impress. And it does. The tourist should take the vaporetto

(Linea 1) that proceeds down the canal, sitting near the bow so that you can be mesmerized by the kaleidoscopic sequence of churches and palazzi. The canal runs eastwards to curve towards the Rialto, the elegant bridge that marked the original commercial heart of Venice; its course continues south and then to the east and at length commands the celebrated view of Santa Maria della Salute and the Dogana, with the Molo.

The Molo was the scene of many of the ceremonies of the Venetian republic: to the right is the prodigious Gothic ducal palace, to the left Sansovino's majestic Libreria. The Piazzetta between these is dominated by the rebuilt campanile and by the spectacular lateral view of the many domed Basilica di San Marco. The basilica is the spiritual, indeed the emotional, centre of Venice. The wonderful drama of its façade and

San Marco: the Tetrarchs.

domes, and the measured rhythm of the interior, impress immediately; the remarkable mosaics take much longer to digest. The magic of the place is most palpable in the early morning, when those who want to pray can visit the north transept. But return later as a tourist to wonder at such miracles as the Pala d'Oro, the jewel-studded altarfront. The treasury must be the most remarkable in Italy, and the panels by Paolo Veneziano in the museum mark the highpoint of Gothic painting in Venice. The galleries above the nave, alas, are less accessible than in the past; and admirably as these are now displayed, it is a poor commentary on our polluted and polluting world that the great classical bronze horses from Byzantium have had to yield their places on the façade to replicas. That the bronzes, like the inscrutable Tetrarchs of porphyry in the Piazzetta, were spoils from the Fourth Crusade of 1204 makes one feel a little less resentful of the depredations Venice would suffer in her turn.

The Piazza San Marco faces the west front of the basilica. It is flanked by the Procuratie Vecchie, to the south, and the Procuratie Nuove, the last begun about 1585. Tourists now outnumber Venetians under the loggias. Yet of the piazza itself one never tires.

Even when crowds mean that the basilica and the ducal palace are untempting propositions, the piazza is a logical place from which to set out. My choice depends on the time. In the mid-afternoon I would make east for San Zaccaria, hoping to catch the sun on the inexorably beautiful late altarpiece by Giovanni Bellini. I might then go on to San Giorgio degli Schiavoni, the confraternity of the Dalmatians; in the lower hall, in their original positions at the

San Zaccaria: Giovanni Bellini, The Madonna and Child Enthroned with Saints (detail).

height the artist intended, are Carpaccio's celebrated canvasses that are among the masterpieces of Venetian narrative taste in the Renaissance. Ruskin at one time considered the *Triumph of Saint George* the finest picture in the world, while Sir George Sitwell would create a room inspired by the *Vision of Saint Augustine*; and any observant child will delight in, for example, the detail of the *Saint George and the Dragon*.

One of the pleasures of Venice is trying to lose the way. I like to wander. An early start from the piazza might take me in a northerly arc, by way of the campo of Santa Maria Formosa, to Santa Maria dei Miracoli, the most exquisite church of Renaissance Venice, built in 1481–9 to the design of Pietro Lombardo. Further north is the Gesuiti, with a dramatic masterpiece of Titian's maturity, the *Martyrdom of Saint Lawrence*. Beyond is the

Fondamenta Nuove, where Venetians still outnumber their visitors. There are boats to the cemetery island of San Michele, to Murano and to Torcello, with its matchless Romanesque cathedral. But I might prefer to resist these temptations and to make on, keeping as near to the lagoon as possible and crossing at least five bridges, for the Madonna dell'Orto. This is a majestic late Gothic brick church, memorable not least for its pictures. Cima's *Saint John the Baptist with other Saints* is as sharp in detail as any relief by the Lombardo and perfectly controlled in colour, while Tintoretto is found at his most cerebral – in the *Presentation of the Virgin* – and at his most visionary – in the *Last Judgement* of the choir.

There are few more charming areas of Venice to linger in. But the more committed sightseer will take one of the

Accademia: Giovanni Bellini, Donà delle Rose Lamentation (detail).

bridges over the canal and find his way, passing perhaps the Ghetto Nuovo, to the Canareggio canal. Across this is the most abused of the great churches of the city, San Giobbe. The right wall of the nave is lined with the altar frames of masterpieces by Basaiti, Bellini and Carpaccio, all long since immured – as if in a sanitized hospital ward – in the Accademia.

The Accademia must take pride of place among the museums of Venice. For there, as nowhere else, the miraculous kaleidoscope of Venetian painting from Paolo and Lorenzo Veneziano to Rosalba Carriera and Guardi can be surveyed. Go early and linger for as long as possible in the small rooms with the Bellini Madonnas, his Donà delle Rose Pietà and Giorgione's Tempesta. But do not neglect the less intimate masterpieces, Bellini's San Giobbe

altarpiece, the haunting late Titian Lamentation, the major works by Veronese and Tintoretto, or Carpaccio's grandest achievement, the sequence of canvasses of the life of Saint Ursula.

Venice's civic museum, the Museo Correr, is also remarkable: the Bellinis there can still be seen in natural side light, as the artist would have expected. The Ca' d'Oro is the most elegant of early fifteenth-century Venetian palaces. Alas, the ruthless recent reorganization of the collection means that one can no longer sense the tact with which Barone Franchetti treated the house. The institu-

Opposite: Accademia: Vittore Carpaccio, Return of the English Ambassadors, from The Legend of Saint Ursula (detail).

tional fate of Ca' Rezzonico, the greatest of the eighteenth-century palaces, also on the Grand Canal, has been kinder: the collection of Settecento pictures, furniture and sculptures perfectly complements the building.

Remarkable as the resources of these institutions are, the achievement of the great Venetian artists is best understood by seeing works of art that remain in context. Within a triangle marked by the Frari, San Sebastiano and the Gesuati, opening hours and the whim of sacristans permitting, an astonishing sequence of masterpieces can be experienced.

At the apex is the vast late Gothic Franciscan church of Santa Maria Gloriosa dei Frari. The building is well named, its brick apses without rival, the campanile only exceeded in height by that of Saint Mark's. The sustained richness of the interior is almost impossible to describe. The choir is dominated by Titian's triumphant *Assumption*, a work of unparalleled ambition. Later, by 1526, the artist would supply his equally remarkable – and in some ways more influential – altarpiece for the Pesaro family. The two pictures were potent statements of an artistic revolution that owed so much to the painter's early mentor, Bellini, whose incomparable triptych of 1488 in the sacristy, still in its proper frame, had in turn been revolutionary in its day. Other major Venetian churches are rich in sculpture, but none competes in range perhaps with the Frari, for impressive state monuments to public figures are complemented by Donatello's spare *Saint John the Baptist* and Canova's pyramidal memorial to Titian.

Behind the Frari is the Scuola di San Rocco, grandest of Venetian institutions of the kind. The building was begun in 1515, but in view of its scale it is hardly surprising that work proceeded slowly. The lower hall, vast and tenebrous, is adorned with a series of eight canvasses by Tintoretto, all but two drawn from the New Testament. Tintoretto was also responsible for the ceiling compartments and twelve further scenes from the life of Christ of the upper hall and the ceiling and Passion scenes of the adjacent hostel, culminating in the prodigious *Crucifixion*. Tintoretto as a portrait painter was truthful and objective; as a religious master he is no less truthful. He has a force that demonstrates that his study of models after Michelangelo had not been vain. But his sense of drama is his own. And his technical abilities were perfectly calibrated for the project.

It is not easy to look at any work of art after brooding with Tintoretto at San Rocco. So it is as well that there is a short walk to Santa Maria del Carmelo, where a supply of coins is necessary to illuminate Cima's tender *Nativity* of c.1509 and Lotto's *Saint Nicholas in Glory* with its irresistible landscape. If a sacristan is about, ask to see the bronze relief of the *Deposition* with portraits of members of the Montefeltro family by the Sienese Francesco di Giorgio in the right apse.

From there it is a short way to San Sebastiano, built between 1505 and 1545, where the third giant among Venetian painters of the time worked over a long period from 1555. Paolo Caliari, il Veronese, lacked perhaps the spiritual fervour of Tintoretto, but at San Sebastiano he demonstrates his full range, although the large *Last Supper* from the refectory was among the pictures removed by the French to Milan and so is now in the Brera. The organ shutters and, not least, the main altarpiece, the *Virgin in Glory with Saints Sebastian, Catherine* and *Francis*, express the qualities that secured Veronese's lasting fame: his elegant types, his dazzling highlights and assured use of architecture.

Veronese's enduring legacy can be experienced nearby. Cross the canal and turn right for the Zattere, with its ever shifting views to the island of the Giudecca and Palladio's great church of the Redentore. Near a vaporetto stop is the most ambitious church of eighteenth-century Venice, Massari's Santa Maria dei Gesuati. The ceiling was frescoed by Giovanni Battista Tiepolo, whose three compositions perfectly complement the architecture and stucco decoration. For altarpieces the three dominant masters of the time were called in. Sebastiano Ricci's *Pius V with Saints Thomas Aquinas and Peter Martyr* on the left is a late tribute to Veronese. This was followed by Piazzetta's luminous and subtle *Saints Vincent Ferrer, Hyacinth, Louis and Bertrand*, the restrained colour of which reads almost like a rejection of Ricci's homage to the Venetian past. Tiepolo's beautiful *Madonna and Child with Saints Catherine, Rosa of Lima and Agnes*, above the first altar on the right, is perhaps his happiest statement as a religious painter. The Gesuati perfectly demonstrates that Venice was no artistic backwater when the Serenissima fell so suddenly to the force of revolutionary France in 1797.

Scuola di San Rocco: Jacopo Tintoretto, Nativity.

21

CASTELFRANCO

FOR THOSE who love Renaissance painting it is always satisfying to see pictures by artists in their native towns. The choice on the Venetian terra firma is wide: Bassano with its unrivalled holding of early works by Jacopo da Ponte, who took his name from the town, in the Museo Civico; wall-protected Conegliano, with Cima's great high altarpiece in the Duomo; Feltre, where the less familiar Morto da Feltre painted his masterpiece – a fresco of the *Transfiguration* – in the sacristy of the Ognissanti; Pordenone and its territory in which one can follow the early development of that towering figure, Giovanni Antonio de'Sacchis, il Pordenone; or indeed San Daniele del Friuli, where Pordenone's most spirited Friulian contemporary, Pellegrino da San Daniele, worked in the church of Sant'Antonio Abbate. Few names in the history of western art are more resonant than that of Giorgio da Castelfranco, whom we know as Giorgione. And so it is to his town, Castelfranco, that we go.

Castelfranco was founded in 1199 by the Trevisans, but despite the ostensible strength of their fortress it fell to the Paduans a mere sixteen years later. It was not until 1339 that the place was secured by Venice. When I first knew it, Castelfranco still seemed almost rural. But there has been much development on the fringe of the town. At its heart is the Castello, in reality a small fortified town, quadrangu-lar in plan with a remarkably complete circuit of walls reinforced at regular intervals by towers and surrounded by a moat. In the centre is the piazza, with the elegant Settecento church dedicated to San Liberale. Here, in the chapel to the right of the presbytery, is the altarpiece of the *Madonna and Child* enthroned with Saints Liberal and Francis, which is one of the few pictures more or less unanimously recognized as being by Giorgione. Subtly asymmetrical paving draws us to the saints, the armoured Liberal with his lance, Francis moving his hands in mute communication, both below the level of the foot of the throne – the base of which is so high that the Virgin must have required help, human or divine, to mount it. At either side is a plausibly continuous landscape, suffused by a golden glow. For Giorgione was above everything a painter of mood.

The visitor is kept at some distance. We can absorb the painter's message without sensing too closely the vicissitudes this masterpiece, for masterpiece it is, has undergone. For neither time nor the restorer has been considerate to the Castelfranco altarpiece. King George III's early mentor, Lord Bute, was not altogether impressed in 1773; and, unable as we are to inspect Giorgione's touch, we have, if we expect to begin the comprehend the picture, to respect the sense of silent, absolutely silent, contemplation that the painter so clearly intended to convey. When we have absorbed this, we begin to know why Giorgione had so profound an influence on his contemporaries.

22

MASER

❖

NORTH-WEST of Castelfranco, on a ridge between hills, outliers of the Monte Grappa, is Asolo, a small town overhung by a small fortress that enjoyed a brief moment of greatness as the seat of Catarina Cornaro after she had surrendered the kingdom of Cyprus to Venice in 1489. The road below Asolo is fringed by villas that once had uninterrupted views across their productive agricultural estates. It is from this that the finest, Maser, built in the 1560s, should be approached. The road turns slightly to reveal the Tempietto, the chapel designed by Palladio, a subtle reinterpretation of the Pantheon; on the left the statued terraces of the villa itself come into view, the central block projecting from the hillside framed by arcaded wings, the stucco painted a buttery cream that glows in the sunlight.

Palladio's patrons were Daniele Barbaro, Patriarch of Aquileia, and his brother Marcantonio; the former was one of the most civilized Venetians of his generation, a statesman and translator of Vitruvius. The architect's genius was to take advantage of the retention of an existing structure at the core of his building and to understand so well how to turn a steeply sloping site to advantage. At the Villa Rotonda the challenge had been to achieve a building that could be seen from every angle, at Fanzolo to design a villa approached on a central axis: at Maser the position of the public road meant that lateral views were of particular importance. The Barbaro were practical men. Their villa was to be the centre of a working farm, but it was also to represent an ideal, inspired by the writings of such classical writers as Pliny. For the piano nobile, the first floor of the central block but at ground level on the back, they employed a painter of exceptional distinction, Paolo Veronese, whose work was complemented by plaster decoration attributed to Andrea Vittoria, but apparently designed by Marcantonio Barbaro himself.

You arrive at the east end of the arcade. Where this reaches the central block, external stairs lead up into the cruciform gallery, the Sala della Crociera, at the heart of the projecting block. Veronese's landscapes on the longer walls, leading to the central window commanding the terraces and the farm beyond, are compromised; but the murals of the shorter lateral sections, sophisticated trompe l'oeils with servants at false doors flanked by statuary, show how brilliant a decorative painter he was. In the rooms at the outer corners, the Stanza di Bacco and the Stanza del Amor Coniugale, each with an elegant stucco chimneypiece, Veronese can be seen at work. He follows rough incisions in the plaster, but never slavishly. The spectator is captivated by the monochrome animals of the dado, the happy optimism of the landscapes and of the humans and animals that move in these, by the bright highlights of the fabrics which are so characteristic of the painter, and by the very confidence of his figures. The frescoes imply the intended function of the rooms, and when I first stayed in the house in 1966, the Stanza di Bacco was still used as the dining room, its counterpart as a drawing room.

The Sala dell'Olimpo is very different in scale. This opens from the north end of the Crociera, and the walls are deco-

Villa Barbaro: Paolo Veronese, Sala di Bacco, fresco (detail).

rated with yet more landscapes, impeccably preserved, in one of which the villa itself is seen transposed to a very different terrain. Above, on trompe l'oeil balconies, are patricians, members of the Barbaro family perhaps or the patriarch's guests and their dogs, below the soaring vault with the most ambitious of all Veronese's frescoes in the house, the gods on Olympus. On either side of the Sala dell'Olimpo are balancing enfilades of rooms, of which the nearest, the Stanza della Lucerna and the Stanza del Cane, were decorated by Veronese with yet more landscapes and, above, opposite the windows, fictive canvasses of the *Madonna and Child* as tender as any of the artist's independent pictures of the kind. The eye is drawn through these rooms to the splendid mural of a gentleman returning from the hunt at the east end of the enfilade and the less well-preserved lady at the opposite end, their presence expressing the purpose of the rooms as stanze di letto (bedrooms), so judiciously preserved by Contessa Marina Luling Buschetti when she restored the house in the 1930s. These rooms are all lit from the north and open onto a terrace across which is an equally remarkable survival, the Nympheum, a fountain flanked by stucco figures and – much damaged by exposure – a further ceiling by Veronese, or 'Paolo' as the contessa used, with affectionate familiarity, to call him.

Among Palladio's villas it was only at Maser that Palladio's contribution was matched by those of a painter of equal distinction. And it is the seamless harmony of their contributions that makes the house the most perfect secular statement of Venetian patrician taste of its time.

23
POSSAGNO

❖

AS MASER is the finest statement of a domestic ideal of the sixteenth century, so Possagno, hardly fifteen kilometres across the hills to the north, is a *locus classicus* of Italian neoclassicism. It was here, in a valley below the southern flank of the Monte Grappa, some seventy-five kilometres north-east of Venice, that the last outstanding Venetian artist, Antonio Canova, was born in 1757. The greatest Italian sculptor of his time, Canova had an international celebrity. He dominated the artistic world of Rome for over a generation, and still deserves the gratitude of his country for the skill with which he superintended the return to the Italian states after 1815 of most of the works of art appropriated for the Louvre.

Canova's house, near the centre of the small town, might be that of a successful merchant or lesser nobleman. But what distinguishes it is the gallery constructed to display the full-scale plaster models for many of the sculptor's most celebrated marbles. The early *Theseus*, the uncompromising *Madame Mère*, the heroic *Napoleon*, the poignant *Magdalen in Penitence* and a constellation of others express the artistic and indeed the political preoccupations of Canova's time. Together these models constitute a secular memorial to the sculptor. Nearby, in contrast, is a well-lit modern wing in which many smaller works, including Canova's unexpectedly delicate models in terracotta, are most intelligently displayed. In the more modest rooms of the original house are his less successful efforts as a decorative

Antonio Canova, the Tempio.

painter. One leaves with some understanding of the range of the man.

Above the town, with its back to the steep hillside, is the Tempio, a vast circular church with a commensurate portico of massive Doric columns, a building that seems to increase in scale as one walks up towards the platform on which it stands. The design was conceived by Canova himself. Work began in 1819, three years before his death, but was only completed in 1830. The church is an uncompromising masterpiece, inspired by both the Pantheon and – for the portico – the Parthenon. It is at once powerfully effective in its restatement of the neoclassical ideal, and yet convincing as a religious statement of a counter-revolutionary age when the Veneto was under Habsburg rule. The position of the Tempio reminds us that Canova was not only a idealist but also a visionary, with the Romantic's understanding of the way so rigorously academic a structure would work in his clear native air, its meticulously cut stone in sharp contrast to the windswept trees that seem to tumble down the hill behind.

Friuli

26 Udine • • Cividale del Friuli 27

• Palmanova 25
• ——— Aquileia 24

• Trieste 28

Grado 24

24
AQUILEIA AND GRADO

❧

THE DISTANT prospect of the campanile across the coastal plain does little to prepare the visitor for great basilica of Aquileia. The Roman city, founded in 181 BC, became an important Christian centre and the seat of a bishopric in the early fourth century, but was sacked by Attila in 452. It was only in the early ninth century that a grant from Charlemagne led to the construction of a new church on the site of the one founded soon after 313 by Bishop Teodoro, and the present basilica was constructed during the long patriarchate of Popone (1019–42). His successors were to rule much of the former duchy of the Friuli until their temporal powers passed to Venice in 1420. In 1509 Aquileia itself, with part of the Friuli, was returned to

imperial rule; except during the Napoleonic occupation it remained under Austrian control until 1915.

To the west of the basilica, approached from the portico through the so-called Chiesa dei Pagani, is the octagonal Baptistery, much restored. The structure of the church is due to Popone, but as the positions of the bases of the columns of the arcades flanking the nave show, the floor level was originally roughly a metre higher, covering the remarkable mosaic pavement of Teodoro's time. While the mosaic is the glory of the church, it also boasts contributions from its Venetian rulers: the elaborate tribune in the raised presbytery and the altar of the Sacrament to the right, both by the Ticinese carver Bernardino da Bissone, and, in the right transept, an admirably lucid altarpiece of 1503 by the Friulian painter Pellegrino da San Daniele. The ninth-century crypt under the presbytery, built for Patriarch Maxentius, is notable for its relatively well-preserved early Trecento frescoes of

Aquileia, Basilica: Cripta dei Scavi, mosaic floor, snails (detail).

scenes from the life of Saint Mark and the *Passion of Christ*. A door on the left of the church leads to the Cripta degli Scavi, a substantial section of Teodoro's shrine that has been excavated round the base of the campanile. Fragmentary walls suggest the scale of the complex, and there are more mosaics, including representations of fruit, chickens and, more unusually, snails. The campanile itself was apparently built partly of spoil from the Roman amphitheatre. What survives of the Roman town has indeed been severely robbed, and is perhaps principally of interest to the archaeologist, although the finds in both the archaeological and Christian museums are of some importance.

Aquileia and Grado are only eleven kilometres apart. The fort on what was then the island of Grado was originally an outpost of its greater neighbour and with the collapse of Roman rule was much more easily defended. By the seventh century Grado had been drawn into the orbit of Venice, and even now visitors to the old town sense that they are in the territory of La Serenissima. The centre of the town round the port is relatively unscathed. There are three early churches, of which the most distinguished is the basilica of Sant'Euphemia, built under Elia, who was Patriarch of Aquileia in 571–87, and consecrated in 579. The fine original mosaic pavement survives; so does the gilded silver paliotto on the high altar that was sent from Venice in 1372. But the basilica is perhaps most memorable for the harmony of its parts. Beside it is a yet earlier, if restored, octagonal Baptistery. The charm of Grado is that its Venetian core has not been degraded by the modern coastal resort that has grown up round it.

25

PALMANOVA

❖

THE CONFIDENCE of Venetian Renaissance art and architecture may seem oddly at variance with the political imperatives that confronted the republic. The subtle reports of her ambassadors imply one aspect of the prodigious efforts that were necessary to secure the interests of La Serenissima. But the role of the military was even more important. Far more was spent on fortifications throughout Venice's territories than on religious or civic buildings: the carved maps of some of these on the façade of Santa Maria del Giglio at Venice must have served as an uncomfortable reminder of republican responsibilities. That Venice's empire could only be maintained at considerable cost is obvious, for example, in the great fortress at Famagusta on Cyprus. Nearer to hand, some twenty kilometres east of Udine, is Palmanova, one of the most complete monuments of late sixteenth-century military architecture and, not insignificantly, one of the few places in the republic that early seventeenth-century visitors on what was later to be termed the Grand Tour chose to see.

The threats posed by both the Holy Roman Empire and the Ottomans meant that it became necessary to reconsider the defence of the Venetian terra firma, and in 1593 the decision was taken to erect a fortress on the site of the town of Palmada, under the control of Giulio Savorgnan and with the assistance of a number of architects including Scamozzi. Palma, as the place was renamed, was a state of the art proposition, embodying the most up to date views about defence. The fortress, on which work continued for some twenty years, takes the form of a star with nine points. There are three gates opening to straight streets that end in alternate sides of the central hexagonal Piazza Grande; subsidiary streets radiate from the remaining sides.

Planting a garrison proved easier than establishing a self-sufficient town, and even now the piazza with its statuary and inscriptions has a somewhat theatrical air. The main buildings are the Duomo and the Palazzo dei Provveditori Generali, the former like the three gates by Scamozzi. But it is not for its individual components that Palma, or Palmanova as it was renamed in 1807, is remarkable. It is as a whole – albeit one that was reinforced with additional bastions in the late seventeenth century, and with an outer circuit of these under Napoleon – that Palmanova is unique. The evident strength of the defences makes it seem the more ironical that the most delicate Venetian draftsman of his generation, Giuseppe Bernardino Bison, was born there in 1762.

Vincenzo Scamozzi, the Porta Aquileia (top) and the Porta Cividale.

26

UDINE

❖

THE ISOLATED hill crowned by the Castello of Udine was granted by the Emperor Otto II to the Patriarch of Aquileia in 983, and in the thirteenth century this became the main residence of several of his successors as they sought to enforce their temporal rule. In time the Venetians emerged as the patriarchate's main adversaries in the Friuli and Udine fell to them in 1420, her subsequent fate depending upon that of Venice itself. The central Piazza Libertà is the paradigm of a Venetian public space, with the mid-fifteenth-century loggia'd Palazzo del Comune and opposite the elegant arcade of San Giovanni of 1533, with the associated clock tower designed by Raphael's versatile associate, Giovanni da Udine, in 1527. At the north end of the arcade a gate designed by Palladio leads to the late Gothic covered way that climbs up towards the church of Santa Maria del Castello. This seems modest enough beside the mass of the Castello, an outsize Renaissance palace begun in 1517 and finished in 1595. Now the museum, it houses a substantial collection of pictures including Carpaccio's serene Blood of the Redeemer.

From the south end of the piazza, the Via Aquileia leads to the much-restored Duomo. Two of the altarpieces on the right, the Trinity and Saints Ermagorus and Fortunatus of 1738 and 1737 respectively, are by Giovanni Battista Tiepolo, as are the earlier frescoes (1726) of the Chapel of the Sacrament. The east end of the Duomo was transformed with a riot of stucco, sculpture and murals in the eigh-

teenth century at the expense of the richest family of the area, the Manin, builders of the outsize villa at Passariano. Monuments to the Manin are placed above carved choir stalls of astonishing virtuosity. Facing the south wall of the Duomo is the small Oratorio della Purità of 1757. The relatively modest height of the ceiling means that one can relish the ostensibly effortless touch of the mature Tiepolo's fresco of the Assumption of the Virgin. The frescoed Immaculate Conception above the altar is also by him, while the Old Testament scenes on the lateral walls are by his son, Domenico.

Not far to the east is the Palazzo Arcivescovile, begun in the sixteenth century. The Venetian patriarchs of Aquileia may have lost the temporal powers of their medieval predecessors, but nonetheless had considerable resources at their disposal. The palace is princely in scale. Patriarch Dionisio Delfino was a discriminating connoisseur, calling in the young Tiepolo in 1726 to decorate the ceiling of the staircase with a fresco of the Fall of the Rebel Angels framed by stucchi and grisaille compartments. In the two summers that followed, Tiepolo decorated the first floor Galleria degli Ospiti with scenes from the Old Testament. The artist was just thirty, but there is nothing immature about his wonderfully inventive compositions. The nearly toothless Sara kneels at the door of a wooden shack by which the Angel has alighted; Abraham bows in prayer; Isaac is open-eyed in surprise as the Angel stays his father's sword. Tiepolo's narrative intelligence is marched by his chromatic range. This is emphasized by the contrast between the three richly coloured mural compartments and the grisaille scenes framing the central Jacob and Laban and the fic-

tive niches with statues of female prophets at either side and between the windows on the opposite wall. We are close enough to see Tiepolo's incised underdrawing and thus experience something of his creative process. He was to paint more ambitious schemes later in the career that took him to Wurzburg and to Spain; but there is a freshness about the frescoes in the Galleria that Tiepolo would never surpass, and indeed did not altogether match in the ceiling of 1728 in the nearby Sala del Tribunale.

27
CIVIDALE DEL FRIULI

❈

THERE are few places in Italy where the post-Roman world seems more palpable than Cividale, the successor of the frontier town of Forum Julii on the right bank of the river Natisone that took the name of its founder, Caesar. Here as everywhere else in Italy the death throes of the western empire brought chaos. But in 568 the Lungobards, or Lombards, who had occupied Pannonia to the east for two generations, migrated though the mountains and set out to conquer much of the peninsula, choosing Cividale as the capital of a duchy that controlled much of the Friuli. Lungobard rule ended with the defeat of the wonderfully named Rotgaud in 776. The duchy passed to Charlemagne and his successors, of whom Lothar founded a school at Cividale in 825; in 1077 Henry IV granted the Friuli to the patriarchs of Aquileia. They effectively held Cividale until 1419, when it fell to Venice.

The medieval city lies within the line of the Roman walls. The most dramatic approach is from the south, over the Ponte del Diavolo across the deep gorge of the Natisone. The road rises steeply to the L-shaped Piazza del Duomo. The front of the Duomo is on the right, a restrained Renaissance replacement of its predecessor destroyed in an earthquake of 1448, with, above the high altar, the pala of Patriarch Pellegrino II (ruled 1195–1204), who is shown before the Madonna and Child. To the right of the Duomo is the Museo Cristiano, with two remarkable survivals of the eighth century, the octagonal Baptistery of Patriarch

Opposite: Oratorio della Purità: Giovanni Battista Tiepolo, Assumption of the Virgin (*detail*).

Callisto (737–56) and the altar of Duke
Ratchis (734–7), carved with vigorous
reliefs of Christ in Majesty, the Visitation and
the Adoration of the Kings in an idiosyncratic
linear style. With the exception of Pordenone's Noli me Tangere, the pictures are of
marginal interest.

The piazza beyond the Duomo is
dominated on the east by Palladio's
Palazzo dei Provveditori Veneti. This now
houses a substantial archaeological collection. Opposite the lateral façade of the
Duomo is the Palazzo de Nordis, with
remarkable medieval works of art including an enamel associated with one of the
Lusignan kings of Jerusalem and the veil
of the Beata Benvenuta Boiani; embroidered in white on a white ground with
the Crucifixion and representations of Saint
Ursula and her virgins, this remarkable
survival is of about 1300.

Return towards the river and take the
turn to the left before the bridge. Ask in
the bar at the corner for the keys to the
'Celtic Hypogeum' just up the road on
the right; cut from the rock, this has now
been identified as a place of purification
for Cividale's Jewish community in the
medieval period. The narrow street
climbs towards the lane from which the
Lungobard tempietto is now entered
through a later convent. The Lungobards
were often content to make do with the
buildings of their Roman and Byzantine
predecessors, and although relatively
modest in scale the tempietto is perhaps
the most distinguished of their monuments. The interior is remarkable above
all for the elongated figures of female
saints in stucco high on the original
entrance wall, which are now said to be
of about 760. Pause outside and follow
the path to the cliff edge, to look out
across the bend of the river to the picturesque Borgo di Brussana towards the
encroaching mountains.

Museo Cristiano: Altar
of Ratchis, Visitation,
734–7.

28

TRIESTE

❖

AMONG the cities of Italy, Trieste is an anomaly. For it lost its economic raison d'être when, in 1918, it ceased to be the main Mediterranean port of the Austrian empire and, severed from its Istrian hinterland, became part of Italy. Originally settled by the Veneti, who gave the town its name, Trieste became a walled Roman colonia under Octavian; long held by Byzantium it subsequently was a commune. Pressure from Venice led the city to appeal to the Duke of Austria in 1368, and thereafter it was drawn into the Austrian orbit. But it was not until 1719, two years after he had challenged Venetian control of the Adriatic, that the Emperor Charles VI declared Trieste a free port.

Before surveying the modern city, it makes sense to search out the evidence of its predecessor on the hill behind. The walk uphill could take in the scruffy husk of the Roman theatre, which must once have had breathtaking views over the gulf, and the elegant Triumphal Arch, built for Octavian, the future Emperor Augustus, in 33 BC. The way climbs steeply uphill between the Museo Civico and the atmospheric Orto Lapidario, with numerous Roman inscriptions, to the cathedral. Dedicated to the local martyr, San Giusto, this takes the place of a Roman temple, parts of the foundations of which can be seen to the north. The jambs of the main door are sections of a Roman stela with portraits of men of the Barbia family; to the left of the front is the campanile, which was remodelled in 1337–43. The church is unexpectedly wide, the central nave flanked by four

Cathedral, jamb of the west door, incorporating Roman portraits of the Barbia family.

aisles. The mosaic of the left apse is of the twelfth century. In a chapel of 1364 on the extreme left, behind an elegant baroque wrought-iron screen made in Ljubljana, is the treasury: on the west wall is a distinguished *Crucifixion* by an artist close to Paolo Veneziano. The detailed account of the walls of Jerusalem in this remind us that the cathedral itself was protected in turn by the Roman walls and by those of the medieval Rocca, now replaced by the formidable Castello built in phases by the Emperor Frederick III from 1470 and under his successors over a period of some two centuries.

The commercial centre of the city has long been on the lower ground beside the sea. A walk might start by the Canal Grande, dug in 1756, dominated at the landward end by the late neoclassical church of Sant'Antonio. Heading southwards down the Riva there are two fine neoclassical buildings, the Palazzo Carciotti, built in 1802–5 for a Greek merchant by an architect of German extraction, and the slightly earlier Teatro Comunale. A little way behind the latter is the Piazza della Borsa, with the Borsa Vecchia of 1806–9 by the Marchigian Antonio Molari, who interpreted classical models to particular effect. A road from the piazza leads to the east corner of the rectangular Piazza Unità d'Italia. The name belies the fact that this was the centre of the Austrian city. The ambitious Fountain of the Continents at the eastern end is of 1751, but the huge buildings that line the piazza (except to the northwest where it is open to the sea) are an orchestrated statement of prosperity in the last phase of imperial rule. The procession of neoclassical palazzi continued southwards along the Riva.

The importance of Trieste to the later Habsburgs is expressed in the Castello di Miramare, some eight kilometres up the coast. Built in 1856–60 for the ill-fated Archduke Maximilian by the German architect Karl Junker, this seems to grow from a low cliff above the water. It is substantially larger than one might at first imagine. The archduke's taste was that of his time and rank, and enough of the original contents survive for us to leave with a clear idea of this. It is touching that his wife, Charlotte, chose in 1857 to be painted in Milan wearing the costume of the Brianza by Jan Frans Portaels

(whose *Jewess of Cairo* serves to remind us of the religious tolerance of the Dual Monarchy), for within two years both Milan and the Brianza had been lost to Italy. The archduke's journey to Smyrna is commemorated by a series of pictures, but we are shown nothing of the tragedy of his attempt to win an empire in Mexico.

Antonio Molari, Borsa Vecchio, 1806–9.

Emilia-
Romagna

Piacenza 32

• Parma 33

• Ferrara 30
29 Pomposa •

• Bologna 34

31 Ravenna •

35 Cesena •

29

POMPOSA

✤

DRIVING to Pomposa on the main road from Chioggia to Ravenna, it is at first almost impossible to believe that the area was once a wilderness. But even now, particularly when approaching from the south, as the prodigious brick campanile rises above the poplars that now flourish on reclaimed land, one has a sense that the great Benedictine monastery was indeed a place apart. Apparently founded in the seventh century although not recorded until the ninth, Pomposa flourished in the eleventh century and became a notable centre of intellectual life. The abbots exercised temporal power over a considerable area from the eleventh-century Palazzo della Ragione, altered in 1396, opposite the monastery, which now serves as the ticket office. Decline began to set in during the thirteenth century; the area became unhealthy and the last monks left in the sixteenth century. The buildings were abandoned to agricultural use and only restored in the late nineteenth century.

To the left of the church is the campanile, in nine sections and forty-eight metres high, which was under construction in 1063. The brickwork is relieved by marble and by friezes, also in brick, and most unusually by circular Fatimid plaques, presumably imported from Cairo. The relationship of the openings of the upper levels is particularly happy. The body of the church, dedicated to the Virgin, was completed in the ninth century, but subsequently extended west-

wards by two bays, to which the atrium was added before 1026 when the building was reconsecrated. The front is richly decorated, and the frescoes of the nave constitute the most extensive extant scheme of the kind of the mid-four-teenth-century school of Bologna. The *Last Judgement* is shown on the entrance wall, and scenes from the Old and New Testaments and the Apocalypse in three tiers above the lateral arcades. The imaginative detail of the Apocalypse scenes is particularly striking. The apse of the raised presbytery was frescoed in 1352 by the most winning and sinuous of the Bolognese of the time, Vitale da Bologna, with *Christ in Majesty* above representations of the *Evangelists*, the *Doctors of the Church* and the *Life of Saint Eustace*.

To the south of the church is a large court, with the chapter house on the east side with frescoes of the *Crucifixion*, of saints and of prophets by a painter strongly influenced by Giotto, whose work was familiar to the emergent painters of the city of Rimini further down the coast. One of the noblest, Pietro da Rimini, was called in, about 1318, to supply three murals for the refectory on the south side of the court-yard: the *Madonna with Saints* between the *Last Supper* and the *Miracle of San Guido degli Strambiati*. Because so much has been lost at Rimini itself, these rank with Pietro's cycle in the Cappellone di San Niccolò at Tolentino among the most ambitious extant schemes of what was, if only rather briefly, a significant local school. Distinguished as the murals are, it is less for these than for the scale of the complex, and the way this rises up from the inexorable level expanse of the plain as it nears the coast, that Pomposa is most memorable.

Abbazia, façade, detail of a window, and the Campanile (below).

30

FERRARA

FERRARA, in the heart of the level valley of the Po, a few kilometres south of the river, has always been of strategic importance. For some 400 years it was held by the Este – of whose line the House of Hanover is a junior branch. Their great brick Castello, begun in 1385 for Niccolò II d'Este by Bartolino da Novara, is the geographical and historic centre of the city, which was significantly extended to the north and east by Borso d'Este (ruled 1450–71) and his half-brother Ercole I (1471–1505). Two blocks to the south is the cathedral, most memorable for its accurately restored Romanesque main portal and Guercino's trimphant *Martyrdom of Saint Lawrence* in the right transept. The cathedral's other treasures are shown in the new museum in the nearby church of San Romano: beau-

Below: Cathedral and Campanile.
Opposite: Castello Estense, remodelled by Girolamo da Carpi from 1554.

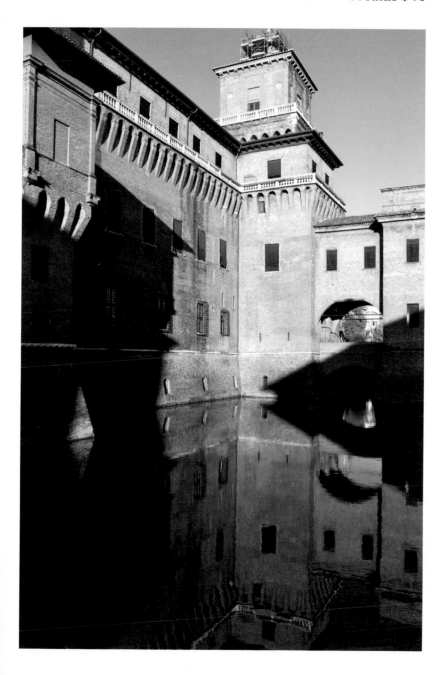

tifully displayed illuminated choirbooks; Romanesque reliefs removed from the façade; the Madonna of the Pomegranate by that subtlest of Sienese Gothic sculptors, Jacopo della Quercia; and masterpieces of 1469 by the greatest painter of fifteenth-century Ferrara, Cosmè Tura, the dramatic Saint George and the Dragon and touchingly nervous Annunciation, respectively the outer and inner shutters of an organ.

The Este were deeply cultivated. An illegitimate son, Baldassare, himself became an accomplished painter. Much has been lost, and the major altarpieces of Quattrocento Ferrara have been dismembered. So the Palazzo di Schifanoia, in the eastern part of the town, is a most precious survival. Begun in the late fourteenth century by Alberto d'Este and subsequently enlarged under Borso d'Este and Ercole I, this is most celebrated for the Salone dei Mesi. Only seven of the original murals of the months survive. These are by Tura's contemporary, Francesco del Cossa, and the young Ercole de'Roberti. Their imaginative and discursive compositions capture the world of Borso's court, its extravagance and dynamism, its douceur de vivre. They remind us too of the inextricable links between Renaissance towns and the rural life that supported them. Piero della Francesca had worked for the Este. And there are echoes of his art in the Schifanoia frescoes, but their painters had very different aesthetic preoccupations than that austere genius. They sought to delight and to divert. And so they do.

There are other notable Renaissance palaces. Biagio Rossetti's unfinished Palazzo di Ludovico il Moro, built for Ercole I's ambassador to Milan, to the south of the Palazzo di Schifanoia, now houses the archaeological museum.

Better known is the Palazzo dei Diamanti, on the Corso Ercole d'Este, north of the Castello. This was begun about 1493 by Rossetti for Sigismondo d'Este. The spectacular façade with blocks of white diamond-pointed marble still clamours for attention. The type spawned a considerable progeny in Italy, Spain and as far afield as Crichton Castle in Scotland.

The palace now houses the Pinacoteca Nazionale, with a comprehensive holding of Ferrarese pictures. There are fragments of Tura's lost altarpiece of 1474 from Sant'Andrea and panels by his contemporaries. The High Renaissance is strongly represented. Interest now focuses on Dosso Dossi, a wayward genius whose poetic landscapes reveal the fascination of the plainsman for the hills. But it was not always so, and works by Benvenuto Tisi, il Garofalo – for example, the central panel of his Costabili altarpiece from Sant'Andrea – show why that artist was considered a northern Italian counterpart of Raphael. The later masters of Ferrara are also appealing: Scarsellino, consistently enchanting, particularly on a small scale; and Carlo Bononi, individual in colour and subtle in his interpretation of the artistic revolution of the Carracci at Bologna.

On the death of Alfonso II d'Este in 1597, Ferrara reverted to papal rule, the Este retaining their duchy of Modena. Ferrara paid a heavy artistic price, losing such masterpieces as the Bellini Feast of the Gods now in Washington, DC, and the early Titian Bacchanals in Madrid, not to mention the London Bacchus and Ariadne. But despite what it has suffered, Ferrara retains a strange magic. Bicyclists happily still outnumber drivers, and as the sun clears the morning mist one can imagine that Borso and his courtiers might be preparing to set out for the chase.

31
RAVENNA

❖

PROTECTED by the marshes of the Po Valley, Ravenna was for some two centuries the outstanding artistic centre on the Italian peninsula. There was a town here long before the Emperor Augustus chose the site of his new naval port of Classe, and the growing city was walled by Claudius. Its relative security was the reason why in 402 the Emperor Honorius chose this as the capital of his western empire in place of Milan. His sister and heir, Galla Placidia, was in turn succeeded by Valentinian III. When the empire was destroyed by the barbarian Odoacer in 476, he too made Ravenna the capital of his kingdom. He in turn was defeated by Theodoric the Goth (ruled 493–526), who also retained Ravenna as his capital and became an advocate of what its critics termed the Arian Heresy. Theodoric's successors were vanquished in 540 by the forces of the Byzantine Emperor Justinian. Ravenna remained the capital of the Byzantine Exarchate until the Lungobard conquest of 751. Thereafter her significance waned. Long a pawn in the struggle between the Holy Roman Empire and the papacy, Ravenna was controlled by Venice – her painters echoing their patrons' political allegiance – from 1441 until 1509, when Pope Julius II reasserted papal rule. The letters written at Ravenna by Lord Byron, intent on his affair with Teresa Guiccioli, give some idea of the dull prosperity that papal control engendered. And it was only well into the nineteenth century that the importance of the great monuments of Ravenna was recognized.

The city is not large, and for the visitor who has time it makes sense to see the great buildings and study their mosaics in a roughly chronological order. Two of the most remarkable are entered through the courtyard of the Museo Nazionale. Resist the temptation to commence with the church of San Vitale, however elated you may be by the wonderful sense of space, and cut through it to the so-called Mausoleum of Galla Placidia that was apparently built, not long before 450, by the empress. The plan is a Latin cross. The astonishingly well-preserved mosaics are coeval with the building and represent a natural evolution from earlier Roman work in the medium. The dominant colour is a deep nocturnal blue against

Mausoleum of Galla Placida, mosaic decoration of soffit.

San Vitale: apse mosaic, Christ with two Archangels, San Vitale and Bishop Ecclesio with a model of the church.

which the white robes of the saints stand out in a luminous manner.

Then return to San Vitale, which was consecrated in 547. The plan was novel, an octagon with a central cupola, and the architecture is perfectly complemented by the remarkable cycle of mosaics in the eastern section. The apse and the vault above, with the lateral walls, are resolved into a wonderfully unified whole in which green predominates, with gold and, once again, white. In historical terms the most revealing compositions are those with, respectively, the Emperor Justinian and his empress, Theodora, flanked by their attendants. Seeing these no contemporary onlooker could have doubted the reality of Byzantine power.

Some way to the south, near the late baroque cathedral, is the octagonal Orthodox Baptistery, whose mosaics are

of not long after 450. The great cupola was treated in three tiers, a circular *Baptism* in the centre, apostles under a canopy and, below these, altars flanked by decorative panels. The cathedral contains two unusually fine sarcophagi from Ravenna's heyday, and there are fine mosaics in the small Cappella di San Giorgio now accessed through the associated museum. Further east, beyond the central piazza, is the Baptistery of the Arians, build under the Goths early in the sixth century; here too the cupola is crowned by a mosaic of the *Baptism*.

A short walk southwards down the Via Roma leads to Sant'Apollinare Nuovo, the remarkable church built by the Arian King Theodoric. The splendid round campanile is of the ninth century, but the tremendous cycle of mosaics in the nave is largely of Theodoric's time. Again there are three tiers, the uppermost of scenes from the life of Christ, then prophets and saints, and, below, views of Theodoric's palace with male martyrs paying homage to Christ, balanced by a representation of the port of Classe, with virgins preceded by the Magi adoring the Madonna and Child. Theodoric's palace lay behind the church. Taking Via Alberoni just beyond this and turning left after going under the railway, or approaching from the north by following the walls of the Renaissance Castello Brancaleoni, it is a short walk to the king's other major monument, his mausoleum. Significantly this is of a traditional Roman type, the successor of the great circular mausolea of antiquity. The recent restoration is exemplary but antiseptic.

The last outstanding building of early Ravenna is outside the walls sadly encroached upon by modern roads. Sant'Apollinare in Classe was built near the port that was so vital to Ravenna's power. Consecrated in 549, it is the close contemporary of San Vitale, but altogether more ambitious in scale. The splendid detached campanile is a later addition, perhaps of the tenth century, and the brick church itself has been much restored. The scale of the interior is most impressive; and one senses something of its original richness from the marching grey and white veined columns, although much of the marble facing was appropriated for reuse at Rimini by Sigismondo Malatesta in 1449. The eye is drawn to the apse with the magnificent sixth-century mosaic of the *Transfiguration*, in which Christ is represented by the Cross. Below is Saint Apollinaris in episcopal robes, flanked by twelve lambs, symbolizing the faithful, and a representation of Paradise, with stylized trees, plants and flowers among small rocks. Here again green is used to almost mesmerizing effect.

With the fall of the Byzantine Exarchate, Ravenna ceased to be a capital. The campaniles of Sant'Apollinare Nuovo and Sant'Apollinare in Classe are the great monuments of Romanesque Ravenna. In the fifteenth century the Venetians sought to redevelop the city, with some success. Their impact can also be sensed in Ravenna's museum, the former Galleria dell'Accademia. There are serene altarpieces by Niccolò Rondinelli, a Ravenna-born adherent of Bellini. His near contemporaries, the brothers Zaganelli, by contrast veered towards their Ferrarese and Bolognese counterparts. The star of the collection is unquestionably the recumbent funerary statue of 1525 by Tullio Lombardo commemorating the warrior Guidarello Guidarelli.

Sant'Apollinare Nuovo: mosaic, Port of Classe.

32

PIACENZA

❖

PIACENZA, the Roman Placentia, on the right bank of the Po, makes few concessions to the tourist. And although on the Via Emilia, the great Roman thoroughfare that linked Milan with the Adriatic, it is surprisingly little visited. But much remains of the city's glory days, when she belonged to the Lombard League that defeated Barbarossa at Legnano in 1176. Only later was Piacenza subordinated to the Visconti, the Sforza, the French, and – from 1545 – the Farnese, whose Bourbon heirs, briefly ousted in 1734–48, were expelled by the French in 1796. In 1816 the city passed with Parma to Napoleon's wife Maria Luisa; in 1859 it was absorbed in the new Italian kingdom.

The strands of Piacentine history are aptly expressed in the central Piazza dei Cavalli, named after Francesco Mochi's equestrian bronzes of Alessandro Farnese and Ranuccio, his son, unveiled respectively in 1625 and 1630. These are among the masterpieces of baroque sculpture: look up at the restless chargers, with their swinging manes and trampling hoofs. Behind these statements of political power is the Palazzo del Comune, begun in 1280, one of the most convincingly monumental secular buildings of the age, stone below, brick above.

Piacenza is rich in early churches. Sant'Antonino, the original cathedral, was rebuilt in the eleventh century; the hexagonal dome floats above the Gothic Paradiso, the great brick entrance added

Francesco Mochi, *equestrian statue of Ranuccio I Farnese, bronze, 1630 (below) and equestrian statue of Duke Alessandro Farnese, bronze, 1625 (opposite).*

in 1350. The Duomo itself is a little way to the east. Built between 1120 and 1233, this – like almost every Romanesque church in Italy – has been much restored. But the façade, pink below, grey above, is most satisfying, as is the great brick campanile, best seen from the courtyard to the left. To bear the weight of the huge octagonal crossing, lateral piers were necessary, and the last bay of the nave was raised so that the transepts are symmetrical. Morazzone was called in to decorate the dome, but only completed two sections of the vault. He was followed by Guercino, whose frescoes, all but invisible by natural light, must always have lacked the delicacy of the artist's preparatory drawings. Between the Duomo and the station is a third notable church masked by a later arcade, San Savino. The interior has been ruthlessly purged of baroque excrescences. The crypt is notable not least because much of the original black and white pavement survives.

To the north-west corner on the Via di Campagna are two fine churches by the architect of Renaissance Piacenza, Alessio Tramello: San Sepolcro, begun in 1513, and the Madonna di Campagna of 1523–8, the first of conventional Latin cross plan, the second, yet grander, conceived as a Greek cross with a central dome. The great Friulian master Pordenone first worked at Piacenza in 1525, and it is his contribution that makes the Madonna di Campagna so remarkable. The murals of the dome, with God the Father in Glory, and the pendentives of the Evangelists, realized in 1528–31, are effective because Pordenone understood that legibility was of paramount importance. He also decorated the chapels in the angles on the left side of the church, dedicated respectively to Saint Catherine and the Magi, intro-

Madonna di Campagna: Pordenone, Christ among the Doctors, fresco (detail).

ducing Tramello's dome in the background of his *Disputation of Saint Catherine*. How observant Pordenone was is seen in his *Adoration of the Magi*, where the detached timbers are described in affectionate detail and he imagines an audience of watchers from the windows in the distance. His psychological range is evident in the expressions of the doctors whom the youthful Christ confounds, one desperately searching for help in his book.

The Palazzo Farnese, begun in 1538 but never finished, was ruthlessly stripped when the Bourbons left for Naples in 1734. The Pinacoteca deserves to be visited, however, for a little-known masterpiece, Botticelli's *Madonna and Child with the Infant Baptist*. This is among the first and freshest of his tondi, its equilibrium established by a frontal parapet. There is perhaps no more perfect hedge of roses in western art, and the open-eyed Child lies on the purple lining of the Virgin's billowing cloak, which protects him from the red and white roses below. The picture remains in its original frame attributable to Giuliano da Maiano. To be able to see such a masterpiece in peace makes up for the capricious opening times of the Collegio Alberoni, the great treasure of which is Antonello da Messina's hauntingly beautiful *Christ at the Column*.

33

PARMA

❖

FROM PIACENZA, the Via Emilia follows the margin of the Po Valley, skirting
the foothills of the Apennines. The next
town of consequence is Fidenza, with a
fine early cathedral. Parma follows, at the
crossroads of the route from Mantua to
the coast at La Spezia. Like other strategically placed cities, her history is complex. Imperial rule was followed by
republican, as were the Visconti, after an
interval, by the Sforza. The papacy recovered Parma in 1521, but in 1545 Pope
Paul III granted it as a duchy to his
nephew, Pier Luigi Farnese. The Farnese
were succeeded by the Spanish Bour
bons, whose contribution is particularly
evident in the ducal palace of Cologno,
fifteen miles north-east.

The city is divided by the river Parma.
The western section has a sleepy charm.
The great monuments are to the east. The
Piazza del Duomo is in the historic cen-
tre. On the south side is the octagonal
Baptistery begun in 1196, a masterpiece
of the transitional phase when the
Romanesque responds to Gothic forms.
The pink Veronese marble softens the
austerity of the design, with tiered loggias and canopied pinnacles. The sculptor
Benedetto Antelami worked on the
building, both inside and out, to spectacular effect. From the Baptistery the visitor
should go to the church of San Giovanni
Evangelista directly east of the Duomo.
This was an early building, but was
reconstructed at the turn of the sixteenth
century. Antonio Allegri, il Correggio –
the painter of the Parmese school – was
called in. He designed the fictive frieze of

the nave, and his *Vision of Saint John* in the
cupola was in every sense a visionary
work, the saint shown in a nimbus of
golden light surrounded by the apostles.

The Duomo is a Romanesque structure, although the campanile is Gothic.
In the right transept is Antelami's masterpiece, the remarkable relief of the *Deposition* dated 1178. The cupola was
decorated in 1526–30 by Correggio. A
natural sequel to his work at San Giovanni, Correggio's *Assumption of the Virgin*
was a conception of dazzling, indeed
vertiginous, ambition. Trained in the tradition of Mantegna, the painter devised
a language of expression that helped to
inspire the baroque. The visitor should
advance slowly up the nave and watch as
the campaign of illusion is revealed. Very
different in character is the third of Correggio's mural schemes at Parma, in the
Camera di San Paolo, ordered in 1518 by
the abbess of the monastery of that
name. The vault is of sixteen compartments, with ovals of pairs of putti. Below
these are delicate monochrome lunettes
of classical themes.

Correggio's counterpart among the
painters of High Renaissance Parma was
Parmigianino. Correggio was the master
of restraint, an Emilian Raphael in his
ability to codify a personal canon of religious expression – he was not responsible for the 'smirking correggiosities' of
which George Eliot once complained in
Middlemarch. Parmigianino was his
equal in delicacy of expression. But his
line has a nervous vigour of its own. His
subtle qualities are perfectly expressed
in the extraordinary decoration of the
Bramantesque church of the Madonna
della Steccata, finished in 1539. Frescoes
and stucco play equal parts in a scheme
of immense sophistication, alas unfinished.

San Giovanni Evangelista: Correggio (Antonio Allegri), Vision of Saint John, *dome fresco, 1522–3.*

The vast Palazzo della Pilotta was begun by the Farnese. Of the original interiors the most impressive was the enormous Teatro Farnese, severely damaged by bombing in 1944. The picture collection of the Accademia, founded in 1762 by Filippo Bourbon, Duke of Parma, and enlarged when expropriated pictures were returned from Paris in 1815, was augmented by Napoleon's widow, Maria Luisa of Austria, who ruled Parma as duchess from 1816 until 1847.

Inevitably Correggio is the focus of interest. The two lateral canvasses from the del Bono chapel at San Giovanni Evangelista, the *Martyrdom of Four Saints* and the *Deposition*, are both works of charged drama. Viewed diagonally in their intended setting, the two must have seemed startlingly realistic. *The Madonna of Saint Jerome* and the *Madonna della Scodella* are rivalled among the artist's major altarpieces only by those at Dresden. The enduring popularity of these *tours de force* is due to Correggio's ability to match the intimacy of his drawings and smaller panels on a large scale. Their ostensible simplicity masks a lifetime's absorption of ideas, visual and iconographic, Italian and of the north.

The city has much else to offer. Later churches include Ferdinando Galli Bibbiena's Sant'Antonio Abate, with its theatrical façade. Neoclassicism is represented by the Teatro Regio, near the Palazzo Ducale, begun in 1821 for Maria Luisa by Nicola Bettoli, whose discipline of detail is impressive. The duchess also commissioned a late masterpiece by the great Florentine sculptor Lorenzo Bartolini, the monument of 1840–1 to her lover, Count Neipperg, in the Steccata.

Parma's political and artistic developments were both determined by her position on one of the major arteries of the Roman road network. To sense this, proceed onwards down the Via Emilia. Modena is the next major city, long a seat of the Este with an outstanding early cathedral and a distinguished museum. Next comes Reggio, another prosperous and confident town, with the ambitious Madonna della Ghiara, begun in 1597, in the left transept of which is an outsize masterpiece, Guercino's *Crucifixion*.

34
BOLOGNA

❧

BOLOGNA is not the most immediately lovable of major Italian cities. Her enduring prosperity is partly due to her position at the point of the Via Emilia where the historic route over the Futa Pass from Florence debouches from the Apennines to the vast plain of the Po. And to understand Bologna it is best to approach from the successors of the Via Emilia: from the Via Ugo Bassi to the Piazza Porta Ravegnana, which overlie the decumanus of what was already a major town. With the collapse of the Roman empire, Bologna's importance dwindled only to recover dramatically in the period after 1164, when she joined the Lombard League. The struggle between the empire and the papacy was finally resolved in favour of the latter. When the signoria of the Bentivoglio family was suppressed in 1506, papal rule was ruthlessly reimposed. This, contrary to what might be supposed, ensured the consistent wealth that made it possible for Bologna to support the most influential school of painters in post-Renaissance Italy. Their achievement was what attracted most northern travellers to visit Bologna in the age of the Grand Tour. And as Ruskin was the high priest of the generation that dismissed the Carracci, Reni and their followers, it is appropriate that another Briton, Sir Denis Mahon, did more than anyone else to rehabilitate their reputation in the twentieth century.

The Carracci would recognize much of the centre of Bologna: the brick arcades of the streets, which Sir Denis also loved, benign alike in rain and sun;

the two leaning towers, the Torre degli Asinelli and the Torre Garisenda, already seen as symbols of the city; the major public buildings that flank the Piazza Maggiore; and not least, dominating the latter, the monumental façade of the cathedral, San Petronio, with the wonderful doorway by the Sienese Jacopo della Quercia, whose bas-reliefs express at once the lyricism and the languor of the late Gothic. In the adjacent Piazza Fontana is a later masterpiece, the bronze Fountain of Neptune completed in 1566 by another brilliant outsider, Jean de Boulogne, for whom it earned the name by which we know him, Giambologna.

Although Bologna could claim a notable indigenous school of painters and miniaturists, her patrons were never parochial. The career of the late fifteenth-century sculptor Niccolò da Bari, otherwise Niccolò dell'Arca, perfectly illustrates this. An arch in the portal of the south-east corner of the Piazza Maggiore leads to the narrow Via Clovature, with, on the left, Santa Maria della Vita. To the right of the high altar is Niccolò's extraordinary terracotta group of the Pietà, almost northern in dramatic tension.

Niccolò owed his sobriquet to his contribution to the arca of Saint Dominic in the great basilica of San Domenico, 250 metres to the south, reached more directly from the second turning to the right off the Via Clavature. The church was begun in 1221, the year of the saint's death, and the façade, although restored, is original. The Dominicans were determined patrons. Giunta Pisano supplied the great Crucifix in a chapel off

the left aisle, while Nicola Pisano, who relied in part on assistants, executed the reliefs of the saint's tomb in his chapel on the right. Two hundred years later, in 1469, Niccolò da Bari was called in to supply a cimasa with free-standing statues. His candelabrum-bearing angel on the left is among the most delicate sculptures of the Quattrocento, and is not outshone by the pendant supplied in 1494 by the youthful Michelangelo. The later decoration of the chapel is also remarkable, with Guido Reni's powerful *Apotheosis of Saint Dominic* in the cove of the apse.

From the Piazza Porta Ravegnana, the Via Zamboni runs at a diagonal to the grid of the early town. On the right is one of Bologna's major churches, San Giacomo Maggiore, another thirteenth-century foundation. At the east end is the Bentivoglio Chapel, consecrated in 1486. The altarpiece is by the most influential painter of Renaissance Bologna, Francesco Francia, who was trained as a goldsmith and evolved a restrained classical style. The murals of the lateral walls, in one of which Giovanni II Bentivoglio and his family appear, are by his equally accomplished contemporary, Lorenzo Costa.

Three hundred metres beyond the church, on the left, is the Pinacoteca Nazionale. Here you can study the long development of the Bolognese school from the fourteenth century onwards, as well as pictures by artists from elsewhere painted for the city – from the late Giotto altarpiece to Raphael's heroic *Saint Cecilia* originally in San Domenico. There are outstanding altarpieces by the three Carracci, Annibale, Agostino and Ludovico, of which Annibale's early *Baptism* is the most appealing; these are complemented by familiar masterpieces of Guido Reni – the greatest master of Seicento Bologna –

Opposite: Giambologna, Fontana di Nettuno, bronze, 1566.

San Domenico: Niccolò dell'Arca, Angel.

including the majestic *Pala dei Mendicanti* and the powerful *Crucifixion* of 1617, and the wonderfully subtle *Saint William of Aquitaine* by the youthful Guercino. The later Bolognese also repay attention: Creti, particularly on a small scale, is exquisite in touch; Giuseppe Maria Crespi impresses for the humanity of both his genre scenes and his religious commissions; while the Gandolfi leave one in no doubt of their almost physical relish for their chosen medium. The vigour of later Bolognese painting was no isolated phenomenon; this was paralleled in the enduring vitality of the ancient university, where the curious can still see the alarmingly well-observed waxes of foetuses used for instruction in the medical school.

35
CESENA

❖

FROM BOLOGNA the Via Emilia continues south-eastwards below the line of the Apennines. The sequence of towns continues: Imola, still dominated by a remarkable fortress; Faenza, famous for her maiolica and with a worthy museum that celebrates it; Forlì, whose museum boasts the masterpieces of that seducer of the Emilian Seicento, Guido Cagnacci; then Cesena, and finally, where the road reaches the coast, Rimini, memorable above all for the Franciscan church, the Tempio Malatestana, designed by Alberti for that most grasping of Renaissance despots, Sigismondo Malatesta.

Cesena is a comfortable town. It lies at the northern end of the main route through the Apennines from the upper valley of the Tiber, and has been occupied since prehistoric times. Contended for by the Church and others, it was granted by Pope Urban VI in 1379 to Galeotto Malatesta, whose family held it until 1460. Cesena subsequently reverted to the Church, and for obvious strategic reasons was chosen in 1500 by Cesare Borgia as the capital of his short-lived duchy of the Romagna. The town was the birthplace of successive popes, Giovanni Angelo Braschi, Pius VI (1775–99), and Barnaba Chiaramonti, Pius VII (1800–22), who survived the indignities to which he was submitted by Bonaparte to regain his sovereign status and be portrayed by Sir Thomas Lawrence for the Waterloo Chamber at Windsor. A patient man, he was the last pope to create a great palazzo for his family, vying with the mansions of the local plutocracy.

The cathedral and churches of Cesena are not of especial interest. Nor perhaps is the Rocca Malatestiana, begun for Galeotto, continued by his successors, and strengthened from 1466 by the papal governor. But the Biblioteca Malatestiana is one of the great libraries of Europe. The neoclassical front of the Palazzo delle Scuole gives no hint of what lies behind: a stair leading to the long corridor to the Biblioteca Comunale. Here a door surmounted by a pediment with the elephant of the Malatesta opens to the Biblioteca Malatestiana. Commissioned by Malatesta Novello, who ruled Cesena from 1429 to 1460, and inspired by the library Cosimo de' Medici had commissioned for the Dominican Observants of San Marco in Florence, this was built in 1447–52 as the library of the Franciscan convent. The architect was Matteo Nuti, who also worked on the Rocca. The library is an aisled room eleven bays in length; the central barrel-vaulted section is higher than the cross-vaulted aisles and divided from these by arcades resting on fluted columns. One's first impression is of beautifully controlled light, distributed through the pairs of smallish arched windows in each bay of the lateral walls and the octofoil window high on the end (east) wall. The reading desks in the aisles were thus served by natural sidelight. No fewer than 136 of the manuscripts ordered by Malatesta remain in the Biblioteca, which is thus the oldest humanist library of the kind to survive at least substantially intact, largely because after Malatesta's death the Franciscans preserved it until their convent was suppressed. The exterior's purpose is beautifully expressed in the rows of almost pointed windows set in stone frames high on the brick walls.

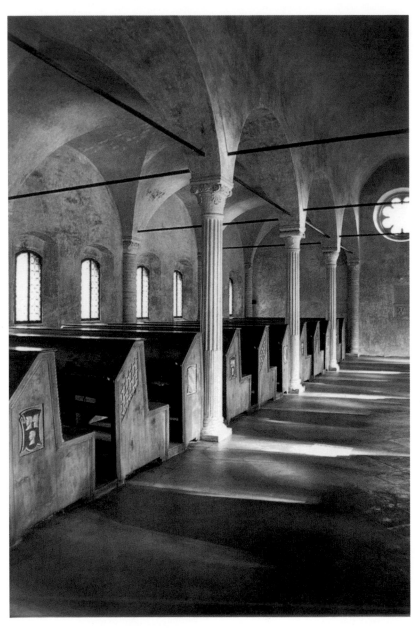

Cesena: Matteo Nuti, Biblioteca Malatestiana.

Tuscany

38 Pistoia •

Poggio a Caiano 37

• Lucca 39

• Florence 36

• Pisa 40

48 La Verna •

49 Borgo San Sepolcro

• San Gimignano 42

Volterra 41

46 Arezzo •

• Siena 43

47 Cortona •

44 Pienza •

45 Sant' Antimo •

36

FLORENCE

❧

THAT we think of Medicean Florence as the artistic epicentre of the Renaissance world owes much to the writing of the sixteenth-century artist-cum-propagandist Giorgio Vasari. But Florence's greatest writers, Dante and Boccaccio, lived before the banking dynasty rose from obscurity, and the city had a long history. Strategically placed beside the river Arno, Florentia was a major Roman city; she came to prominence again in the eleventh century and was subsequently at the heart of the long struggle between papacy and empire, between Guelf and Ghibelline, its respective adherents. The commune was succeeded by a republic. Commerce and banking greatly enriched the city, although the Black Death of 1348 dramatically affected growth. Political divisions and aristocratic rivalries were assiduously exploited by the Medici, and from 1434 Cosimo il Vecchio effectively controlled Florence. His grandson Lorenzo il Magnifico consolidated the family's position, exercising a tight control over the expanding territory that Florence controlled. Lorenzo's successors were driven out in 1494 and again in 1527, only to return in 1530. Lorenzo's illegitimate great-grandson Alessandro became duke in 1531, and his cousin and heir Cosimo I was elevated as Grand Duke of Tuscany in 1569. On the death of his descendant Gian Gastone in 1737, the grand duchy passed to Francis, Duke of Lorraine, consort of the Empress Maria Theresa. Ferdinand III was expelled by the French in 1799, but recovered Tuscany in 1815; he and his

son Leopold II were the most enlightened Italian rulers of their time. The grand duchy was in 1860 absorbed in the new kingdom of Italy, of which in 1865–71 Florence was the capital. Despite losing this status to Rome, Florence long continued to be the most cosmopolitan city of Italy, with a large number of expatriate residents, many of whom left their mark on her institutions and monuments.

When I first was in Italy, in 1966, Ester Bonacossa pronounced that May was the month for Florence – and for fireflies. Alas, except perhaps in deep November or early February, the tourist cannot now hope to escape his kind. A queue snakes outside the Uffizi, and even now that a more sensible ticketing system has been introduced, the obvious highpoints of the collection – the early Florentine pictures, the extraordinary Botticellis and the two early Leonardos – are under constant siege. Moreover, the new galleries do less than justice to celebrated masterpieces by Raphael and the great Florentines of the High Renaissance, and the choice of background colours is bizarre. At the Accademia groups surround Michelangelo's *David* although almost no one looks at the early altarpieces. The same goes for the Museo Archeologico, which houses such treasures as the *Chimera of Arezzo* and an outstanding collection of Attic black-figure vases. By contrast, the steps of the Duomo are crowded and a long line leads to the visitors' entrance. If you wish to study the bronze doors of the Baptistery that remain in situ, on the south with reliefs by Andrea Pisano of 1330 and their counterpart to the north of 1403–24 by Lorenzo Ghiberti, go at dawn, when you may also share the Piazza della Signoria with the pigeons who breakfast on the last night's horse droppings. If you wish to examine the incredible sixteenth-century sculptures in the piazza, Donatello's heroic Judith or Giambologna's *Rape of the Sabines*, you will have to ignore the exhausted tourists who settle round these.

Yet with a little patience, the magic of the city exerts itself. My favourite approach is from Pian dei Giullari to the south. The narrow Via San Leonardo twists between the unyielding walls of a sequence of villas, some more modest than others. At length the Forte Belvedere looms on the left; ahead is the Porta San Giorgio, to the east of which is a well-preserved section of the medieval city wall. Within the gate, the Costa San Giorgio descends steeply. As it curves there are changing views towards the centre of the city on the further bank of the Arno. Make to the left for the church of Santa Felicita, in a small piazza stepped back from the Via Guicciardini. Nothing quite prepares one for the Capponi Chapel immediately to the right of the entrance.

The altarpiece, the *Deposition* by Pontormo (1528), is the most distinguished picture of the period in Florence to remain in its intended setting, and thus to be seen at the level the artist intended. The body of Christ has been taken from the Cross, and is borne by two youths as the Maries grieve; the emotional conviction of the design is given a deeper poignancy by Pontormo's hauntingly beautiful colours, his idiosyncratic range of blues and reds and pinks: colours which, if the eye is given time to adjust, sing more surely by the filtered daylight than when artificially illuminated, and must have been yet more eloquent in flickering candlelight.

The Via Guicciardi to the left leads to the Piazza Pitti with, on the east, the vast, partly rusticated façade of the Palazzo Pitti, seat of the Medici and their successors. The grand ducal collections were by any standard prodigious, and the Galleria Palatina in the series of staterooms with outstanding Seicento frescoes and stucco is a remarkable survival: an early nineteenth-century arrangement of pictures

Baptistery, South Door: Andrea Pisano, Hope *(left) and* Humility *(right), gilt-bronze, 1330.*

Santa Felicita: Pontormo, Deposition
(detail).

in a traditional hierarchical tiered hang.
The Medici would be astonished by how
little attention is now paid to the two
breathtakingly beautiful altarpieces of the
Assumption of the Virgin by Andrea del Sarto,
which they bought in 1602 and 1639
respectively. Other masterpieces, not least
the portraits by Raphael, his *Madonna della
Sedia* and the wonderful Titian portraits,
still keep their place in those contemporary halls of fame – the postcard stalls –
but some former stars, Cristofano Allori's
intent *Judith* or the Carlo Dolcis for example, are the preserve now of the art his-
torian.

Happily the descendants of the
Medicis' subjects continue to enjoy the
Boboli Gardens that stretch behind
the palace to the city wall. Begun for
Eleonora of Toledo, so familiar to us from
Bronzino's portrait in the Uffizi, to a
design of 1550 by Niccolò Tribolo, these
were developed over the following hundred years as successive waves of grand
ducal taste demanded. There is much

sculpture, including an explicit Cinque-
cento masterpiece, Vincenzo de'Rossi's
Paris and Helen of 1560, and Giambologna's
Venus rising from the Bath in the Grotta di
Buontalenti.

Opposite the Pitti narrow streets cut
westwards towards the church of Santo
Spirito, which is in some ways the most
characteristic religious building of
Quattrocento Florence. The architect was
Filippo Brunelleschi – most famed, of
course, for his astounding dome of the
Duomo that is in so many ways the
symbol of the Florentine Renaissance
and floats majestically above the city.
Santo Spirito is of traditional cruciform
plan with subsidiary aisles. The exterior

*Boboli Gardens, Grottoes of Buontalenti:
Vincenzo de'Rossi, Paris and Helen, marble,
1560.*

Santa Trinita: Lorenzo Monaco, Flight into Egypt.

is of sober stucco, a honeyed cream. Within, one is struck by the visual coherence of the architecture and of the many late Quattrocento altarpieces and altarfronts still in place round the transepts. Patrons and painters compete, but on strictly complementary terms. The later altarpieces – of which the most memorable are by that narrator of near genius Aurelio Lomi – are more ambitious in scale.

Two blocks to the west is another celebrated church, Santa Maria del Carmine. The Corsini Chapel in the left transept is perhaps the most completely satisfying monument of baroque Florence. But it is not for this that the tourist-pilgrim comes. Your objective is the Brancacci Chapel opposite, which alas can no longer be entered from the body of the church, with the revolutionary frescoes of the short-lived Masaccio that heralded the Tuscan Renaissance in painting, their softer, more lyrical counterparts by his associate Masolino, and the courageous scenes by Filippino Lippi that completed the cycle.

From the Piazza del Carmine it is a short walk to the Arno. The view from the south bank as one makes for the Ponte Santa Trinita has not materially changed since it was depicted by Zocchi and Patch in the eighteenth century, although traffic has deserted the river for the lungarni – and motorcycles are noisier than boats. Across the bridge is the church of the same name, an ancient foundation that remains a convincing place of prayer. Behind a grill in its original setting on the right is a haunting masterpiece by the last great painter of Gothic Florence, the *Annunciation* by Don Lorenzo Monaco, with the Angel and Virgin in profile and, between, a stand of trees with trunks silhouetted against the gold ground of the panel; below, the Christmas narrative is continued in predella panels of almost unprecedented delicacy. Nearby is the Sassetti Chapel with Ghirlandaio's altarpiece and the admirably controlled fresco cycle which explain why he was so dominant an influence in late fifteenth-century Florence. Like his Medici masters, Francesco

San Marco: Fra Angelico, Annunciation, fresco (detail).

Sassetti knew what he wanted.

The visitor with time will want to see more of the great churches that now, like the Duomo, charge for admission: Santa Maria Novella, with its wonderfully arro-gant façade, for Masaccio, Orcagna and Ghirlandaio; San Lorenzo for Donatello, Verrocchio and, above all, Michelangelo, whose expression of a personal architectural language in the adjacent Laurentian

Library is arguably as remarkable as the Medici tombs in the New Sacristy; cold Franciscan Santa Croce, that Valhalla of the Florentines, for Giotto and the Gaddi, Taddeo and Agnolo, not to mention Donatello's relief of the *Annunciation* and the chaste tomb of Bonnie Prince Charlie's widow, the Countess of Albany, and that incomparably pure masterpiece of the Quattrocento, Brunelleschi's Pazzi Chapel. Then find your way to the medieval Bargello, which with its prodigious holdings of Tuscan sculpture has been, except where Michelangelo is concerned, spared the tyranny of trendy display. The concentration of works by Donatello and his successors has no equal, but is most nearly rivaled in the Museo del Opera del Duomo, where the justly famous cantorie by Donatello and Luca della Robbia complement earlier sculpture from the cathedral, and have now been joined by Ghiberti's celebrated reliefs from the Porta del Paradiso of the Baptistery and by Michelangelo's late *Pietà*.

It is in quieter places that it is more easy to understand the successive waves of Florentine taste: at Orsanmichele, where Daddi's altarpiece glows by candlelight in Orcagna's massive tabernacle of 1349–59; in the Convento di San Marco, where the genius of Fra Angelico is seen in the museum but most perfectly expressed in the frescoes of the cells – I must declare an interest as it was a Christmas card of the upright *Annunciation* that opened my eyes at the age of nearly six; in the Badia, with its monuments by Mino da Fiesole and Filippino Lippi's beautiful *Vision of Saint Bernard*; at Santa Maria Maddalena dei Pazzi, where Perugino's silent *Crucifixion* (accessible only on Tuesdays and Thursdays) remains so

compelling a religious image; in the Ognisanti, where Botticelli and Ghirlandaio contend; in the Annunziata, where Andrea del Sarto and his contemporaries continued the decoration of the atrium and he returned to fresco his overdoor of the Madonna del Sacco in the cloister; or the Chiostro dello Scalzo, with Sarto's admirably inventive grisaille frescoes of the life of Saint John the Baptist.

One of the pleasures of sightseeing in Florence is the way that the city, as if unwittingly, discloses its past. Tourists searching for a fashionable gelateria may sense that the curving walls of a huddle of buildings represent the line of the Roman amphitheatre west of the Piazza Santa Croce; a maze of narrow streets and the Palazzo della Signoria tell of the medieval republic already rich from banking, and the façades of the many Renaissance palaces in, for example, the Borgo degli Albizi still demonstrate the prosperity of Medici rule. Moreover, we can survey the city from certain viewpoints, Bellosguardo or the walk up to San Miniato al Monte, which glows in the evening sun.

Our understanding of what Florence meant to earlier generations of visitors is enhanced in the Museo Horne, formed by Herbert Horne, whose monograph on Botticelli has had no rival in English for over a century. Across the Arno the Museo Bardini, with the collection assembled by the leading Florentine dealer of the same period, has a complementary message. Florence can seem a forbidding city of uncompromising grey stone, but despite the depredations of Bardini and his predecessors her treasures are literally inexhaustible.

37

POGGIO A CAIANO

❧

THE political power of the Medici was underpinned by their vast territorial possessions. And many of their villas survive to demonstrate their predilection for rural life. Among these Poggio a Caiano is the most remarkable. The sprawling town is not perhaps prepossessing. But we are in a different sphere once through the gate to the villa Giuliano da Sangallo devised for Lorenzo il Magnifico. This crests a low eminence. The elegance of its line, with open loggias and on the first floor a wide portico in antis crowned by a stretched pediment, is not diminished by the later belfry; and the innovative layout of the square structure can still be appreciated despite subsequent interventions, of which those of the Savoys were particularly unsympathetic.

The villa was still unfinished on Lorenzo's death, and work was interrupted when his son Piero was banished in 1494. After the Medici returned in 1512, the project was revived, and it was given an added impetus by the election of Lorenzo's son Giovanni as Pope Leo X a year later. The huge central hall was intended to celebrate the Medici, as the emblems on the barrel vault remind us, and the pope's friend Paolo Giovio devised the iconographic programme for the decoration of the room. Andrea del Sarto and Franciabigio were entrusted with the decoration of the two longer walls, while the much narrower lateral ones were allotted to Pontormo. At the time of the pope's death in 1521, Pontormo had supplied his remarkable mural of Vertumnus and Pomona in the upper part of the right-hand wall, while Franciabigio had completed the lower part of his Return of Caesar from Exile, and Sarto had realized much of the Tribute to Caesar diagonally opposite. There are

Villa: Giuliano da Sangallo, detail of façade.

beautiful passages in both narratives, but neither has the magic of Pontormo's fresco, which is among the masterpieces of secular decoration of the time. Alessandro de'Medici, who regained his inheritance in 1531, attempted to revive the scheme, but it was only completed after Alessandro Allori was enlisted in 1578. Allori did his best to respect what he found, for he was well aware that his own uncle and mentor, Bronzino, had been a pupil of Pontormo.

For a contrasting view of Pontormo's genius, go on to the little town of Carmignano, some five kilometres to the west. On the right wall of the parish church is his altarpiece of the *Visitation*, touching, as the iconography demands, charged with emotion and characteristically inventive in colour. Only the wayward nature of the artist can explain why the panel was not borne off by the Medici or Napoleon's agents.

A few kilometres to the south, high on a ridge, is Artiminio, the substantial villa divised for Grand Duke Ferdinando I in 1594 by Bernardo Buontalenti. The architect evidently took Poggio a Caiano as his model, and, at least from a distance, his façade floats majestically above the olive groves. At Artiminio even more than at Poggio a Caiano the Medici could escape from the machinery that ensured their rule, and it cannot be wholly coincidental that the most interesting of the interiors is the small bathroom decorated by Bernardino Poccetti.

38
PISTOIA

❖

THE medieval Florentines did not always deal kindly with their neighbours. Like her larger neighbour Prato, Pistoia – with agricultural and commercial wealth and banks – was a rival; conquered in 1294, Pistoia became a protectorate in 1329 and in 1530 was absorbed in the Grand Duchy of Tuscany.

The town is on the northern margin of the plain of the Ombrone, backed by the rising mass of the Apennines. The parallelogram of the late walls implies Pistoia's importance. Near the centre is the Piazza del Duomo, hemmed in by buildings of surprisingly consistent interest: the thirteenth-century cathedral, the Gothic Baptistery, the Palazzo del Podestà, begun in 1367, and the impressive Palazzo del Comune. The cathedral's most celebrated treasure is the silver altarpiece of San Jacopo, begun in 1287 and progressively augmented in the ensuing century. Of the numerous reliefs the finest are arguably the scenes from the life of the saint of 1367–71 by Leonardo di Giovanni. For the student of the Renaissance, two works on the opposite – left – side of the church are of particular interest. The altarpiece on the right of the chapel at the end of the left aisle was ordered from Andrea del Verrocchio. The executant was his pupil Lorenzo di Credi, and the vigour of such details as the fringe of the carpet demonstrates why Verrocchio's studio was so influential an artistic powerhouse. Just inside the main door is another undertaking of Verrocchio, the tomb of Cardinal Niccolò Forteguerri, who died in 1473; this would, if completed to the original scheme, have been the most distinguished mural monument of the age.

The pulpits of Pistoia are very remarkable, and it makes sense to see them in chronological sequence. Leaving the Piazza del Duomo at the north-east corner, continue to the church of San Bartolomeo in Pantano. The unfinished façade is of Pisan type. The pulpit of 1250 is by Guido da Como, whose narrative reliefs already reflect the advances of contemporary Pisan sculpture. The second of the great Pistoiese pulpits is in San Giovanni Fuorcivitas, on the south side of the Via Cavour – the first major road south of the Piazza del Duomo – which represents the line of the medieval wall. The Romanesque church has been restored and the façade was not finished. Inside you come first to the splendid water stoop, itself attributed to Giovanni Pisano. The pulpit is by Fra Guglielmo da Pisa, a follower of Nicola Pisano, and was finished in 1270.

The most beautiful sculpture in the church is of a different stamp. The glazed terracotta *Visitation*, usually attributed to

Cathedral, Romanesque façade with portico added in 1311.

Sant'Andrea: Giovanni Pisano,
pulpit, marble (detail).

Andrea della Robbia, is one of the very
few free-standing works of serious distinction in the medium. I first saw it with
John Pope-Hennessy, who lit candles
so we could see how these gave life to
the white glaze – as the artist so clearly
intended. Tender in expression yet restrained to the point of austerity, the
group is as moving on its own terms as
Pontormo's picture some twelve kilometres to the south at Carmignano.

The last – and noblest – of the Pistoiese pulpits is at Sant'Andrea, north-
west of the Piazza del Duomo. The
arcaded façade – again of Pisan type – is
enriched by a central portal with reliefs
of 1166. The nave and aisles are relatively
narrow. On the left is the pulpit of 1296–
1301 by Giovanni Pisano, son of Nicola,
whose great pulpit of 1260 in the Baptistery at Pisa had heralded nothing less
than the rebirth of Italian sculpture as an

intellectual force. Of all the pulpits of
the age, that at Sant'Andrea is perhaps
the loveliest. Giovanni understood his
father's achievement and knew what he
had learnt from classical example. He
respected, too, his father's narrative discipline. But the son is an artist of the
highest order in his own right. His forms
have a sinuous Gothic generosity, his
reliefs a rhythmic conviction. Few works
of their generation still speak with equal
eloquence.

The Trecento marked the zenith of
Pistoia's prosperity, as the large Franciscan and Dominican churches confirm,
but the Renaissance left its contribution
in the small church of Santa Maria delle
Grazie, often attributed to Michelozzo
but probably by an indigenous architect, and in the loggia of the Ospedale,
adorned with a polychrome frieze.

39

LUCCA

❖

THE majestic walls of Lucca, with their sequence of eleven formidable bastions built between 1504 and 1645, offer visual evidence of the city's long independence from the Grand Duchy of Tuscany. Her strategic position and the fertility of her territory ensured the survival of the Roman town. In 1119 Lucca became a free commune; a period of great prosperity – and church-building – ensued. After a phase of political turbulence, the city recovered independence in 1369. Paolo Guinigi held the signoria for thirty years until 1430, but thereafter Lucca prospered as an increasingly aristocratic republic until the French invasion of 1799. Granted by Bonaparte as a principality to his sister Elisa and her husband Felice Baciocchi, Lucca was in 1817 awarded to Napoleon's wife, Maria Luisa of Parma, and only passed to Tuscan rule in 1847.

The eighteenth-century tragedian Vittorio Alfieri recollected of his first visit to Lucca that a day there had seemed like a century. Few will agree. While the walls testify to Lucca's determination to preserve her independence and the innumerable villas in the hinterland imply the sustained wealth in later centuries of her leading families, many of the outstanding buildings in the city itself date from the period of the free commune. The church of San Michele in Foro, at the very heart of the grid of the Roman town, epitomizes the Pisan Romanesque. Ruthless restoration does not disguise the richly decorated texture of the façade; the apse is also distinguished. Passing this,

and making north-west, turn right and then left on the Via Fillungo; beyond the bend, to the left, is the great church of San Frediano, largely built between 1112 and 1147. The mosaic of the *Ascension* on the façade is, alas, much restored, but the interior is particularly satisfying. The decoration of the second chapel on the left is the masterpiece of that most eccentric of Bolognese Renaissance painters, Amico Aspertini, whose classicism is informed by a kleptomaniac's accumulation of detail. Further on is the Cappella Trenta, with a sculpted polyptych, dated 1422, by Jacopo della Quercia.

Leave the church and cross the Via Fillugo to the Roman amphitheatre. The centre has been cleared and serves as a playground; houses are built into the structure. However, its form and scale can still be sensed. We can only be grateful that it has been spared by the archaeologists. As Lucca retains so much of the early street plan, it is relatively easy to head south for the Duomo. Founded in the sixth century by San Frediano, this is the most ambitious of the Romanesque churches of Lucca. The upper part of the façade was constructed by Guidello da Como and bears the date 1204; the elaborately decorated portico was begun in 1233. Entering the church, one is immediately impressed by its scale and height. In the left aisle is the octagonal shrine devised in 1482–4 by the local sculptor Matteo Cividale to contain the revered Volto Santo, a Romanesque effigy of Christ on the Cross in a robe enriched with Gothic jewellery. Mentioned by Dante, the Volto Santo was – and remains – the religious symbol of Lucca. An early copy is at Borgo San Sepolcro, and the image appears on an early sixteenth-century English cope at Stonyhurst. The people of Lucca still pay it far more atten-

Cathedral: Fra Bartolommeo, Madonna and Child with Saints Stephen and John the Baptist, *1509.*

tion than the two Renaissance masterpieces in the church.

The earlier and better known of these, in the left transept, is Jacopo della Quercia's extraordinary funerary image of Ilaria del Carretto, wife of Paolo Guinigi. She died in 1405 and the tomb was delivered in 1408. The effigy is placed on a sarcophagus decorated with putti supporting a splendid festoon. The young and exquisitely beautiful consort lies in her eternal sleep, a lapdog at her feet. Fluidly carved in flawless pale marble, the sculpture exerts an irresistible appeal. The most recent restoration has been irresponsibly criticized. Behind the monument, to the left of the presbytery, is the Chapel of the Sanctuary. The altarpiece of the *Madonna and Child with Saints Stephen and John the Baptist* was supplied by Baccio della Porta, Fra Bartolommeo, in 1509. One of the purest achievements of the Florentine High Renaissance, exqui-

site both in its equilibrium of composition and subtle clarity of colour, this is one of the few major works by the painter which can still be seen in an appropriate setting.

Lucca repays the persistent. There are other early churches. And a wonderfully detached impression of the town and its campaniles can be gained from the walls. The Museo di Villa Guinigi houses a substantial museum, including a sensitive portrait of a diffident youth by Pontormo, while the Palazzo Mansi retains the collection of that family. Those with time should try to see at least some of the villas of the Lucchese and their gardens, but will need to check opening times. Of the gardens, the most magnificent are those, impeccably maintained, of the Villa Reale di Marlia, once inhabited by Elisa Baciocchi. The eighteenth-century topiary theatre is a particularly happy survival.

40

PISA

❖

PISA owes much to its position astride the river Arno as it approaches the sea: a major port under the Romans, the city subsequently had a key role in defending the coast, not least from the Saracens whom it drove from Sardinia in 1015–16. As a free commune which was already a major trading power in the Mediterranean, Pisa became an archiepiscopal see in 1092, and obtained substantial possessions both in Italy and in Sardinia in the ensuing century, taking advantage of the weakness of the Crusaders to demand commercial concessions in their ports. Always in uneasy competition with Florence, Pisa lost ground when local families contended for the signoria in the early fourteenth century; Sardinia was lost in 1327, and in 1399 the city was sold to the Visconti of Milan, and finally occupied by the Florentines six years later. Florentine rule was benign, and the Medici took a responsible interest in what became their second city, fostering public institutions and works, including the canal linking it with Cosimo I's successor port of Livorno.

The great monuments of Pisa's glory days are within the north-west angle of the walls: the huge Duomo, begun in 1063; the Baptistery to the west, commenced in 1152 by a builder of genius, Diotisalvi, but not completed for over 200 years; the Campanile, or Leaning Tower, to the east, begun in 1173 and finished in the mid-Trecento; and the

appropriately sombre Camposanto, or cemetery, to the north, on which work started in 1278. The buildings are not aligned, yet the sense of space that flows between them was evidently not accidental. And each successive structure was clearly intended to respond to what was already built, so the richly decorated texture of the circular Baptistery, most sophisticated of medieval rotundas, answers the west front of the Duomo, while the columned tiers of the Campanile seem to float above us, not just because these lean but because they seem so weightless by comparison with the massive bulk of the Duomo. The builders of Pisa understood the properties of light, as one can see when the movement of the sun diminishes and then draws out the shadows cast by the narrow pilasters of the façade of the Camposanto.

To understand the achievement of the great sculptors of medieval Pisa, the Pisano, it makes sense to begin with the Baptistery. Here again the builders express a lightness of touch. On the left is the prodigious pulpit begun in 1260 by Nicola Pisano. This is decorated with scenes from the life of Christ, personifications of the Virtues, and, in the spandrels of the arches, the Prophets. Nicola's genius was to learn from classical statuary how to give life to his forms. The revolution he started, and on which his young son Giovanni collaborated, was to transform the development of Italian sculpture. Nicola strove for the plausible, while Giovanni's taste was more lyrical: his great pulpit of 1302–11 in the Duomo, reconstructed in 1926, is a highpoint of the Italian Gothic. There is a wonderful harmony between the structure itself and Giovanni's sinuous

Opposite: Camposanto.

sculpted forms. It takes a little time to realize how successful the interior of the Duomo is; the nave is flanked by double aisles, the cupola of the crossing borne on arches that imply a knowledge of Muslim architecture. Later accretions, individually distinguished but cumulatively almost oppressive, crowd in, and it is not even easy to concentrate on the five saints by Andrea del Sarto on the pilasters of the presbytery.

The Camposanto suffered gravely in 1944. It is lined with a notable series of funerary monuments, including that of the connoisseur Count Francesco Algarotti, paid for by Frederick the Great of Prussia, and a large number of classical sarcophagi, as well as a vase in Parian marble, the figure of Dionysius which was used by Nicola in his pulpit in the Baptistery. The murals are of yet greater interest. Francesco Traini's *Triumph of Death* and *Last Judgement* were the most arresting achievements of the greatest Pisan painter of the Trecento. By contrast, the scenes from the Old Testament by Benozzo Gozzoli strained even that discursive master's narrative abilities.

Pisa is well endowed with churches, the Dominican Santa Catarina, with notable Trecento sculpture and painting, now rather outshining the rivals' San Francesco, although this contains an impressive *Baptism* by Jacopo da Empoli. At the heart of the northern section of the city, on Piazza dei Cavalieri, is San Stefano dei Cavalieri, planned by Vasari as the church of the Order of Knights of San Stefano founded by Cosimo I. Banners taken from the Turks are ranged on the walls. Continuing southwards you reach the Arno, lined by houses that have changed relatively little since the early nineteenth century when Byron and other English visitors were drawn to the city. On the opposite bank, near the Ponte Solferino, is the quintessential monument of the Pisan Gothic, Santa Maria della Spina of 1323. Wholly harmonious in detail, this must always have seemed exiguous beside the great river.

On the north bank by the east end of the Lungarno Mediceo is the Museo Nazionale di San Matteo. Here, as nowhere else, you can survey the evolution of painting at Pisa. For the Pisano did not function in isolation. Nicola's older contemporary, Giunta Pisano, was the great protagonist of Dugento painting in central Italy, and his signed *Crucifix* is a work of capital significance. His followers are comprehensively represented. Pisa's relative economic eclipse in the Trecento was reflected in that of local painters, and so the great masterpieces in the collection henceforward tend to be by outsiders; among these are the Sienese Simone Martini's pentaptych of 1319 and the *Saint Paul* from Masaccio's altarpece of 1426 from Santa Maria del Carmine.

Like other great Italian cities, Pisa did not exist in isolation. The finest church in the vicinity, some five kilometres south-west, is the Romanesque San Piero di Grado, which marks the spot where Saint Peter disembarked. The isolated setting means that there is nothing to disturb our appreciation of the intelligent use of contrasting tufo and black and white stone from nearby San Giuliano, and the sharp detail of the mouldings. On the flank of the hills to the east of the city is the Certosa di Pisa, largely rebuilt in the Seicento and nobly positioned. Staying regularly nearby at Agnano, I developed an exaggerated affection for the Napoleonic aqueduct that brought water to the city.

41

VOLTERRA

❖

OTHER Italian cities cling to ridges; Volterra straddles a mountain top, dominating the cascading ridges and balze of the hinterland. The site perfectly fulfilled the requirements of the Etruscans, whose city of Velathri was defended by walls, some seven kilometres in circuit, that enclosed both the high ground, which would be occupied by the medieval town, and the three ridges descending to the north. Stretches of the walls survive. Roman Volaterrae was also a place of some consequence, as the theatre tucked under the medieval wall near the Porta Fiorentina reminds us. The medieval commune contended with neighbouring San Gimignano and was first briefly occupied by the Florentines in 1254. But it was only in 1472 that Volterra became a Florentine dependency, of which the formidable fortress at the east angle of the city is only the most obvious statement.

Why Volterra mattered to Lorenzo il Magnifico and his successors is self-evident however Volterra is approached. On the road up from Pentedera there are tantalizing glimpses. While it may be easier to park near the Porta Fiorentina, I prefer to enter from the west at the Porta San Francesco. Just within the gate, to the left, is the Franciscan church, austere and bare, but to the right is the large Cappella della Croce di Giorno, frescoed in 1410 by Cenni di Francesco with scenes from the life of Christ and the story of the True Cross. Cenni was little more than an efficient follower of Agnolo Gaddi, but he rose to the challenge; we are left in no

San Francesco. Cenni di Francesco, Massacre of the Innocents, fresco (detail).

doubt that the Innocents were massacred and that Saint Helena did find the right Cross.

The Via San Lino rises steeply to the heart of the city. At an obvious fork, take the right-hand street for the irregular Piazza San Giovanni. The fine Romanesque façade of the Duomo masks a very successful sixteenth-century internal reconstruction. Albertinelli's *Annunciation* apart – memorable for what is perhaps the most beautiful of his landscapes – the lateral altarpieces are by later sixteenth-century masters, including a gifted local man, Niccolò Circignani, a suave Florentine, Santi di Tito, and a gifted northerner, Pieter de Witte, il Candido. Opposite the Duomo is the thirteenth-century octagonal Baptistery, with a font by Andrea Sansovino. Some way behind the Duomo is the Piazza dei Priori, most notable for the Palazzo dei Priori, completed in 1254, ironically the year of the first Florentine occupation.

The best views of the palazzo's tower and the campanile of the Duomo are from the Parco Archeologico at the high point of the hill, with the eroded remains of the Etruscan acropolis. The immense accumulation of Etruscan material excavated at Volterra is shown in the Museo Etrusco on the Via Don Minzoni in the shadow of the Fortezza.

Guaranteed by that emphatic complex, the prosperity of Medicean rule is implied by the many palaces of the city. That of the Inghirami, patrons of Raphael, is just below the archaeological park, but there are many more. One, the Palazzo Viti in the Via dei Sarti, is now open to the public. Near this is the former Palazzo Minucci, which now houses the Pinacoteca Comunale. There are fine late Gothic altarpieces by Taddeo di Bartolo, the most forceful Sienese master of the early Quattrocento, and his near contemporary, Alvaro Portoghese, who adapted to Florentine taste. The late

Quattrocento Sienese Benvenuto di Giovanni responds to the balze west of the town in the grey and white landscape of his Nativity. Of the three altarpieces supplied for the town by the Cortonese Luca Signorelli, two are here – the third is in London. No Italian of his time painted books with greater enthusiasm, so it is entirely characteristic that the Virgin in his chromatically charged Annunciation has dropped hers. To modern taste Signorelli is outshone by Rosso Fiorentino, whose deeply emotional Deposition can be read as an inspired rejection of the altarpiece recently supplied by Signorelli's erstwhile associate, Perugino, for Santissima Annunziata in Florence, where Rosso had worked in the atrium. After looking at a great masterpiece it is difficult to attend to less clamant pictures. But do not pass by the Deposition or the Nativity by Pietro Candido: both perfectly express the pyrotechnical brilliance as a colourist that were to stand him in such stead as a designer of tapestries at the court in Munich in the late sixteenth century.

Pinacoteca Civica: Luca Signorelli, Annunciation (detail), 1491.

42
SAN GIMIGNANO

❖

SAN GIMIGNANO is the paradigm of a medieval Tuscan city. The walls are intact and we still enter through the original gates; the defensive towers of local families which were obsolete even before the imposition of Florentine rule between 1348 and 1354 bristle like porcupine quills on the hill that was settled in early times. Named after a bishop of Modena, San Gimignano had become a free commune in the twelfth century. As in other Tuscan cities, the struggle between Guelf and Ghibelline was prolonged. Commercial links with Siena were strong in the fourteenth century and their artistic ramifications can still be experienced.

Much of the fabric of the medieval town survives. At its heart is the Piazza della Cisterna, flanked by a number of early houses and linked to the irregular Piazza del Duomo, which is dominated by the loggia'd Palazzo del Podestà, begun in 1239 and enlarged in 1337, by the restrained front of the Collegiata and by the towering Palazzo del Popolo, started in 1288, extended in 1323, and now the monument in which we are closest to the pulse of the medieval city. Communal pride is clearly expressed in the so-called Sala di Dante, where the poet urged the city fathers to adhere to a league of Tuscan Guelfs in 1300. The room is dominated by Lippo Memmi's *Maestà* of 1317, which follows the pattern of Simone Martini's fresco in the corresponding position in Siena; the lateral sections were tactfully restored by Benozzo Gozzoli in 1467. The Pinacoteca

Civica is housed in the palace. The roundels of the *Annunciation* by Filippino Lippi are breathtakingly beautiful, and are placed on either side of the miraculously preserved tempera panel of the *Madonna and Child with Saints* by Pintoricchio. Most tourists rush by, intent on climbing the tower, which offers an unequalled view of the town.

The Collegiata is now entered from the courtyard to the south, through a vaulted loggia with a fresco of the *Annunciation* by Sebastiano Mainardi, Ghirlandaio's brother-in-law and pupil. The cruciform interior is notable for its frescoes. On the wall of the right aisle is the prodigious sequence of scenes from the *Passion of Christ* which are traditionally attributed to Barna da Siena. Probably of before 1340, these are the grandest achievements of mid-Trecento Sienese painting. For Barna's lyricism of line was matched by his narrative acuity and interest in emotion. On the opposite, left, wall is the slightly later cycle of Old Testament scenes by the most forceful and compositionally innovative of Barna's immediate successors, Bartolo di Fredi. The entrance wall was decorated in 1465 by Gozzoli, whose *Saint Sebastian*, punctured by no fewer than thirty-six arrows, is flanked by pigmented statues of c.1421 representing the *Annunciation* by Jacopo della Quercia; Gozzoli's respect for these is implied by the fictive settings he devised for them. San Gimignano boasted its own saint, Fina. Her chapel, the last on the right, decorated by Ghirlandaio, is a perfect statement of disciplined late Quattrocento taste.

Despite the tourists and the shops catering for them, linger in the Via San Matteo, to the north of the Piazza del Duomo, which is lined with medieval houses. Before the Porta San Matteo turn

Sant'Agostino:
Benozzo Gozzoli,
Crucifixion, fresco,
1464.

to the right for the austere barn-like church of Sant'Agostino. Gozzoli's frescoes of the life of the saint in the choir are particularly well preserved. He is an engaging artist with a genius for anecdote, and it no doubt suited him to work for patrons whose taste was somewhat outmoded by Florentine standards. He also decorated an altar on the left wall of the church with a mural of *Saint Sebastian* and, below this, a small fictive devotional panel of the *Crucifixion*. The high altarpiece, the *Coronation of the Virgin*, is by Piero del Pollaiuolo, younger and weaker brother of Antonio, here straining at the limits of his abilities.

The supply of water is essential to any town, and San Gimignano was no exception. The Porta dei Fonti leads downhill to the Fonti, a medieval arcaded structure built against the hillside, with, at a lower level, a further arcaded basin. Where women once came for water and to contend with their laundry, an abandoned Vespa is now the only sign of life.

Palazzo Pubblico, with the arms of the Medici and the badge of San Bernardino.

43
SIENA

MOST visitors approach Siena from the north – the road from Florence – their sense of anticipation heightened by the sight of her great fortress of Monteriggioni, thrown up in 1203 to repel the Florentines. But it is from the south that one has the most memorable views of the city. High in the centre is the great campanile of the Duomo, below it, to the east, the elegant Torre del Mangia of the Palazzo Pubblico. Other churches can be seen above the tremendous circuit of the walls that defined the limits of the early town and defended what was in artistic terms perhaps the most self-sufficient centre of the early Renaissance.

This artistic individuality reflected the political position. Although of Etruscan origin, Siena only became a place of importance in the early medieval period. Long the rival of Florence, Siena was a major commercial and banking centre that jealously preserved her independence and republican institutions. Pandolfo Petrucci gained power in 1487, but his sons failed to ensure the succession and in 1530 Siena fell to the army of Emperor Charles V. In 1552 the city rebelled against his son, King Philip II of Spain. After a long siege, Siena surrendered in 1555, to be granted in 1559 to Cosimo I, Grand Duke of Tuscany. Medici rule was moderately benign, but Siena's enduring medieval character owes much to the fact that she became a backwater.

The fan-shaped Piazza del Campo is at the heart of the town. The great façade of the Palazzo Pubblico, begun in 1297, is, as it were, the stage set of a wide theatre, its audience the façades of the palaces on the circumference. It was in the piazza that San Bernardino preached his austere message in the mid-fifteenth century, and it is there that the annual drama of that great historic Sienese event, the Palio – or horse race – is still played out. The saint's badge is seen above the arms of the Medici on the Palazzo Pubblico, which despite the risk of crowds must be visited. In the vast Sala del Mappamondo are two defining masterpieces of Simone Martini, his frescoed *Maestà* and the extraordinary equestrian portrait of the condottiero Guidoriccio Fogliani silhouetted against an undulating horizon of hills punctuated by bristling fortresses. Equally remarkable are the frescoes of Simone's contemporary, Ambrogio Lorenzetti, in the Sala della Pace. That of *Good Government* celebrates the life of the medieval commune: the town is ordered, its territory peaceful and productive. No earlier Sienese landscape offers so compelling a portrait of contemporary agriculture. The fresco of *Bad Government* is, of course, altogether different in mood – a stark warning of the consequences of anarchy.

As the palazzo was the centre of communal rule, so the Duomo, higher to the west, best approached by one of the narrow streets above the Via di Città, was at the heart of its religious life. The striped Gothic structure must always have impressed those who saw it. It does so still, although the façade sculptures by Giovanni Pisano have been moved to the nearby museum, the Opera del Duomo, and are replaced by copies. After seeing the façades of the cathedral and the incomplete skeleton of what was intended as the nave of its successor, it makes sense to visit the Opera del Duomo. For this now houses most of the components of the epicentral masterpiece of medieval Siena, the *Maestà* of Duccio di Buoninsegna. This double-sided altarpiece was installed on the high altar of the cathedral on 9 June 1311. The *Madonna and Child* with numerous saints, raised on a predella, faced the body of the church; on the reverse were scenes from the life of Christ. No Sienese painter for over a century evaded the influence of the *Maestà*. And it is not difficult to see why. For in this prodigious complex Duccio codified a religious language which owed much to his immediate local predecessors – whose achievement is only now being recognized – and to Byzantine influence, but nonetheless was without precedent in its visual coherence and narrative force. While Duccio did not himself paint all the subsidiary panels and pinnacles, he exercised so close a control over those who did that their individual contributions cannot be determined.

The interior of the cathedral is as arresting as the façade, with the massive banded piers of the hexagonal crossing. Despite the removal of the *Maestà* – and of Giuseppe Mazzuoli's baroque sculptures of the Apostles now in London's Brompton Oratory – the riches of the cathedral continue to astonish. And it is altogether impossible to do justice to these in a hurry. The building is vast, its scale only emphasized by the attentions the Sienese lavished upon it. The wonderful pulpit of 1265–8 in white marble is by Nicola Pisano and represents a development from its precursor in the Pisan Baptistery. The remarkable stained glass of

Cathedral: Francesco di Giorgio, pavement border.

the central rose window was designed by Duccio himself.

Not content with adorning walls, the Sienese decorated the pavement of the cathedral with compositions of inlaid marble. Usually covered, the pavement is now visible for two months from mid-August. The earliest sections are of 1369 and many major artists were involved, including Francesco di Giorgio Martini, Matteo di Giovanni and Neroccio di Bartolomeo Landi, the protagonists of late Quattrocento Sienese art. The designers were responsible not only for their compositions but also for the borders framing these, of which those by Francesco di Giorgio are particularly satisfying. Their High Renaissance successor, Domenico

Beccafumi, made a virtue of the challenge the medium imposed: his sections of the pavement, including the *Moses striking the Rock* and the wonderfully animated decorative friezes, exploit its linear potential to the full. Beccafumi, like other Sienese masters, was versatile. His bronze statues of angels in the choir – with their bases of masks of men with flowing hair – are of a compelling plasticity.

The left aisle of the Duomo is particularly rich. The Petrucci apart, no Sienese family could match the Piccolomini, two of whom became popes, Pius II (1458–64) and Pius III (1503); their altar in the fourth bay is by the Roman sculptor Andrea Bregno, but three of the statues,

Saints Gregory, Paul and Peter, are by the youthful Michelangelo (1501–11). It was indeed at Siena that Michelangelo and his younger contemporary Raphael were first in indirect competition. Immediately beyond the altar is the entrance to the Piccolomini Library, commissioned by Francesco Piccolomini to celebrate the career of his uncle, Pope Pius II. The vast frescoes are by the Perugian Benedetto Betti, il Pinturicchio, but, as surviving drawings establish, at least two were designed by Raphael. The compositions are seen through a trompe l'oeil loggia in a perspective that allows for the height at which these are placed. Pinturicchio's star has faded since the Victorian era but his narrative gifts have rarely been surpassed. Of equal interest are the illuminated miniatures on display in the cabinets below. These have no rivals of their date, the 1460s, and are by two outstanding north Italian masters, Liberale da Verona and Girolamo da Cremona. Of the two, Liberale is the more emotionally intense, Girolamo the more cerebral and conscious of the classicism of Mantegna's generation.

Leaving the cathedral, follow its east side and go down the splendid flight of steps to the Baptistery. The façade is more austere than that of the cathedral, the interior unexpectedly high. In the font, begun in 1417 by Jacopo della Quercia, one can see how the late Gothic dissolves into the classicism of the early Renaissance. Although only a decade separated Jacopo's *Expulsion of Zaccarias* from the companion reliefs by his younger Florentine contemporaries Ghiberti and Donatello, the significance of the intellectual revolution they represented is not in doubt.

South-west of the piazza, on the Via di San Pietro, is the Pinacoteca Nazionale.

Modern notions of display have not been allowed to disturb traditional arrangements. The collection of Sienese pictures has no rival. Duccio's tiny *Madonna dei Francescani* is followed by significant groups of pictures by Simone Martini and the Lorenzetti and their later fourteenth-century successors. The Quattrocento is represented in depth, with rooms devoted to Sassetta and that idiosyncratic visionary, Giovanni di Paolo; to Sano di Pietro, the most productive native master of the mid-century; to the languorous Madonnas of Matteo di Giovanni and to the lyrical Neroccio. High Renaissance Siena was no backwater. Sodoma, who arrived from Lombardy, was by any standard a major artist, while Beccafumi was a magician both in his lyricism of line and in his use of colour. Spare a moment, too, for their contemporary Girolamo del Pacchia's beautifully expressed *Visitation*.

Proceeding south from the Pinacoteca, the road emerges before the much-reconstructed church of San Domenico. On an altar on the right is Perugino's *Crucifixion* of 1506, commissioned by the powerful Sienese banker Agostino Chigi, while in the Cappella Piccolomini is what has some claim to be Sodoma's masterpiece, his *Adoration of the Magi*. The only other Sienese altarpiece of the time still in situ that rivals it is in San Martino, south of the east corner of the Campo: Beccafumi's *Nativity*, which is of a breathtaking beauty, visionary in design and thrilling in chromatic range.

At San Martino you may be alone. This will not be the case in the sanctuary of Saint Catherine to the north-west of the city. The saint died in 1380 and her house was adapted as a shrine in 1464. As John Addington Symonds observed, the sanctuary preserves much of its orig-

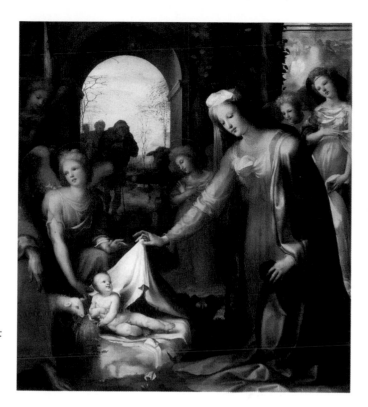

San Martino:
Domenico
Beccafumi,
Nativity
(detail).

inal character – and on that account alone is a remarkable survival. In the Upper Oratory are a series of pictures of the life of the saint by the most gifted masters of late sixteenth-century Siena, including Francesco Vanni, whose *Canonization of Saint Catherine* perfectly exemplifies his delicate taste.

Many of Siena's major churches lie at or near the extremities of the original urban area: Santa Maria del Carmine with Beccafumi's *Saint Michael*; Santa Maria dei Servi with the impressive *Madonna del Bordone* of 1261 by Coppo di Marcovaldo; austere San Francesco; its more splendid counterpart, San Domenico, high on the ridge above the medieval Fonte Branda,

with a constellation of early altarpieces and Sodoma's persuasive *Saint Catherine in Ecstasy*; and, opposite the cathedral, Santa Maria della Scala, which boasts the outstanding sculpture of mid-Quattrocento Siena, Lorenzo Vecchietta's moving bronze of the *Risen Christ* of 1476, placed alas too high for its subtlety to be easily appreciated. All are worth visiting, not least for the pleasure of walking through the city. So, below San Domenico, is the medieval Fonte Branda. Changes of level mean that almost every turn discloses an unexpected view of medieval brickwork or the façade of a Renaissance palazzo, with so often at least a glimpse of open country in the distance.

44

PIENZA

❧

THE Piccolomini family held the village of Corsignano, spectacularly placed on a long hill, in still untrammelled country between the towns of San Quirico – on the Roman Via Cassia south of Siena – and Montepulciano. Enea Silvio Piccolomini was born there in 1405; humanist, poet and diplomat, he was elected to the papacy in 1458, taking the name Pius II. Within a year his project to transform the place into a modern city, renamed in his honour, was begun under the direction of the Florentine architect Bernardo Rossellino. The project was far from finished at the pope's death in 1464, but Pienza remains the finest fifteenth-century planned city in Italy.

The approach is from the west – the road from both Siena and Rome. The Via del Corso leads to the central piazza, with a well of 1462 by Rossellino. On the right is the façade of the cathedral, which was completed in the same year. This is flanked by the episcopal palace adapted for Cardinal Rodrigo Borgia, the future Pope Alexander VI, and the Palazzo Piccolomini, built between 1459 and 1463 by Rossellino in the most up-to-date Florentine mode; opposite are the much-restored Palazzo Comunale and the palace built for the pope's friend, Cardinal Giacomo Ammannati.

The cathedral replaced a Romanesque priory. Like so much Sienese architecture and painting of its period – 1459–62 – this is still Gothic in taste. The structure was too massive for the site and buttresses were needed to support the choir, which was built out to the very extremity of the hill. The interior is restrained,

Bernardo Rossellino, Palazzo Piccolomini, 1459–63.

with elegant choir stalls, again of 1462, also of Gothic form. The five altarpieces were all painted in Siena between 1461 and 1463. The most remarkable is in the chapel to the left of the high altar, Vecchietta's *Assumption of the Virgin*. Sculptor-cum-painter Vecchietta was an artist of deep originality, aware of, but not over-awed by, the achievement of Florentine contemporaries. The other altarpieces are more conventional. One is by the consistently individual Giovanni di Paolo, another by that most predictable Sienese master of the age, Sano di Pietro, and two are relatively early works of Matteo di Giovanni, who was to influence most of the emergent Sienese artists of the next generation. Seen together in their proper setting, the five pictures offer a microcosm of Sienese painting of the period.

The episcopal palace now houses the Museo Diocesano. The great treasure is the fourteenth-century *opus anglicanum* cope presented to the Duomo by the pope and now named after him. England was famous for her medieval embroidery, and the Pienza cope, with its scenes from the lives of Saints Catherine of Alexandria and Margaret of Antioch and of the Virgin, shows why. The vigorous detail parallels that of contemporary illuminated manuscripts. Pictures include an exceptionally well-preserved *Madonna* by Pietro Lorenzetti and an impeccable early triptych by Sano di Pietro.

Had Pius II reigned longer more palaces would have been constructed by favoured cardinals. As it is, there is a happy contrast between the buildings at the heart of the city which he willed into existence and the more modest houses lining the main street. There are marvellous views over the surrounding country, where, alas, traditional methods of agriculture are in retreat.

Two nearby churches deserve to be seen. The unassuming Romanesque Pieve di Corsignano – with the font in which Pius II was christened – is a kilometre or so to the west. Rather further, north of the road to San Quirico, is the monastery of Sant'Anna in Camprena. Opening times are capricious, but if they can be seen, the spirited frescoes by Sodoma more than justify the detour.

Museo Diocesano: Sano di Pietro, Saint Catherine of Alexandria *(detail of triptych).*

45

SANT'ANTIMO

❖

SANT'ANTIMO must be the most luminous Romanesque church in Italy. The Benedictine abbey may not have been founded, as was long believed, by Charlemagne, but is first recorded in 813. Set in a narrowing valley just west of the pilgrim route to Rome, the Via Francigena, that followed the ancient Via Cassia, the abbey became exceedingly rich in the early medieval period.

First seen across fields, the church with its beautiful apse and tall companile makes an indelible impression. Begun in 1117, it is built of travertine enriched with alabaster from nearby Castelnuovo. The west front is austere, the central door opening to the nave which is flanked by columns of varying size, with fine capi-tals; the finest of these, the second on the right, represents *Daniel in the Lions' Den*. Particularly in the morning, the light draws us forwards. The presbytery is set within an ambulatory with three radiating chapels, a scheme implying a knowledge of the great abbey at Cluny. But there is no such precedent for the liberal use of alabaster, the translucence of which gives the ambulatory a magical quality. To the south is the sacristy, overlying the crypt of the earlier ninth-century church; opposite is a smaller cruciform space within the lower stage of the campanile.

Many early churches in Italy have been ruthlessly restored. This is not the case at Sant'Antimo, because the monastery fell into decline and was suppressed by that most civilized of popes, Pius II, in 1462. As a result neither the Renaissance nor the baroque left its mark, and little survives of the monastic buildings. So the great church stands in unintended isolation.

Sant'Antimo
from the east.

46

AREZZO

❖

AREZZO is a confident city. Its ancient core, the successor of the Umbrian and Roman Arretium, descends the west-facing slope of an outlier of the hills to the east. The town is at the intersection of ancient routes – that from the north from the Valdarno running southwards down the side of the Val di Chiana, and the road across the mountains from the Adriatic – and Arezzo was the natural entrepôt of a productive agricultural area.

The approach from the west is not prepossessing. For the walls now protect the city from the enemy of our times, intensive development. The driver should use one of the car parks outside the southern section of the wall, and cut across to the central Corso Italia. The tourist with limited time will rush on to San Francesco. But the secret of sightseeing is to make time. So I would begin with the beautiful and well-restored Santa Maria della Pieve, on the right of the street, a paradigm of the Tuscan Romanesque with its tiers of columns, its tympanum and its splendid detached campanile. The interior does not disappoint. The high altar – with an admirable and appropriate polyptych by Pietro Lorenzetti – is raised above a generous crypt. Leave by the side door to see the external treatment of the apse from the Piazza Grande.

Continue up the Corso Italia, passing the shield-studded Palazzo Pretorio, and follow round to the Via Ricasoli with the lateral façade of the cathedral on the right. This major Gothic building has also been restored. Few Italian churches are richer in early sculpture, and none perhaps boasts finer early sixteenth-century glass than the sequence of windows of 1520–6 by the French-born Guglielmo de Marcillat. Piero della Francesca's static *Saint Margaret* is on the left wall by the door to the sacristy, in one of the rooms of which is a detached fresco of *Saint Jerome in the Wilderness* by an outstanding local artist of the following generation, Bartolomeo della Gatta. Bartolomeo never disappoints. Saint Jerome is set in his rock-strewn vision of the desert of Calchis.

The importance of Arezzo to the Medici is implied by the statue of Grand Duke Ferdinando I beside the cathedral; designed by Giambologna, it was executed by his assistant, Pietro Francavilla.

Cathedral: Bartolommeo della Gatta, Saint Jerome, *fresco (detail).*

Continue northwards and take the first turn to the right for the least well known of the great churches of Arezzo, San Domenico. The front offers no hint of what is within, an unrivalled series of murals by Aretine masters of the late medieval period, notably Spinello Aretino and his son Parri Spinelli. Spinello is unfailingly efficient, while Parri evolved an idiosyncratic Gothic idiom suggesting an obstinate indifference to the artistic preoccupations of his Tuscan contemporaries. The greatest work of art in the church, suspended above the choir, is the Crucifix by Cimabue, one of the signal masterpieces of the late Dugento.

On leaving the church, turn right and take the second street on the left. Almost immediately on the right is the Casa di Vasari, where works by the Aretine writer-cum-artist have been assembled. There are further pictures by Vasari in the Museo Civico just to the right of the further end of the street. The museum also houses one of the finest public collections of maiolica in Italy. Diagonally opposite the museum is the Via Cavour. Follow this, passing a small piazza with the church of Santissima Annunziata, with an external fresco of the subject by Spinello, and the Badia, with a high altar by Vasari that was originally in the Pieve, for the piazza of San Francesco.

Arezzo-centric as Vasari was in the *Vite*, which has left its mark on all later accounts of early Italian art, he would be surprised by our reverence for Piero della Francesca. San Francesco is an austere barn of a church. Flanked by lateral chapels is the choir. Lorenzo di Bicci had been called in to decorate it in 1447, but fortunately had only completed the vault when he died in 1452. Piero was subsequently called in. His was a rare intelligence. He understood what he could achieve and what he could not, and how the play of light could infuse his nobly static forms. The legend of the True Cross is related in three tiers of compartments flanking the central window and on the lateral walls, which are visually anchored in their setting by the vividly coloured fictive marble facings below. Influenced in youth by Fra Angelico, Piero was an artist of conviction: the Virgin accepts the announcement of her impending death from the Angel with an impassive composure; the Emperor Constantine dreams, oblivious of his servants; and the Queen of Sheba's bearing is echoed by the deportment of her attendants. We witness the melée of two battles, with the trampling of hoofs and the lowering of lances; we see the resolve of the just victors and the fear of the fallen, yet share the painter's detachment from them. Like other of the greatest artists, Piero carried his style to its logical conclusion. As one can see elsewhere in the church, his example certainly overwhelmed his follower Lorentino; it must also have puzzled Vasari, and evoked little wider interest until the mid-nineteenth century. Piero's reputation now rests on his very restraint, on the subtle logic of his compositional architecture, and above all on the classic integrity of his types.

47
CORTONA

✣

THE old road south from Arezzo follows the line below the hills that flank the Val di Chiana. This passes the town of Castiglion Fiorentino and the spectacular castle of Montecchio Vesponi, once owned by the English *condottiero* Sir John Hawkwood. Then the ancient city of Cortona comes into view. The main road twists up the hillside, passing the greatest of the Cortonese villas, built for Cardinal Silvio Passerini. It is no longer possible to drive through the Porta San Domenico, so the motorist should follow round the town walls to the left, your reward a

splendid section of Etruscan polygonal masonry. A short walk from the Porta Colonia leads to the Piazza del Duomo.

The cathedral itself is not particularly remarkable, but the Museo Diocesano in the former church of the Gesù opposite most certainly is. Among Tuscan museums of the kind, only that at Asciano, admittedly much smaller, boasts so high a proportion of masterpieces. Fra Angelico's *Annunciation* from the church of San Domenico is indisputably the finest of his several altarpieces of the subject. The Angel is inexorable in his message, the Virgin perfect in her submission to this. The predella too is of the utmost refinement; in the *Visitation* the painter shows the view from the town, with hills to the left, the level valley on the right and in the distance Lake Trasimene. The frate's

Museo Diocesano: Fra Angelico, Saint Dominic raising Napoleone Orsini, *predella panel (detail).*

own monastery was associated with San Domenico, for which he also supplied a polyptych, which happily survives with its predella. Cortona had for over a century turned to Sienese painters, including Pietro Lorenzetti. This tradition was represented by the polyptych of the mid-1430s, also from San Domenico, by Sassetta. He was well aware of the challenge posed by Fra Angelico and rose to it with his innate poetic conviction.

The Cortonese could claim no artistic school of their own. The sculptor of the font by the *Annunciation*, which used to be attributed to the wonderfully named Ciuccio di Nuccio, would hardly have been employable in Florence. But the town can boast one painter of genius, Luca Signorelli. Downstairs is a room with a significant group of late altarpieces by him, the finest his *Deposition of*

1502. Nearby is the remarkable cope with embroidery designed in 1525 for Cardinal Passerini by no less an artist than Andrea del Sarto. The frescoes in the lower church were an early project of the Aretine Giorgio Vasari, who in his childhood had known Signorelli.

There is much to see in the town. The Accademia Etrusca in its eighteenth-century heyday received self-portraits from Zoffany and Northcote. Although Fra Angelico's altarpieces have gone, there is a frescoed lunette by him at San Domenico. And the church contains an exceptionally complete late Gothic altarpiece by Lorenzo di Niccolò – supplied second-hand by the Medici – as well as a masterpiece of Signorelli's early collaborator, Bartolomeo della Gatta. The *Assumption of the Virgin*, like the frescoed *Saint Jerome* of the cathedral at Arezzo,

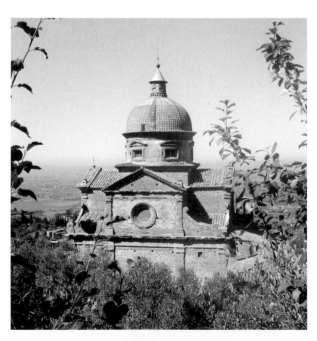

*Giorgio Vasari,
Santa Maria Nuova.*

shows that Bartolomeo came close to being a painter of genius.

The energetic can walk uphill, passing several small palaces and a good bust of one of the Tomassoni, for porticoed San Niccolò with its *Dead Christ with Saints* by Signorelli, simple yet of power. Higher still is the ugly sanctuary of Santa Margarita of Cortona, redeemed by the saint's sculptured tomb of 1362 and by a late masterpiece of the Sienese Counter-Reformation, Francesco Vanni's visionary *Immaculate Conception*. At the apex of the hill is the well-named Castel del Girifalco (gyrfalcon).

Below the walls of the town, respectively to the south and the north, are two domed churches, Santa Maria del Calcinaio (lime-worker) and Santa Maria Nuova. The former, of Latin cross plan, was begun in 1485, apparently to the design of that most versatile of Sienese artists, Francesco di Giorgio; with its crumbling pietra serena enrichments, this exemplifies the controlled classicism of the late Quattrocento. Santa Maria Nuova, by contrast, is centrally planned. The design was due to Vasari, but the executant mason was a local man, Cristoforo Infregliati. Built in 1550–4, the church deserves to be open more regularly than it is. Foundations of the kind mushroomed in the area during the Renaissance, as towns competed to commemorate miraculous visions like that of the Cortonese lime-worker who saw an image of the Virgin. Externally by far the most impressive is the Bramantesque Santa Maria della Consolazione below Todi, but this, alas, was only completed internally after a long interval. Sangallo's San Biagio outside Montepulciano is much larger than either of the miracle churches at Cortona, yet lacks their charm.

48

LA VERNA

❖

THE religious have always been drawn to remote places, and the visitor to Tuscany should try to see some of the monasteries that made so important a contribution to spiritual life. South-east of Florence, on the flank of the Pratomagno, is Vallombrosa, which gave its name to the monastic order instituted by San Giovanni Gualberto and haunted the imagination of Milton. Across the hills to the east is Camaldoli, where the order of that name was founded by Saint Romuald. Further south is La Verna, then a wild fastness, to which Saint Francis withdrew in the company of Fra Elia (Brother Elias), who witnessed his stigmatization there on 17 September 1224.

The main approaches from Bibbiena and Pieve Santo Stefano climb steeply, for the mountain is 1,283 metres high. It takes its name from the dense woodland that crowns the Monte Penna. Inevitably La Verna became a place of pilgrimage, and this it very much remains, with a cluster of small buildings often crowded with the devout.

The visitor now enters through an arch and follows a passage, eventually arriving in the irregular central court by the main church. Cross this to the modest gate to which pilgrims formerly climbed. Their first sight on entering, ahead and to the right, was the small church of Santa Maria degli Angeli, first built in 1216–18 by Count Orlando dei Cattani, who had given the mountain to Saint Francis. The interior is subdivided by lateral altars with polychrome glazed

Chiesa Maggiore: Andrea della Robbia, Annunciation, *glazed terracotta.*

terracotta reliefs by Giovanni della Robbia that contrast with the restrained tonality of Andrea della Robbia's main altarpiece of the *Virgin entrusting her Girdle to Saint Thomas.* To the right of the church is a corridor that leads to the small museum, with a handful of pictures and a collection of vestments. The processional route continued to the Chiesa Maggiore, begun in 1348. Nowhere perhaps is Andrea della Robbia, the gifted son of his father Luca, seen to better effect. The grandest of his reliefs in the church is the *Ascension,* but Andrea's genius as a religious artist is more perfectly expressed in two ostensibly less ambitious compositions, the *Adoration* and the *Annunciation,* in both of which his disciplined palette, predominately of blue and white, is particularly successful.

From the chapel the pilgrim proceeds through the Corridor of the Stigmata to the small Chapel of the Stigmata dominated by the glazed altarpiece of the *Crucifixion* by Andrea della Robbia that has some claim to be his masterpiece. Certainly this is among the most compelling religious images of its time.

La Verna remains a place of rare beauty, not least in September when the woods are carpeted with pale pink cyclamen. It has, too, an unexpected magic when mist shrouds the unpretending buildings.

49
BORGO SAN SEPOLCRO

❧

THE most northerly major town of the Tiber Valley, Borgo San Sepolcro lies at the junction of two great historic routes, that from the Romagna in the north to Perugia and eventually to Rome, and the road that crosses the Trabaria Pass to the east, linking the Adriatic coast with the Tuscan heartland. Fought over by local families and powers, and controlled by the papacy for much of the fifteenth century, the town was a major prize when it fell to Florence in 1515.

Massive fortifications attest to Borgo's importance as a frontier fortress. That the town had long acclimatized itself to Florentine taste is demonstrated by the career of its outstanding artist, Piero della Francesca, whose mentors were Fra Angelico and Masaccio. Piero, so long overlooked, has now been a cult figure for almost a century. His sphere of activity was, to a remarkable extent, dictated by geography. His major commissions were all for places in direct reach of his native town: Rome and Perugia to the south, Ferrara to the north, Arezzo to the west, and to the east Urbino and Rimini. Furthermore, Piero's Riminese patron, Sigismondo Malatesta, obtained Citerna – hardly ten kilometres from Borgo – which overhangs the cemetery of Monterchi, from which Piero's fresco of the *Madonna del Parto* was recently hijacked by the authorities of that town. The prodigious fresco cycle at Arezzo is his grandest achievement. Yet it is surely at Borgo San Sepolcro that he is best understood.

The Palazzo Comunale is sadly no longer entered from the Via Matteotti but from a side door. The visitor is advised to move briskly through the first rooms. Piero's polyptych of the *Madonna della Misericordia* was an early commission, although it was not completed until about 1460. The Madonna is of an elevated beauty, and the spectator was not intended to doubt that the citizens and their women who sheltered beneath the mantle were right to trust to her protection. The flanking saints have, perhaps, a more tentative quality, and certainly lack the tension of the *Crucifixion* which originally surmounted the Madonna and is now at Naples. But it was only in the predella that Piero subcontracted to assistants.

The *Resurrection* is the symbol of Borgo San Sepolcro – the observant will already have noticed Niccolò di Segna's Ducciesque interpretation of this in his polyptych in an earlier room. Piero's cel-

Pinacoteca Comunale: Piero della Francesca, Resurrection, *fresco (detail), c. 1463.*

ebrated fresco of the subject thus had an especial significance for his townsmen. Our eye moves upwards from the sleeping soldiers to Christ. He rises, as if by an inexorable force, from the sarcophagus, his face at once impassive and serene. Behind stretches the landscape that Piero knew so well, living and verdant on the right, desiccated like that he would have seen on the Bocca Trabaria to the left. Inexorable in logic and timeless in message, the Resurrection is Piero's absolute masterpiece.

Dazed, and perhaps humbled, the tourist leaves. The town has more to offer. Diagonally across the Via Matteotti is the cathedral, with an early copy of the Volto Santo at Lucca, a fine example of the early medieval pigmented wooden sculpture of which so much survives throughout Italy.

Borgo San Sepolcro is laid out on a grid plan. Leaving the cathedral, turn left and keep straight on, until forced a block to the right, passing a particularly fine crumbling palace and other substantial houses. At the opposite side of the town is San Lorenzo, a church that is often closed, but where a nun from the adjacent monastery is usually in attendance.

On the altar is a picture that was as compellingly original as Piero's *Resurrection*, the *Deposition* by that visionary genius of the Florentine High Renaissance, Rosso Fiorentino. Like other major artists of his generation, Rosso gravitated to Rome. When it was sacked by the imperial forces in 1527 he withdrew to Umbria, designing altarpieces for Perugia and the miracle church at Castel Rigone, high above Lake Trasimene, and himself painting that of the cathedral at Città di Castello. The *Deposition* was painted

San Lorenzo: Rosso Fiorentino, Deposition.

in 1528–30. It is a deeply pondered drama, wrought to an extraordinary emotional pitch, for Rosso's charged colour is matched by the intensity of his figures. His was a restless spirit which found a supreme expression in this altarpiece, painted for a relatively obscure setting in a lesser provincial town. We are fortunate that it remains there. For the fervent dynamism of the *Deposition*, reflecting an inner turbulence that must have been sharpened by circumstance, only enhances our understanding of the spiritual confidence of the impassive Resurrection. Both pictures convey that sense of the inevitable which is a characteristic of the very greatest works of art.

Umbria

• Città di
Castello 50

51 Gubbio •

• Perugia 52
• Assisi 54

• Panicale 53
• Città della Pieve 53

55 Montefalco •
Montesanto 56 •

• Orvieto 58
• Spoleto 57

50
CITTÀ DI CASTELLO

❖

THE successor of the ancient Umbrian
Tifernate and the Roman Tibernium,
Città di Castello was a commune, free at
times but at others subject to the papacy,
to Perugia and to Florence. Braccio Fortebraccio of nearby Montone took the
city in 1422 and later the Vitelli family
secured the signoria. Papal suzerainty
was reasserted by Cesare Borgia, but the
Vitelli remained in effective control for
much of the Cinquecento. The place paid
a heavy price during the French occupation, losing Raphael's *Marriage of the Virgin*,
which was taken to Milan, and other
masterpieces. But there is still much to
see within the irregular rectangle of the
brick city walls to the north-east of the
river Tiber.

The civic and religious heart of Città di
Castello is the Piazza Gabriotti. The
Gothic Palazzo Comunale of 1334–52 by
Angelo da Orvieto was never completed,
and is memorable not least because so
much of the eroded rusticated masonry
is original. Beside it is the much-remod-
elled Duomo, with a beautiful Gothic
sculptured portal on the north front
facing the square. The interior was reconstructed during the Renaissance. The
cathedral museum contains the remarkable twelfth-century silver-gilt altar front
associated with Pope Celestine II, as
well as early Christian silver found at
Canoscio. Rosso Fiorentino's visionary
Transfiguration, painted with evident haste
after the Sack of Rome in 1527, formerly
almost inaccessible in the transept, loses
in impact now that it can no longer be
seen from below.

Cathedral, north door (detail), relief of
Mercy.

Just within the southern line of the
town wall is the Palazzo Vitelli alla Can-
noniera, built for Alessandro Vitelli, who
initially called in the younger Sangallo,
between 1521 and 1532; it now houses
the Pinacoteca Comunale. The museum
used to be little visited, and the custodian
got so accustomed to my turning up
alone or with fellow guests that he just
handed me the keys. Things now are very
different. The collection is admirably displayed, and justice is done to some very
remarkable things: the noble *Maestà* by
one of Duccio's most intelligent associates, known appropriately as the Master
of Città di Castello; a fine *Madonna* by
Spinello Aretino; Signorelli's dramatic
Martyrdom of Saint Sebastian; and the standard

that is the only one of the commissions awarded to the young Raphael painted for this to remain in the city. Recent additions include the Ruggieri collection with de Chirico's *Piazza d'Italia*. Much of the original decoration of the palace survives, including a series of accomplished coastal landscapes set in grotteschi by Cristoforo Gherardi, who came from Borgo San Sepolcro, in the salone. The sgraffito decoration of the garden front is a rare survival.

Elegant as the palace is, it was evidently upstaged by the much larger Palazzo Vitelli a Porta Sant'Egidio, the city's main east gate, which was designed for Paolo Vitelli by Vasari. The Bolognese Prospero Fontana was called in to decorate the main salone with appropriately pompous scenes from the history of the family. Altogether more congenial are the murals in a loggia of the annexed Palazzina, now used by a bank whose officials are, at least in my experience, tolerant of sightseers; these also are by Gherardi.

Those who are drawn to the area for the work of Piero della Francesco may wish to see the only signed panel by Giovanni da Piamonte, on the basis of which he has been identified as an assistant of the master at Arezzo. Dated 1456, this shows the *Madonna and Child between Saints Florido and Filippo Benizzi*. Generally covered as an object of veneration, this is in an oratory in the church of Santa Maria delle Grazie in the northern part of the town.

Pinacoteca: Luca Signorelli, Martyrdom of Saint Sebastian (detail), c. 1498.

51

GUBBIO

N O great Italian city is more palpably medieval than Gubbio. The town stands on the southern flank of the Monte Ingino, commanding what must always have been a productive plain. Her Roman past is seen in the much restored theatre below the town and in the Eugubine tablets — laws recorded on sheets of bronze in the museum. But the city, as we see it, dates largely from the twelfth and succeeding centuries.

Entering by the Via Matteotti, you reach the Piazza dei Quaranta Martiri between the loggia of the Arte della Lana, the wool guild, and the thirteenth-century monastery of San Francesco. Narrow streets rise steeply towards the centre of the town, where the great Palazzo dei Consoli is clearly visible on its terrace; but the main road turns to the left and then bends twice to the right to reach the Via dei Consoli, and its procession of medieval houses with their *porte degli morti* — doors of the dead — raised above the street level. The pink stone façades reveal their past, as one can see where doors and windows have been blocked and moved.

The Piazza della Signoria is the heart of the town, built out over a giant blind arcade. On the right is the Palazzo dei Consoli, emphatically masculine despite its elegant loggia high above. The palace was designed by Angelo da Orvieto and built in 1332. The door opens to a vast hall, from which a narrow stairway mounts to the upper floor, now the civic museum, as rewarding architecturally as

Palazzo dei Consoli, south façade.

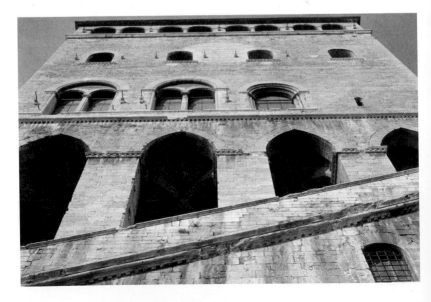

for its pictures – for sadly there is nothing by Neri da Gubbio, the Eugubine miniaturist whom Dante consigns to his Inferno. In the archaeological section, the Eugubine tablets have pride of place. On the north side of the piazza is the long neoclassical brick front – oddly thought to be in the English taste – of the Palazzo Ranghiasci. Below this, a passage leads steeply up to the Duomo. An oddly unsatisfactory building, it is most notable for the decoration of a small chapel on the right by an underrated realist of the baroque, Antonio Gherardi da Rieti. Opposite and a little below the Duomo is the ducal palace. The Montefeltro gained the signoria of Gubbio in 1384, and the palace rebuilt by Federico di Montefeltro was a smaller counterpart to that at Urbino. The courtyard remains a space of great elegance, with crumbling facings of grey pietra serena, but the marquetry of the studiolo is in New York, its pictures divided between London and Berlin. Still higher up the hillside is the medieval aqueduct, which can be followed for a mile or so as it curls round the flank of the Monte Ingino to the north-west. The views down over the tiled roofs of the town are memorable.

One Eugubine painter, Mello, an early Trecento follower of the Lorenzetti, is adequately represented in the museum of the Duomo and in the Palazzo dei Consoli. A century later Gubbio produced one of the more engaging figures of the international Gothic movement, Ottaviano Nelli. His masterpieces are in two churches on the east of the town. In the Madonna del Belvedere at Santa Maria Nuova the *Virgin and Child* are seen with angels under a baldachin supported on thin spiral columns up which putti crawl. The fabrics are sumptuous. Nearby, but outside the walls, is Sant'Agostino,

Sant'Agostino: Ottaviano Nelli, Life of Saint Augustine, fresco (detail).

whose choir Nelli decorated with episodes from the life of the saint. His narrative is discursive, and his depiction of potentates and their attendants tells us something of the extravagance of contemporary patrician taste.

With the extinction of the della Rovere line in 1624, Gubbio reverted to papal rule. Two churches below the town evoke this period. The elliptical *Madonna del Prato*, outside the Porta Romana, was decorated by the local painter Francesco Allegrini and has a provincial charm. Eighteenth-century San Benedetto, below the Porta Castello, is of a different order. This too is elliptical. The original furniture is almost miraculously intact. And the high altarpiece, Agostino Masucci's *Immaculate Conception*, exemplifies the restrained classicism of early eighteenth-century Rome at its purest; the lateral altarpieces by Sebastiano Conca and Francesco Mancini are equally effective.

52

PERUGIA

LIKE so many ancient cities, Perugia has long outgrown her early walls, and much of the new town is remorselessly ugly. For that reason, the most appealing approach is from the north-east, the steep ascent from Ponte Rio, which rises to the earliest of the great monuments of the city, the Etruscan Arch of the inner enceinte. Through this, climb the narrow street to the flank of the cathedral and the piazza on the further side which is the true centre of the city. This is an irregular space, sloping downwards from the lateral façade of the church. At the centre is Giovanni Pisano's Fontana Maggiore, begun in about 1275 and one of the masterpieces of its age, and beyond is the vast medieval complex of the Palazzo dei Priori, long the administrative hub of the city. Like so many Italian cities in the Middle Ages, Perugia was fought over by internal factions and external powers. Her dramatic history is implied by the loggia added to the cathedral by Braccio Fortebraccio from Montone, who in the 1420s came so close to carving out an Italian kingdom for himself, by the external pulpit at which San Bernardino of Siena preached, and by the superlative bronze statue of 1555 by the Perugian sculptor Vincenzo Danti of Pope Julius III, symbol of the authority that for over three centuries exercised a firm political control.

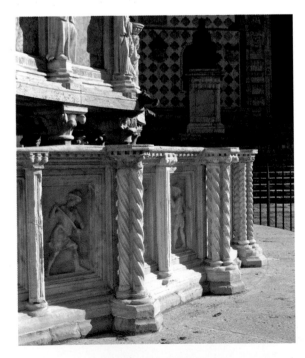

Nicola and Giovanni Pisano, Fontana Maggiore, 1275–7.

Vincenzo Danti, Pope Julius III, bronze, 1555.

Perugia is a palimpsest. A quietly baroque façade may mask a medieval building, which in turn might overlie an Etruscan structure – as the Palazzo Sorbello does the remarkable Etruscan well. The churches, too, have for the most part been adapted to successive waves of taste; and because Bonaparte's lieutenants had so clear an understanding of the importance of the greatest local painter, Pietro Vannucci, il Perugino, the city suffered grievously from their depredations. Thus it is that the two great altarpieces in the cathedral are both by outsiders, Signorelli from Cortona and Federico Barocci from Urbino, whose great *Deposition* must rank as one of the major masterpieces of the Counter-Reformation: their erstwhile companion, Perugino's *Marriage of the Virgin*, is now at Caen.

The French could not bear off Perugino's frescoes of the Collegio del Cambio,

just beyond the Palazzo dei Priori. The decoration of the Audience Chamber, with the *Nativity* and *Transfiguration* flanked by classical heroes and sibyls under a vault of grotteschi of classical deities, is complemented by the equally meticulous woodwork; the painter's direct and unpretending self-portrait in a fictive frame is set between his lines of heroes. High in the Palazzo dei Priori is the recently rearranged Galleria Nazionale dell'Umbria, which offers a matchless survey of painting in Perugia from the late thirteenth century. Nowhere else are such artists as Giovanni Boccati, Benedetto Bonfigli, Bartolomeo Caporali and Fiorenzo di Lorenzo so well represented, and the eight panels of miracles of San Bernardino painted in 1473 by Perugino, Pinturicchio and others are among the happiest achievements of the Umbrian Quattrocento. Masterpieces by artists from Tuscany, Duccio and Fra Angelico and Piero della Francesca, testify to the range of Perugian patronage, but the loss of so much to the Vatican and the museums of provincial France means that the story is incomplete.

From the central hill on which the Etruscans originally built, Perugia extended a tentacled grip over the ridges to north and south. From the Porta Sole – near the church of San Severo with Raphael's earliest extant fresco – you can see the northern area of the city; the ground falls away to the walls and the Etruscan Arch. Opposite this is the large Augustinian church and then the long ridge beyond, with monasteries where nuns will show their treasures and the huge brick Porta Sant'Angelo near the – much restored – early circular church of that saint. The young Raphael placed *Saint Jerome* before this view in a drawing now at Oxford.

Perugia's most dramatic street is the narrow Via dei Priori that plunges northwards under the Palazzo dei Priori: there are houses, the uppermost now shops; a few palazzi; the unexpectedly coherent baroque Chiesa Nuova with an unfamiliar masterpiece, Francesco Trevisani's *Annunciation*; the Oratorio of the Disciplinati di San Francesco, one of the confraternities by the membership of which the noblemen of Perugia set such store; a small Renaissance chapel, the Madonna della Luce; and not least, nestling beside the pink and white mass of the former church of San Francesco al Prato, the Oratorio di San Bernardino. This was constructed in 1457–61 when the cult of the reformist Sienese monk was at its most fervent; its glory is the polychrome façade with reliefs by the Florentine sculptor Agostino di Duccio, who had learnt the precepts of his fellow Florentine, the architect and classical theorist Leon Battista Alberti, but interpreted these with his own lyricism of line.

Another memorable walk takes you from the piazza to its southern counterpart, the Piazza del Sopramuro (now Matteotti) flanked by the long fifteenth-century façade of the Palazzo del Capitano del Popolo. At the south-western corner a street twists downwards, lined now with shops, to the medieval façade of the church of Sant'Ercolano. This has hardly changed since it was depicted in Benedetto Bonfigli's mural of the mid-Quattrocento in the Palazzo dei Priori. Below this, you join the main artery leading south to two of the finest churches of the city. First comes that of the Dominicans, vast and rather bare. The east window boasts some of the most ambitious stained glass of its date – 1402 – in Italy; nearby is the canopied Gothic tomb of Pope Benedict XI. A truncated altarpiece by Agostino di Duccio and fragments of fourteenth-century frescoes show how rich the church originally was. The convent was of commensurate scale and now houses the Museo Archeologico. Etruscan funerary urns may pall, but the reconstruction of the tomb of the Cai Cutu family, found by chance in 1983, does not. And the sixth-century bc bronze fittings of a carriage from Corciano are exceptional survivals.

Further south is one of the least expected monuments of mid-fifteenth-century Perugia, the Porta San Pietro. Inspired by Roman example and designed by Agostino di Duccio, this was the most ambitious Albertian structure of the period in Umbria. Beyond, outside the walls, is the monastery of San Pietro, whose pencil-sharp hexagonal campanile designed by the Florentine Bernardo Rossellino (1463–8) is one of the landmarks of Perugia. The church is reached through an atrium. Basilical in plan, this is richly furnished. The narrative intarsie of the choir of 1536 by Fra Damiano da Bergamo are surpassed by none of their date in Italy. Of Perugino's large high altarpiece, only four predella panels remain, but otherwise the Benedictines were able to preserve most of their treasures. Eusebio da San Giorgio's *Adoration of the Magi* is the only major Peruginesque altarpiece to remain in any Perugian church, although, perversely, its predella is now placed under another picture. Canvasses by the Perugian Giovanni Domenico Cerrini, the Marchigian Sassoferrato, the Orvietan Cesare Sermei and the Roman Giacinto Gimignani remind us that despite strict papal control Perugia was not altogether a backwater in the seventeenth century.

53

PANICALE AND CITTÀ DELLA PIEVE

THE small town of Panicale crowns one of the chain of small hills to the south of Lake Trasimene. There are views down across the lake: to the left, the promontory of Castiglione del Lago with its Cinquecento palace of the della Corgna and, to the right, the Isola Polisena, the church on which boasts the grandest of Perugian Renaissance crucifixes. But it is not for these, nor for the cluster of buildings round the handsome Collegiata, that we have come. A little way to the east is the small church of San Sebastiano. Here in 1505 Perugino painted a fresco of the martyrdom of the saint. Much admired in the nineteenth century, this is hardly à la mode. Sebastian awaits his fate with a calm indifference; the tightly silhouetted archers are more elegant than menacing, balletic almost in their motions. Behind is an arcade of admirably simplicity through which we see the lake framed by descending ridges.

Perugino's idealized forms were matched by his inspired response to the landscape he knew so well, and it was through this that his influence would endure for centuries. Born Pietro Vannucci, the painter belonged to a moderately prosperous family of Castel del Plebis, now Città della Pieve, some twenty-five kilometres to the south-west. When age and changing taste meant that Perugino had fewer commissions from patrons elsewhere, he returned to work in his native territory. The best known of his frescoes at Città della Pieve is the

rather laboured *Adoration of the Magi* set above trompe l'oeil wainscotting in the Oratorio dei Bianchi. More intriguing is what remains of the *Deposition* in the church of the Servites. Perugino himself designed the composition, but asked the sculptor Andrea Sansovino to make a model for this, a rare survival now in the Victoria and Albert Museum. Conscious no doubt of his weakening abilities, the veteran painter was nonetheless determined to give of his best. The early campanile of the Duomo is the only significant structure within the walls that Perugino would recognize. Opposite this is the handsome but unfinished sixteenth-century palace designed by Galeazzo Alessi for a papal nephew, Ascanio della Corgna, who called in Niccolò Pomarancio to decorate some of the interiors. With its elegant door-case and window-frames, the palace stands out in the predominantly brick town.

Oratorio di Santa Maria dei Bianchi: Pietro Perugino and studio, trompe l'oeil wainscotting below the Adoration of the Magi, fresco, 1504.

54

ASSISI

THE first sight of Assisi is unforgettable. The town seems to hang from the Monte Subasio, stretched between the massive basilica at its northern angle and the two medieval fortresses high to the south, the Rocca Maggiore and the Rocca Minore. Controlling the most fertile part of the valley of the Assino and its mountainous hinterland, Assisi has long been a place of some consequence. The portico of the Roman temple, commandeered by an undistinguished church, still dominates the central Piazza del Comune. The wonderful front of the Romanesque cathedral

of San Rufino east of the piazza implies the town's wealth in the eleventh century.

But Assisi as we know it owes its character to one man, Saint Francis. The son of a local noble, born in 1181/2, Saint Francis, after various vicissitudes, became a powerful champion of religious reform. The order that bears his name became a force throughout the western church. Canonization followed his death in 1226 by only two years. And Assisi was quickly established as a major place of pilgrimage. The saint, whose dual commitment to poverty and obedience was genuine, would doubtless have been dismayed by the scale of the monastery his successors created in his name. Built on massive foundations, the church is on two levels and was most probably designed by Fra Elia.

San Francesco, from the north-west.

The pilgrim who walks up through the piazza below it enters the Lower Church by a side door and advances to find the body of it on the left. The church consisted originally of a single nave, from which pilgrims would descend to the crypt where the saint is buried; the side walls were frescoed, about 1270, by the so-called Master of Saint Francis with scenes from the life of the saint that established the iconography of future representations. The addition of lateral chapels means that much of the cycle is lost, but before considering these the visitor should proceed to the right transept and examine Cimabue's fresco of the *Madonna and Child with Saint Francis and Angels* – painted perhaps ten years later than the anonymous master's narratives – and then climb up to the Upper Church.

San Francesco.

Consecrated in 1253, this is a monumental, if austere, Gothic structure. Frescoes on an almost unprecedented scale must have been intended from the outset. Work began in the choir and the transepts, but the murals by Cimabue and others in these have suffered severely in the past.

The nave was decorated in three tiers, the upper two with scenes from the Old Testament by Roman associates of Pietro Cavallini, the least familiar of the major innovative masters of the late thirteenth century. In the lower tier, the life of Saint Francis is narrated in a series of twenty-eight compartments, the rhythm of which is partly defined by the fictive cornices and hangings below them. The traditional view that most of the cycle is by Giotto has been questioned by several Anglo-Saxon art historians but would seem to be valid. The artist was keenly aware of his role as propagandist. His narration is clear and logical, his human forms solid and plausible, his settings subordinate and insubstantial. His rendition of the Temple of Minerva in the Piazza del Comune – before which the young Francis divests himself of his clothes – well illustrates this: the columns are etiolated, their number reduced. Buildings crumble, rooms confine. But it is the saint who holds our interest. Nowhere is this more perfectly expressed than in the celebrated fresco – to the right of the main door – of *Saint Francis preaching to the Birds*, his avian congregation perched on the hillside. The last four scenes on the left wall with their elongated figures are different in approach. The hand is clearly Florentine, that of the so-called Master of Saint Cecilia.

The Saint Francis cycle marked an epoch in the evolution of painting in central Italy. Later, Giotto would return to Assisi. The Magdalen Chapel to the right of the Lower Church was designed, and presumably partly executed, by him; and his was the impetus behind the vault of the crossing of the Lower Church. It was, however, to Siena that the authorities at Assisi turned for further projects. The first chapel on the left, dedicated to Saint Martin of Tours, was assigned to Simone Martini. Partly because Simone also apparently designed the stained glass, the chapel is infinitely satisfying in its visual unity. Simone's refinement is extreme, and it is impossible to imagine a more elegant silhouette than that of the saint as he cuts his cloak in half to clothe the beggar. The Assisi chapel, more perhaps than any of his Sienese commissions, demonstrates why Simone became so attuned to courtly taste, whether in Angevin Naples or at papal Avignon.

Simone's contemporary, Pietro Lorenzetti, was enlisted for the left transept,

Temple of Minerva, late 1st century BC.

where he painted scenes from the Passion, perhaps unfairly criticized by Berenson, and the huge *Crucifixion*, a narrative of almost unprecedented animation. But it is for the frescoes below this that Lorenzetti is more generally remembered, the niche with vessels used to celebrate mass and − above all − the poignant *Madonna and Child with Saints Francis and John*, intended for close − and tearful − contemplation. As an adolescent I was not surprised to see that a survivor from an earlier age, Princess Marthe Bibesco, kept a postcard of it on her writing table.

Places of pilgrimage are meant to attract crowds. But if numbers become too oppressive, there are buildings nearby where one will not be disturbed. A hundred metres up the main street, on the right, is the Oratorio dei Pellegrini, where a nun still prays in the presence of frescoes by local painters of the later Quattrocento, Matteo da Gualdo, Pier Antonio Mezzastris from Foligno and, most probably, Perugino's early associate Andrea d'Assisi. Rather further away, below the walls, is the convent of San Damiano with murals by the Peruginesque Eusebio da San Giorgio in the cloister and an atmospheric candle-stained church, which the stipulations of the Lothian family have protected from tourist exploitation.

For tourism has its price. Saint Francis would still recognize the open downland of the Subasio. The rippling horizons he knew are unimpaired. But even since I first knew it in 1966, the valley below Assisi has been horribly scarred by unsightly development. Nonetheless, much of the town has hardly changed since the late Victorian painter William Blake Richmond wrote about it.

55
MONTEFALCO

THE valley south of Assisi must always have been of strategic importance and supports a number of towns: Spello, with an imposing Roman gate and the church of Santa Maria Maggiore where Pintoricchio's frescoes in the Baglioni Chapel do honour to painter and patron alike; Foligno, where the palace of the Trinci still testifies to the ambition of a family whose signoria was brutally suppressed by the papacy in 1439; and, to the west, Bevagna, with its Gothic Palazzo del Consoli and on the same piazza two unusually successful late Romanesque churches, San Silvestro, begun by Master Binello as is recorded in an inscription of 1195, and San Michele, where he was assisted by a collaborator, Rodolfo. On a

San Fortunato: Benozzo Gozzoli, Madonna and Child, border (detail), *fresco, 1452.*

hill to the south is Montefalco, which was held by the Trinci from 1383 until their fall, and then like Foligno under direct papal rule.

Walled in the fourteenth century, Montefalco boasted its own saint, the Augustinian Chiara di Damiano, whose life is recounted in a fresco cycle of 1333 in her eponymous church. The strength of the Augustinian presence is implied by the large Gothic church of Sant'Agostino, but it is for its Franciscan church that the town is most memorable. Built in 1336–8 and now deconsecrated as a museum, San Francesco is an austere monument. On the right in the first bay is the chapel of Saint Jerome, frescoed in 1450–2 by Benozzo Gozzoli, who had previously acted as Fra Angelico's assistant in Rome; the fictive polyptych is a charming visual conceit, and the conviction of the scheme helps to explain why the artist was retained to decorate the choir with a cycle of scenes from the life of Saint Francis, also of 1452. Benozzo was no artistic protagonist, but his work at Montefalco was to have considerable local repercussions, as is so evident in the plangent mood of the emergent masters of the school of Foligno, Niccolò da Foligno and Pierantonio Mezzastris.

Less than half a kilometre south of the town, still rustic in setting, is the church of San Fortunato, who established Christianity at Montefalco. Benozzo worked here also, painting the beautiful lunette with the *Madonna and Saints* above the portal, and, within the church on the right, a more solemn fresco of San Fortunato himself enthroned as well as a Madonna of which a section has been lost. Outside is the Cappella di San Francesco (or Cappella delle Rose). This was decorated in 1512 with murals of Franciscan scenes and of saints by Tiberio d'Assisi, who understood something of Perugino's spatial formulas. This is more than can be said for his uneven Montefalcan contemporary, Francesco Melanzio, whose provincialism has ensured that most of his oeuvre remains in the churches of his native town. Below the town to the south in the sanctuary of the Madonna delle Stelle, begun by the Perugian architect Giovanni Santini in 1862, is a *Visitation* by the German Friedrich Overbeck that expresses the reverence of the Nazarines for the Peruginesque.

56
MONTESANTO

IT MAY seem eccentric to write about Montesanto. For the place as I first knew it is beyond recall. High on a gently sloping ridge above the valley of the Vigi, south-east of Casenove on the ancient road from Foligno across the Apennines, Montesanto was an outpost of the duchy of Spoleto. The crumbled medieval walls enclose a rectangular area originally laid out on a grid plan. The Touring Club Italiano's guide devoted four lines to Montesanto. I heard of it though Marilena Ranieri, whose mother, Signora dei Vecchi, remembered that her family, the Orfini, migrated every summer from Foligno to what her friend Berenson described as their robber-baron's castle at Casenove, and then, when the heat became impossible, withdrew to Montesanto, which at 753 metres above sea level was always cooler. In extreme old age she asked to be taken back, and was surprised that what had been a day's journey took half an hour. But it was not for that reason that Marilena made me want to go.

Largely abandoned as Montesanto then was, for most of its inhabitants had long since left, there was still at the central crossing a cluster of two or three houses of some consequence. Near these was the parish church. This retained the original late Renaissance and baroque furnishings, an earlier triptych and a number of altarpieces. The finest was a then little-known Nativity by Beccafumi, the tender subtlety of which, both in design and colour, was only the more poignant in so remote a setting. Inevitably the panel seems a little less eloquent now that it is in quarantine at the museum in Spoleto. But at least it is safe. Montesanto is not, for it was not far from the epicentre of the devastating earthquake of 1996. The few houses were shattered and the front of the church fell away. I returned a few months afterwards, on a sharp winter's day, and wept.

The Beccafumi will probably never return. And the ancient walls will continue to crumble. But there is still much for the patient visitor to see in the area. Just south of Casenove, at Serrone, is one of the most touching northern Caravaggesque pictures in Italy, the Holy Family in the Carpenter's Shop. Some miles south of Montesanto the Vigi flows into the Nera. The economic importance of the valley of the Nera as a route through the Apennines is shown by the fortifications at Borgo Cerreto and such local churches as the Romanesque San Felice di Narco.

57

SPOLETO

❖

SPOLETO was an Umbrian settlement but fell to Rome in the third century BC and became a major city, as is shown by the remains of a temple, a theatre, an amphitheatre and an arch dedicated to the younger Drusus. Maintained by the Byzantines, Spoleto was sacked by Attila the Hun, but in 571 under the Lungobards became the seat of a powerful duchy. A long rivalry for control between the Holy Roman Empire and the Church

The Castle and the Ponte delle Torri.

ended with the latter's absorption of the duchy in 1247. Papal rule only ended with the Risorgimento.

The size of Spoleto always comes as something of a surprise, the walls enclosing a large irregular area on the left bank of the Tessino. Approaching from the north, the visitor should pause at two remarkable churches on the opposite bank: San Salvatore is, most remarkably, a late Roman basilica remodelled under the Lungobards and was much studied by Renaissance architects, while Romanesque San Ponziano has a fine crypt with an early Trecento fresco of the Madonna by a local master.

The most powerful symbol of papal rule at Spoleto is the great Rocca (fortress) on a promontory falling away on two sides to the river at the eastern angle of the walls. This was built for the formidably effective Cardinal Albornoz by an equally remarkable architect, Matteo di Giovanello, il Gattapone. Below the Rocca is the Duomo, with an impressive Romanesque front to which a Renaissance portico was appended. From above the central door Bernini's bust of Pope Urban VIII surveys the interior, which was subtly transformed in 1785–92 by an archiect of genius: Giuseppe Valadier. Treasures range from the signed Crucifix of 1187 by Alberto Sozio, the earliest picture by a named Umbrian painter, to the Presentation by Antonio Cavallucci, one of the last exponents of the tradition established by Carlo Maratta. The apse of the first chapel on the right, built for Bishop Costantino Eroli, was frescoed by Pinturicchio in 1497.

Thirty years earlier, when the authorities decided to commission a cycle of ambitious frescoes for the choir in honour of the Virgin (to whom the Duomo is dedicated), they called in not a local painter but the aged Fra Filippo Lippi from Florence. We think of Lippi as a painter of delicate Madonnas and altar-pieces, sensitive and susceptible to female beauty. What distinguishes the Spoleto scheme from Lippi's earlier work is its overwhelming scale: the vast lunette of the *Coronation of the Virgin* vies with the apse mosaics of medieval Rome, and the *Annunciation, Dormition* and *Nativity* below are equally monumental in conception, although more restrained in colour. Even though he employed an équipe of assistants, the project killed Lippi, but his was perhaps not an unworthy death.

Spoleto boasts a wealth of other churches and post-Renaissance palaces, but none of these quite matches three very different buildings in the vicinity. Below the city wall opposite the Rocca is the Ponte delle Torri, a majestic aqueduct-cum-bridge with ten Gothic arches built for Albornoz. Whether or not this was also designed by Gattapone, it rivals as a work of engineering the aqueducts of ancient Rome, and was indeed assumed to be Roman by early travellers, many of whom visited the Temple of Clitumnus, some twelve kilometres to the north. Elements of the decoration of this elegant paleo-Christian structure were copied by Umbrian painters of the Quattrocento; and, as the late Giles Worsley observed, it was the model for the temple in Poussin's *Death of Phocion*, the ultimate Seicento classical landscape. The successor of the Roman Via Flaminia is now too close to the temple for comfort. In this respect fate has been kinder to the splendid Romanesque church of San Pietro on the flank of the Monteluco south of Spoleto. The sculpture of the façade is of exceptional vigour.

58

ORVIETO

✿

THE first impression of Orvieto is unforgettable. The city is perched on a high outcrop, defended by perpendicular cliffs which lour above the valley of the Paglia. The site inevitably attracted the Etruscans, but Orvieto was not, it seems, a town of importance until the sixth century. In the late medieval period, rival families and the papacy vied for control; only in 1450 did the latter finally prevail.

The great striped Gothic cathedral, which was begun in 1290 to celebrate a miracle of 1263, can be seen from the valley. But nonetheless the sheer façade comes as a surprise. The Sienese Lorenzo Maitani superintended the project from 1310 for two decades and oversaw the execution of the remarkable reliefs which encrust the pilasters of the lower tier. The much restored rose window was designed by the great Florentine artist Andrea Orcagna.

No Gothic interior in Italy is more exilarating in its sense of space. In the left aisle is a frescoed *Madonna and Child* of 1425 by Gentile da Fabriano, most refined of the late Gothic painters of central Italy. To the left of the crossing is the trapezoidal Cappella del Corporale, decorated like the choir with much restored murals by the local late fourteenth-century master, Ugolino di Prete Ilario; on the altar, usually invisible within its tabernacle, is one of the great master-pieces of medieval metalwork, Ugolino di Vieri's reliquary of 1337–8, which contains the Corporale. That it cost the almost incredible sum of 1,274 florins

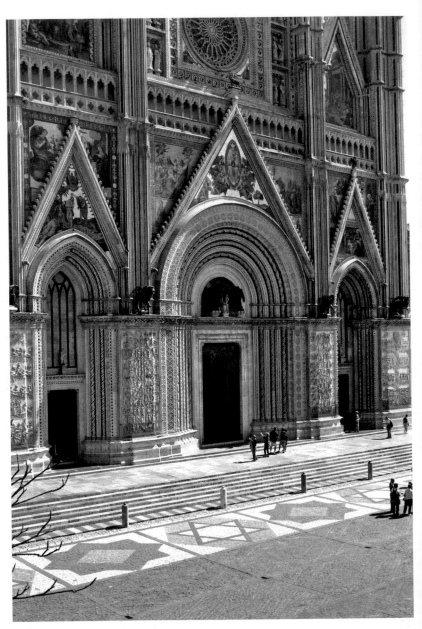

Cathedral, façade projected by Lorenzo Maitani, 1310.

demonstrates how much this relic meant to the Orvietans.

The tourist of today comes to see the Cappella di San Brizio, the Cappella Nuova, opposite. Work on this began in 1409. Fra Angelico was enlisted to decorate the chapel and in 1447 completed, with the help of assistants, two of the eight sections of the vault, *Christ in Glory* and *Prophets*, works of unprecedented

scale in his oeuvre. The frate was then summoned to Rome and did not return to Orvieto. In 1489 Perugino received a contract to complete the scheme. He did nothing, and a year later his contemporary and erstwhile associate, Luca Signorelli, was called in.

While the scale and character of Signorelli's frescoes of the vault were influenced by those of Fra Angelico, his

Cathedral: Luca Signorelli, Lamentation, fresco (detail).

great murals on the walls must have seemed startling in their novelty. The *Preaching of the Antichrist*, the first compartment on the left wall, represents a development from the frescoes of the Sistine Chapel, in which the artist had collaborated; as in the Sistine murals there are obvious portraits. Signorelli's imagination astonishes in the detail of the *End of the World*, which flanks the entrance arch. Yet more extraordinary are the paired frescoes of the right wall, the *Resurrection of the Flesh* and the *Damned*: in the first, two angels blast on their trumpets as the virtuous rise from the dead to their summons; in the second, devils are in undisputed control, the damned concentrated in a heaving scrum, their screams and laments in vain. The cycle continues in the same vein at either side of the altar, with angels respectively despatching sinners to Hell and guiding the elect to Paradise; this concludes, in the second section of the left wall, with the *Calling of the Elect to Heaven*, in which the virtuous are marshalled by a cloud of airborne angels. No other painter of his generation could have acquitted himself on Signorelli's terms; and although few related studies survive, we know enough about his methods to be left in no doubt that every significant figure was carefully worked out from the human model. Signorelli, like Fra Angelico, was a visionary who understood that plausible observation would convince his audience.

The lower tier of the decoration of the chapel also calls for close examination. The elaborate dado includes half-length representations of poets, including Homer, Empedocles, Lucan, Horace, Ovid, Virgil and Dante. Each is surrounded by four grisaille roundels, which read as reliefs and have a spontaneous vigour. On the right wall is a recessed chapel with what is in effect a fictive sculptured altarpiece of the *Lamentation* flanked by two saints, Faustino and Pietro Parenzo, who were buried in the chapel. With characteristic acuity Signorelli shows Christ being carried to the sepulchre in a fictive bas-relief in the background.

The Cappella di San Brizio is in every sense an overwhelming experience. Nothing else in Orvieto is on the same heroic plane. But there are other distinguished things to see. Beside the cathedral are the Palazzi Papali, with a key work by Simone Martini, his Monaldeschi polyptych. On the opposite side of the town is San Domenico, with the partly reconstructed tomb of Cardinal Guglielmo di Braye – who died in 1282 – by Arnolfo di Cambio, greatest among the followers of the Pisano. At the northeast end of the town, by the castle, is the remarkable Pozzo Rocca. This great well was excavated at the order of Pope Clement VII, who took refuge in Orvieto in 1527–8 after the Sack of Rome. It was designed by the Florentine architect Antonio da Sangallo the Younger; there are two stairs, each of 248 steps. Descending one of these, it is not difficult to understand why this most satisfying masterpiece of civil engineering took almost twenty years to complete.

The Marche

• Urbino 59

60 Mondavio •

61 Loreto •

63 Monte San Giusto •
64 Fermo •

62 Servigliano •

65 Ascoli Piceno •

59

URBINO

❧

BALDASSARE Castiglione's Il Cortegiano (The Book of the Courtier) of 1528 offers a uniquely vivid account of the world of Guidobaldo di Montefeltro, and, to an English audience, Urbino and Guidobaldo's father, Federico di Montefeltro, have been synonymous since the publication of James Dennistoun's Memoirs of the Dukes of Urbino in 1851. It is not fortuitous that two of the great masters of the sixteenth century, Raphael and Federico Barocci, grew up in the shadow of the ducal court at Urbino.

The Montefeltro were granted Urbino in 1155. By the fourteenth century they also controlled the nearby towns of Fossombrone and Cagli on the Roman Via Flaminia, one of the key routes from Rome to the Adriatic and its ports. Equally significant was their dominance of the main road to Tuscany in the west across the Trabaria Pass. Most early visitors would have taken this, and then crossed the hills from Castel Durante, now Urbania, long famous for its maiolica. As Lord Clark observed, the backgrounds of Piero della Francesca's portraits in the Uffizi of the successful condottiero Federico di Montefeltro, hereditary Count of Urbino, and his wife, Battista Sforza, were inspired by the views from this road. As it curls downwards towards the city, the twin towers of Federico's palace come into sight – Barocci recorded them from the opposite angle in his astonishing Entombment at Senigallia on the Adriatic coast.

Dominating its hinterland, the palace also looms large above the Piazza Duca Federico. Federico began to build about 1444. In 1465 Luciano Laurana was called in; he left in 1472, and subsequently the Sienese Francesco di Giorgio Martini took over the project. Work had progressed considerably before Federico was elevated as duke in 1474. The entrance from the piazza is relatively restrained. This leads to Laurana's arcaded courtyard, a concept of singular perfection, marred somewhat by the later addition of a third storey. At the north-eastern angle is the great staircase to the domestic apartments. Nowhere were the precepts of Albertian proportions more assiduously respected than in these. The harmony of the spaces is matched by a fastidious use of ornament. Alas, the possessions of Federico's della Rovere heirs left for Florence after the surrender of the duchy to the papacy in 1626. But the intarsie of his studiolo, masterpieces of trompe l'oeil deception, survive; so do some of the panels of philosophers by Joos van Ghent originally placed above them, although others are in the Louvre. Federico's artistic horizons are implied by chance survivals. Joos van Ghent's damaged Institution of the Eucharist shows how quickly that northern master responded to Italian influences when he entered the ducal service. Paolo Uccello's chilling predella with the scenes of the profanation of the host by a Jew reminds us that the morality of Renaissance civilization was very different from our own. Piero della Francesca's peerless Flagellation is a masterpiece of a different order; in recent decades no picture has inspired more self-indulgent iconographical speculation. Opposite is his later Senigallia

Opposite: Ducal Palace, courtyard by Luciano Laurana.

Madonna, remarkable not least for its subtle modulations of colour. Most characteristic of what we think of as Federico's world is the celebrated panel of an ideal piazza; it comes as a surprise to realize that the only signs of life in this majestic architectural fantasy are the two doves who sit on a cornice.

Shorn of most of its indigenous contents, the palace makes a perfect setting for the Pinacoteca Nazionale delle Marche. Among the early pictures, the altarpiece by the Riminese Giovanni Baronzio stands out, not least for the unusual harmonies of green. The beautifully crisp polyptych by Alvise Vivarini hints at Venice's long economic influence on the Adriatic coast. The leading native painter of Federico's time was Giovanni Santi, Raphael's father; his smaller panels have a refinement denied to his more ambitious undertakings. Raphael himself is represented by a wreck once owned by Imelda Marcos and the panel of a lady, '*La Muta*', too often underrated, which is in some ways the most sophisticated of the portraits of his Florentine phase. On the second floor are the later pictures. Here the hero is unquestionably Barocci. His early *Madonna di San Giovanni* is instant in appeal, while the late *Stigmatization of Saint Francis*, of 1594–6, with its nocturnal landscape, is a visionary statement.

To the north of the ducal palace is the cathedral, rebuilt after an earthquake of 1789 by Giuseppe Valadier. The respectable high altarpiece is by that underrated exponent of late Roman classicism, Francesco Unterberger, but it is for two pictures by Barocci that the building is memorable. *The Martyrdom of Saint Sebastian* on the second altar to the right is a precocious exploratory work, more indebted to Correggio than to Raphael. *The Last Supper* in the chapel to the left of the choir is a more considered masterpiece. Every element of the interwoven composition was worked out on paper. We are left in no doubt of Barocci's deep spiritual conviction.

On leaving the cathedral, follow the main street to the Piazza Republica, the hub of the city. Abutting this is the Franciscan church with another moving altarpiece by Barocci. *The Pardon of Saint Francis* was finished in 1576; the saint looks upwards in supplication to the risen Christ. Almost opposite the church, to the right of Via Mazzini, is the narrower Via Barocci, which leads to two remarkable oratories. In the first, the Oratorio di San Giuseppe, is a beautiful stucco *Nativity* by Federico Brendani, Barocci's contemporary, who was also responsible for notable plasterwork in the ducal palace and at nearby Piobbico, the fief of the Brancaleoni family. Beyond is the Oratorio di San Giovanni, one of the high points of the late Gothic in Italy. The interior was frescoed in 1416 by the brothers Lorenzo and Jacopo Salimbeni from San Severino. The *Crucifixion* of the altar wall expresses Lorenzo's vigour; no incident of the gospel narrative is omitted. The murals of the right-hand wall, illustrating the life of Saint John the Baptist, are more inventive, for the artists were less bound by precedent. Emphatically Italian, they bear us to a wonderland they knew, as it were, partly at secondhand, mediated through northern miniatures and French ivories perhaps, yet expressed with conviction in a southern range of colour. The brothers relished the courtly cavalcade and the brave show of contemporary fashion; they were also acute observers. Their Jordan has its complement of fish and a frog, while water pours down from the heads of the couple whom the saint has baptized.

Oratorio di San Giovanni: Lorenzo and Jacopo Salimbeni, Saint John Baptizing, fresco (detail).

60

MONDAVIO

❖

FOR the sightseer who likes to see groups of related buildings or works of art, the Marche is rich in possibilities. Commissions of the rival courts of the Malatesta, the Montefeltro and the Varano can be seen in Rimini, at Urbino and at Camerino. And as such families well knew their need for defence, the area is equally rich in military buildings of the Renaissance.

The most celebrated of these is perhaps the Rocca at Sasso Corvaro, designed by Francesco di Giorgio but altered in the eighteenth century, which seems to float effortlessly above the little town at its feet, and owes its existence to the struggle between the Montefeltro and the Malatesta. Its owners, the Brancaleoni, adhered to the former and would

a century later remodel their ancient castle at Piobbico as a Renaissance palace. Sasso Corvaro's closest rival is the unfinished Rocca at Mondavio, begin in 1482 for Giovanni della Rovere, who sought to consolidate the signoria of nearby Senigallia, which he had received from his uncle Pope Sixtus IV in 1474. Here brick was used by Francesco di Giorgio to brilliant effect. The carefully battered walls, intended to resist artillery, seem to have been cut from butter. How revolutionary the design was is suggested by comparison with the well-preserved walls of nearby Corinaldo, begun in 1366, which had to be reinforced in 1484–90.

For all its originality Mondavio seems almost puny by comparison with Giovanni della Rovere's massive quadrangular fortress at Senigallia. Begun by Luciano Laurana and completed by Baccio Pontelli, this incorporated part of the structure of the town wall of the Roman port and is an emphatic statement of dynastic power and ambition.

Rocca by Francesco di Giorgio, begun 1482.

61
LORETO

A FIRST view of the great sanctuary at Loreto even now takes the breath away. This extraordinary complex, to which many of the great architects and painters of the Renaissance contributed, is as remarkable as the legend it celebrates. In 1291, as the Crusaders lost their hold on Palestine, the house in which the Virgin had been born and in which Christ was brought up after the return from Egypt was miraculously carried by angels to a hill near Fiume. On 10 December 1294 this was borne across the Adriatic to a laurel wood near Recanati, from where it was flown onwards to a farm owned by two brothers; their competing claims led to a final migration to the crest of a ridge on what was a public road, which after all was a not inappropriate site for a place of pilgrimage.

The small town that grew up on the approach to the sanctuary was incorporated within the splendid defensive walls built for Pope Leo X to the design of the younger Antonio da Sangallo and Andrea Sansovino, among others. Enter by the Porta Romana and follow the main street to the Piazza della Madonna, with a central fountain of 1604–14. On my first visit this was crowded with pilgrims, many in wheelchairs; Ursula Corning, who had worked in the New York hospital she helped to re-endow, looked on with a professional interest, trying to work out how many of the sick really believed they might be cured. The presence of ailing pilgrims reminds us that Loreto is in every sense a working shrine. On the left of the piazza is the colon-naded Palazzo Apostolico, begun by Bramante and worked upon by a sequence of later architects from Sangallo to Luigi Vanvitelli. Ahead, flanked on the left by Vanvitelli's campanile of 1750–4, is the rich façade of the basilica itself, begun in 1571, and notable above all for the bronze reliefs of the doors; that in the centre is by the Lombardo brothers, that on the left, of 1596, by Tiburzio Vergelli and an assistant, while its counterpart was begun by Antonio Calcagni from Recanati and finished by other local masters in 1600.

The church is cruciform in plan. It was begun in 1468, and from 1476 the Florentine Giuliano da Maiano was in control, carrying the walls to full height. These were, however, reinforced for defensive purposes for Pope Innocent VIII, under whose Borgia successor, Alexander VI, work began on the octagonal dome designed by Giuliano da Sangallo, but strengthened by Francesco di Giorgio. Further work of consolidation was entrusted to Bramante (1509–11) and to Andrea Sansovino. Within the church it is the white marble Santissima Casa under the cupola that dominates the central axis. Encasing the original building, this was designed by Bramante, and is remarkable for its sculptured decoration. The large narrative reliefs of scenes from the life of the Virgin should be read from the left, north, wall. The most beautiful perhaps are those by Sansovino, the *Annunciation* of 1523 facing the nave and his *Nativity* on the south wall. The bronzes of the doors, by the Lombardo, Vergelli and Calcagni, are also distinguished.

At the angles of the crossing are four octagonal sacristies. That to the south-west, dedicated to San Marco, was frescoed from 1477 by Melozzo da Forlì. In the centre of the vault are the arms of

Basilica, Sacristy
of San Giovanni:
Luca Signorelli,
Evangelists and
Doctors of the
Church, with Angel
Musicians,
fresco (detail).

Cardinal Girolamo Basso della Rovere, surrounded by bands of decoration, including eight compartments with angels holding musical instruments and symbols of the Passion, and below these eight more with prophets. The angels are perhaps Melozzo's happiest achievements. Only one of the projected frescoes of the walls was painted, the *Triumphal Entry to Jerusalem*, much of which is by the young Marco Palmezzano. The south-east sacristy, dedicated to Saint John, is perhaps yet more memorable. Here the car-

dinal, who was responsible for the church from 1476 until 1507, called in the young Luca Signorelli. His arms once again are at the centre of the octagonal vault, in the segmental compartments of which are the *Evangelists* and the *Doctors of the Church*, each seated below a beautiful music-making angel. Below are the *Conversion of Saint Paul, Christ and Saint Thomas*, and pairs of Apostles. The cardinal's arms, supported by paired putti, appear again in elegant grisaille above the door. Signorelli's work at Loreto was no doubt the springboard that led to his selection to contribute to the Sistine Chapel.

A door from the left transept leads to the treasury, housed in the large Sala Pio XI, the ceiling of which, frescoed in 1605–10, is the most ambitious work of that genial late Mannerist painter, Cristoforo Roncalli, il Pomarancio. Although the buildings are annexed, it is necessary to return to the piazza to enter the museum in the Palazzo Apostolico and see the large group of late works by Lotto, who retired as an oblate to Loreto and was buried in the church. The

sequence culminates with his Presentation, the personal and deeply moving last work of a great artist who clearly did have the conviction of his faith. Less appealing perhaps, but equally remarkable, is the massive collection of maiolica from the workshop of Orazio Fontana presented to Loreto by Guidobaldo II della Rovere, Duke of Urbino. Two of the museum's greatest treasures arrived as gifts in the eighteenth century, major cartoons for key commissions by Annibale Carracci and Domenichino.

Basilica, Sacristy of San Giovanni: associate of Luca Signorelli, putto supporting the arms of Cardinal Girolamo basso della Rovere, fresco (detail).

62
SERVIGLIANO

MANY visitors to the Marche search out medieval and Renaissance monuments. And this is wholly understandable. But there is also much of later periods to see. Thus, if the beautiful Barocci at Senigallia is inaccessible, we can always linger in Pietro Ghinelli's circular Foro Annonario, the neoclassical masterpiece of an obscure local architect.

Sometimes it is the less grandiloquent that takes us most surely to the spirit of a lost age. So it is at Penne San Giovanni, birthplace of the still-life painter Mario Nuzzi dei Fiori, where a handful of patri-

cian families supported the Settecento theatre, a happy survival with its prettily decorated boxes, hardly larger than a drawing room. Penne is on a ridge above the valley of the river Tenna. Below, and on the opposite (right) bank, is an unexpected apparition, a small eighteenth-century town. In 1771 the town of Servigliano, a few kilometres to the south, was destroyed by a landslide. A year later Pope Clement XIV ordered that a new town, Castel Clementino, be founded on a lower and less vulnerable site. Work was continued under his successor, Pope Pius VI. In 1863, after the reunification of Italy when it was no longer fashionable to celebrate the legacy of papal rule, the new town was given the name of its predecessor.

Servigliano is a textbook model town of its period, square in plan, entered by three elegant gates, with two main streets that intersect in a generous piazza in front of the handsome church. It boasts no great work of art; it can claim no individual building of particular importance. But it has the merit of being largely intact, and is moreover accessible in the early afternoon when even the most determined sightseer will not be able to gain access to the wonderful polyptych by Carlo Crivelli at nearby Massa Fermana, or those by his son Vittore at Monte San Martino diagonally across the valley.

View northwards from the south gate, with the church on the right.

63
MONTE SAN GIUSTO

THE cities and towns of the Marche have enjoyed a long yet quiet prosperity. A succession of snaking valleys descend gently towards the Adriatic, the Venetian dominance over which has left an extraordinary legacy in the Bellinis at Pesaro and Rimini, and the Titians at Ancona and Urbino. No Venetian recognized the potential of Marchigian patronage more clearly than Lotto. And its legacy endures. One can follow his career from the Recanati polyptych of 1508, by way of the Jesi *Entombment* of 1512, the incomparable *Saint Lucy* altarpiece of 1532 also at Jesi and the visionary *Madonna of the Rosary* of 1539 – with its scattered rose petals – at Cingoli, to the later canvasses at Loreto. The Recanati *Annunciation*, with its cat, is the most familiar of the Marchigian Lottos, but the most prodigious must be the *Crucifixion* of 1531 at Monte San Giusto.

The town stands high above the valley of the Chienti. Like others in the area it is built largely of brick. At its centre is the Palazzo Bonafede built for Niccolò Bonafede, Bishop of Chiusi, between 1504 and 1524. The nearby church of Santa Maria in Telusiano was remodelled by the bishop as his mausoleum, and he

was buried there in 1534. The modest brick façade offers no hint of the interior. This is dominated by the altarpiece, with Lotto's great arched *Crucifixion* in the original gilded frame. Modern lighting means that it is easy to savour the dazzling use of colour that has so important a part in the visual drama. In the foreground is the swooning Virgin, supported by Saint John – who seems almost to project from the painted space – and the attendant Maries. Saint John looks to the left, towards the kneeling bishop. Bonafede's arms are crossed in prayer, his massive head almost disturbingly larger than that of the angel who acts as intermediary. The eye is drawn upwards. The crosses stand out against the evening sky, a dark cloud silhouetting Christ with his billowing loin-cloth, and the thieves, good and bad, their arms tied behind the crossbars. Below is a noisy pell-mell of soldiers, each carefully characterized. Lotto is so individual that one is not at first aware of the range of pictorial experience on which he draws: the clarity of the Venice of Bellini, the classical rhetoric of the mature Raphael, prints by Dürer and other northern prototypes. His digestive power was matched, however, by his visual independence of mind, by an unfailing narrative conviction, and by an almost miraculous sense for colour. The *Crucifixion* is at once deeply moving and breathtakingly beautiful.

Monte San Giusto, Santa Maria in Telusiano: Lorenzo Lotto, Crucifixion, 1531, in the original frame.

64

FERMO

❈

THE artistic riches of the Marche can be experienced in microcosm at Fermo, the successor of the Roman Firmum Picenum, set on a hill some five miles inland from the Adriatic shore.

High above the centre of the town is the Duomo; the front with an elaborate portal survives from the structure of 1227 designed by Maestro Giorgio da Como, but the interior was reconstructed from 1781 onwards. To the right of the entrance, in the surviving west bay of the early church, is Tura da Imola's signed monument to Giovanni Visconti di Oleggio (d. 1366), one of the series of noble men who held the signoria of Fermo in the late medieval period. In a chapel on the right is a much revered eleventh-century Byzantine icon of the Virgin, but the most appealing altarpiece is that of the Cappella del Sacramento, the *Circumcision* by the late Cinquecento Florentine painter Andrea Boscoli, whose melting forms and subtle sense of colour secured him a number of commissions in the area. The great treasure of the Duomo, now in the adjacent Museo Diocesano, is the so-called chasuble of Saint Thomas of Canterbury, which, as an Arabic inscription establishes, was made at Almeria in Spain in 1116.

Fermo's churches and brick palaces cluster happily. And the central Piazza del Popolo is particularly appealing, with the Loggiato of San Rocco of 1528 and, at the north end, the handsome baroque

Duomo, west door (detail).

Palazzo degli Studi opposite the Renaissance Palazzo Comunale, which houses the Pinacoteca. The patrons of medieval Fermo had to look to artists from outside their town; the polyptych of 1369 was supplied by a diligent itinerant, Andrea da Bologna, while the *Madonna of Humility* is by that delicate Fabrianese magician, Francescuccio Ghissi. The eight scenes from the life of Saint Lucy of about 1410–12 by the Venetian Jacobello del Fiore are among the narrative masterpieces of their age. The surprise of the museum is the *Nativity* of 1608 by Rubens. Near this is a Seicento masterpiece, Lanfranco's contemplative *Pentecost*.

65

ASCOLI PICENO

❖

THE Piceno was the Roman name for what is now the southern half of the Marche, and Ascoli was a stronghold of the Piceni who controlled much of this area long before Rome's conquest in 286 bc. Some twenty-eight kilometres from the Adriatic, the city is on a promontory above the confluence of the river Castellano with the Tronto. The Ponte di Solestà across the latter was built early in the imperial era, and much of the plan of the Roman town survives in the tight grid of the existing streets. But is it for its Romanesque churches, built of travertine stone, and her many later palaces that Ascoli is now remarkable.

The Renaissance arcaded Piazza del Popolo lies at the centre of the town. This is dominated on the west by the Palazzo del Capitano del Popolo, a medieval structure which was altered to the design of the local painter Cola dell'Amatrice in 1520 and partly remodelled in 1535; Cola's rusticated door-cases on the west façade are particularly striking. To the north is the flank of the major Gothic church of San Francesco. A circuit beyond this might take in no fewer than four of Ascoli's Romanesque churches, Santa Maria inter Vineos, Santi Vincenzo e Anastasio, San Pietro in Castello and San Pietro Martire, en route for the Ponte di Solestà. Two hundred and fifty metres west of San Francesco is another late Romanesque church, Sant'Agostino, with the fourteenth-century Fabrianese Francescuccio Ghissi's Madonna of Humility on the right. A block to the south is another Romanesque church, San

Venanzio, incorporating the south wall of a Roman temple, with a cerebral if little-known masterpiece of the Roman baroque, Baciccio's Death of Saint Francis Xavier. South of the Piazza del Popolo is the smaller Piazza Roma, dominated by the dignified façade of Santa Maria della Carità, begun in 1532 to the design of Cola dell'Amatrice.

The Piazza Roma is linked to the east by the Via XX Settembre to the Piazza Arringo. On reaching this, turn right, up the narrow Via Tornasecco, to San Gregorio, another Roman temple recast as a Romanesque church. At the further end of the piazza is the Duomo and, on the right, the Palazzo Comunale and the Palazzo Vescovile. The former, an agglomeration of earlier structures, was refronted in the seventeenth century and houses the Pinacoteca Comunale with a notable holding of local works and one exceptional treasure, the opus anglicanum cope. This was given to the Duomo by Pope Nicolas IV in 1288; stolen in 1902 it was returned to Ascoli by the American philanthropist J. Pierpont Morgan three years later. The animated embroidered designs stand comparison with the finest English illuminations and stained glass of their date, soon after 1265. The collection of pictures ranges from the masterpiece of the Quattrocento Paolo da Visso by way of a tender Annunciation by Reni to an Assumption by the nineteenth-century Domenico Morelli. In the Palazzo Vescovile, the projecting wing of which has also been attributed to Cola, is the Museo Diocesano with more Marchigian pictures. Across the piazza is the exemplary Museo Archeologico with exceptional Iron Age metalwork.

The Duomo was enlarged in 1482; the massive façade was constructed to the

Palazzo del Popolo, west façade by Cola dell'Amatrice.

design of Cola in 1529–39. On the left is the free-standing octagonal Romanesque Baptistery, crowned by a loggia. The scale of the church is impressive; the Gothic choir stalls are fine, but much else is best forgotten. In the Cappella del Sacramento, on the right, however, is the splendid polyptych of 1473 by the most eccentric of late fifteenth-century Italian painters, the Venetian Carlo Crivelli, who had settled at Ascoli some years earlier and remained there until his death in 1494/5. This was originally on the high altar and retains its intricate Gothic frame. The main tier shows the *Madonna and Child* between Saints Peter, Jerome, Emidius – the patron of the city – and Paul; above is the *Pietà* and further saints, and below, in the predella, Christ and the apostles. Crivelli's Paduan training is tempered by experience of local painters from Camerino and Foligno. None of his contemporaries knew better how to paint fruit realistically, but realism was not Crivelli's prime objective. His Madonna is at once elevated and poignant, his Child aware – not only from its weight – that the enormous apple he holds is the symbol of the Passion and of mankind's subsequent redemption. As if to intrude on the spectator's space, the left feet of both Saint Peter and Saint Paul project beyond the platform on which they stand. It is unfortunate that this masterpiece is placed too high to be fully appreciated.

The patrons of the Marche were dazzled by Crivelli's proficiency – and by his colours. Until his death in 1495 he had no challenger; his brother Vittore and close follower Pietro Alemanno would adhere to his model until the end of the century. Ascoli is fortunate that its greatest altarpiece survived both the depredations of revolutionary France and later Anglo-Saxon shopping.

66 Viterbo

69 Tuscania

• Bagnaia 67

• Caprarola 68

•Tarquinia 70

•Tivoli 73

• Rome 71

• Ostia 72

• Anagni 74

Lazio

66

VITERBO

❖

VITERBO is the major city of the northern Lazio. There had been an Etruscan settlement, but the place was of little importance until it was fortified in 773; five years later it was granted by Charlemagne to the papacy. Work on the ambitious circuit of the walls, which largely survive, commenced in 1095, and in the thirteenth century Viterbo was the second capital of the popes in their long struggle with the Hohenstaufen, as we are reminded both by the Palazzo Papale and the tombs of Popes Clement IV and Adrian V, who died respectively in 1268 and 1276, in the austere Franciscan church. Thereafter the city dwindled in importance, and as a result much of its medieval core survives. By coincidence Viterbo has two links with the English royal house: in 1271 Henry, Earl of Corn-

Palazzo Papale, the Loggia, 1255–66.

Cathedral from the Loggia.

wall was murdered in the church of the Gesù, and Henry VIII's kinsman Reginald Pole was legate of the patrimony of Saint Peter (the secular governor based in Viterbo) from 1541 until 1555.

The administrative centre of the city, now the Piazza del Plebiscito, is surrounded by public buildings. From its south-eastern angle the Via San Lorenzo winds upwards, crossing the partly Etruscan Ponte del Duomo and passing the early Quattrocento Palazzo Farnese, to the Piazza San Lorenzo. Ahead is the cathedral and to the north the Palazzo Papale, begun between 1255 and 1266, with an elegant open loggia overlooking the lower part of the city. The Cinquecento front of the cathedral masks a handsome twelfth-century structure, with a wide nave separated from the aisles by colonnades. On the left wall there is an altarpiece of exceptional interest, Girolamo da Cremona's *Christ and Four Saints* of 1472, with a trenchant profile of

the donor, Bishop Settala. We think of Girolamo as a miniaturist of genius, and in this altarpiece see that he was a key figure in the interplay of artistic ideas at a decisive moment.

Cross back over the Ponte del Duomo and make to the right for a fine early church, Santa Maria Nuova, and then cut eastwards through the atmospheric medieval quarter that preserves much of its twelfth-century character. Work round to the Fontana Grande of 1206–79. From here the Via Garibaldi runs to the Porta Romana, to the left of which is another good Romanesque church, San Sisto. Outside the gate, turn left and follow a stretch of the well-preserved walls, which now serve to protect the city from a modern enemy, traffic pollution, for some 250 metres, to Santa Maria della Verità. This suffered gravely in the war. On the right is the Gothic Cappella Mazzatosta, justly celebrated for the remarkable cycle of frescoes of 1469 by a short-lived local master, Lorenzo da Viterbo. Although these have had to be detached and thus have lost something of their original power, we are left in no doubt that Lorenzo studied Piero della Francesca's lost frescoes in Rome. But Lorenzo was more than a mere imitator; he had a compelling artistic integrity of his own.

Beside the church is the Museo Civico. The archaeological collection is extensive, but the pictures are of more general interest. Among those by local artists is a more than competent *Nativity* of 1488 by Antonio da Viterbo, the Viterbese follower of Perugino who assisted Pinturicchio in the Borgia Apartments of the Vatican. The masterpiece is Sebastiano del Piombo's *Pietà*, a lapidary masterpiece which exemplifies the artist's close association with Michelangelo.

67

BAGNAIA

❖

PROXIMITY to Rome means that the Lazio is rich in the great houses built for prelates and princely families. Some seek to dominate their territory. The Villa Lante, by contrast, is almost casual in its relation to the small town of Bagnaia, just east of Viterbo, whose inhabitants still seem to live in their narrow streets despite the intrusion of a busy road.

Cardinal Giovanni Francesco Gambara, who became Bishop of Viterbo in 1566 and died in 1587, was a man of subtle taste. For his summer residence he, like his all-powerful neighbours the Farnese at Caprarola, called in an architect of genius, Jacopo Barozzi da Vignola. Work on the formal garden was begun in 1568 using craftsmen previously employed at Caprarola, but not completed until ten years later, when Vignola himself was dead. The design took full advantage of the sloping site, with a sequence of fountains and channels framed by hedges set on three terraces among trees. The contrasts of architectural formality and the inherently informal — water and trees — express the spirit of the Renaissance garden, and the sound of the water is omnipresent. Below are the twin pavilions that constitute the villa. The first — on the right — is contemporary with the garden and was also projected by Vignola; this was Gambara's retreat. Its counterpart, faithfully copied from Vignola's design, was built for Gambara's successor, Cardinal Alessandro Montalto, who held Bagnaia from 1590 until 1612.

The Villa Lante is a magic place. It is difficult to tear oneself away. But many visitors will wish to visit the very different and slightly earlier garden at Bomarzo, some thirteen kilometres to the east. This was conceived by Vicino Orsini, who inherited the cliff-top castle that still dominates the valley in which he laid out his 'sacro bosco'. The site was scattered with natural outcrops of volcanic stone (*peperino*) from which bizarre statues of giants, monsters, animals and other subjects were carved. The modern entrance is unworthy, and the place is disturbing, even oppressive. It is the creation of an eccentric who was touched with genius.

Villa Lante: the 'chain' of water.

Villa Lante: the Fontana dello Quadrato.

68

CAPRAROLA

❖

OF PAPAL *nipoti* of the Cinquecento none had more ruthless political or demanding artistic ambitions than the Farnese, descendants of Pope Paul III. His son Pier Luigi was successively invested with the duchies of Castro and of Parma and Piacenza, which would pass to his own second son, Ottavio. Pier Luigi's eldest son, Cardinal Alessandro (1520–1589), was the greatest patron of the line, and at Caprarola we still can sense his forceful personality. Jacopo Barozzi da Vignola's plans for the palazzo were finalized on 31 March 1559, and as you proceed up the spinal street of the small town you are inescapably aware of the magnitude of the cardinal's intentions.

The villa crowns the ridge as if to challenge the prospect it commands, with the volcanic cone of Mount Soracte rising from the plain and the distant peaks of the Gran Sasso. A great double stair rises to the door in the five-sided substructure, military in aspect, that respected the foundations of the palace which the younger Antonio da Sangallo had begun for the cardinal's grandfather before his election to the papacy. Vignola's genius was to create the towering palace above this. His lateral nine-bay main façade, in which the contrasting colours of brick and stone are exploited to signal effect, answers the angle bastions of the Sangallo scheme.

The ground floor is entered though the vestibule, where Federico Zuccaro's decoration includes the cardinal's arms and views of the villa and other Farnese possessions. Ahead is the door to Vignola's masterly circular court at the centre of the building; this is arcaded on two levels, the masonry below channelled while the piers between the upper arches are enriched with paired Ionic pilasters. The door on the left wall of the vestibule opens to Vignola's beautifully controlled circular staircase, supported on paired columns, the Scala Regia. Decorated in 1580–3 under the supervision of Antonio Tempesta, this leads to the sumptuous apartments of the piano nobile.

The sequence begins with the Salone di Ercole, above the vestibule, the five arches of which are so conspicuous an element of the façade. The arches are answered in the decoration of the room, the murals of which are by members of the équipe brought in when Federico Zuccaro took over the project after the death of his more gifted elder brother, Taddeo, in 1566. Next comes the circular domed chapel, where the frescoes are largely by Federico himself. Beyond is the celebrated Sala dei Fasti Farnesiani, devised by Taddeo at the very end of his life, with scenes celebrating the history of the Farnese, the largest of which show the Troops sent by Paul III to combat the Protestants and King François I receiving the Emperor Charles V and Cardinal Farnese in Paris, with several readily recognizable portraits. The glorification of the Farnese is continued in the adjacent Anticamera del Concilio, Taddeo's *Proclamation of the Council*, which is arguably his most sophisticated fresco in the palazzo. Beyond is the Summer Apartment, hanging over the garden to the north, beginning with the cardinal's bedroom, the Sala di Aurora, decorated like the two rooms that follow by Taddeo to a programme devised by Annibale Caro. The northern Bartholomäus Spranger worked in the projecting Tower Room at the northern angle of the palace. The Summer Apartment is balanced by that intended for winter use, the Appartamento del'Inverno, with three rooms decorated by Jacopo Bertoia. There follows the Sala degli Angeli, frescoed by two of the most appealing of Mannerist masters, Giovanni dei Vecchi and Raffaellino da Reggio. Both painters also worked with a specialist in cartography, Giovanni Antonio da Varese, in the large Sala del Mappamondo, with maps of the world and territories recently claimed for the Faith, that concludes the sequence of the rooms.

Behind the palazzo a commensurate garden was laid out, with an elegant loggia'd Palazzino del Piacere from which a runnel of water descends to a basin flanked by flights of steps. Grand as this is, the garden must always have lacked the charm of that at Bagnaia.

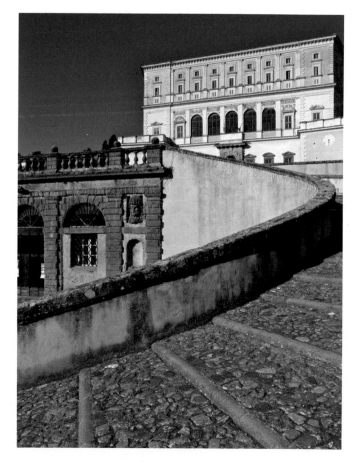

Jacopo Barozzi da Vignola, Palazzo Farnese.

69

TUSCANIA

❧

TUSCANIA is in several ways outshone by her larger neighbour Viterbo; the town boasts no celebrated papal palace and fostered no local school of painters. Yet of the two cities it is perhaps Tuscania that draws one back. The Etruscan Tuscana was absorbed by her Roman successor, which was in turn occupied by the Lungobards in 574. It is to their rule, which ended in 774, that the glory of Tuscania, San Pietro, is due. Tuscania's subsequent history was complicated, but in 1443 Cardinal Vitelleschi finally enforced papal control.

Tuscania's importance diminished, and the medieval city – its confines marked by the extant walls – was larger than its immediate successor. There is abundant evidence of the strata of the town's history – the restrained late Romanesque façade of Santa Maria della Rosa, the medieval Palazzo Spagnoli and the Quattrocento Palazzetto Farnese nearby. The commercial acumen of the painters of Siena is implied by a polyptych by Andrea di Bartolo in the rebuilt Duomo, while the one surviving chapel of San Francesco – the nave of which is now an open-air restaurant – was frescoed in 1466 by the brothers Sparapane from Norcia, provincial masters who here reveal an unexpected affinity with the Sienese Giovanni di Paolo. The later strata too have charm, none more than the stuccoed Supercinema of 1928 with an inscription to remind us that it was built in the sixth year of the Fascist era.

To the south of the town are the two churches that even in the nineteenth century drew visitors to Toscanello, as it was then known. Santa Maria Maggiore is set below the walls, its façade opposite a massive bell-tower. Originally the eighth-century cathedral, the church was largely reconstructed in the twelfth century and reconsecrated in 1206. It is built in a greyish tufa, but white marble was used to effect on the façade. This is enriched by a central lunette with the *Madonna and Child* and other subjects, and surmounted above a blind arcade by a superb rose window. The lateral portals also are richly decorated. Despite the earthquake of 1971 that damaged so many of the monuments of Tuscania, the interior has a timeless quality. For there is nothing to distract us from the early font, the reconstructed pulpit and the partly frescoed ciborium. The whole is dominated by the frescoed *Last Judgement* above the arch of the central apse.

Further south, on a hill upon which the Romans built over the Etruscan settlement, is San Pietro. The way climbs steeply, allowing the eye to linger on the apse, which like that of Santa Maria Maggiore faces north. The visitor passes the complex and then turns into the enclosure. The façade of the church is set back, flanked on the right by the annexed range of the former episcopal palace, which is balanced to the west by two tall towers. Although restored in 1876, the early thirteenth-century façade is thoroughly convincing. The central portal is surmounted by a rose window with symbols of the Evangelists and reliefs which include a particularly disturbing demon. The interior is essentially an eleventh-century remodelling of the original eighth-century Lungobard structure, fusing thus post-Roman with Romanesque forms. The great indented arches of the nave are borne on capitals, some of which were evidently reused – Corinthian, a bastard Ionic and composite – and high above these runs a blind arcade. The late twelfth-century Cosmati floor is unusually well preserved and complements the two earlier ciboria and the intricately decorated marble panels of San Pietro. the screen, survivors of the Lungobard scheme. Below the presbytery is the crypt, with an ordered copse of reused Roman columns. Despite the earthquake, San Pietro remains a wonderfully satisfying building.

San Pietro.

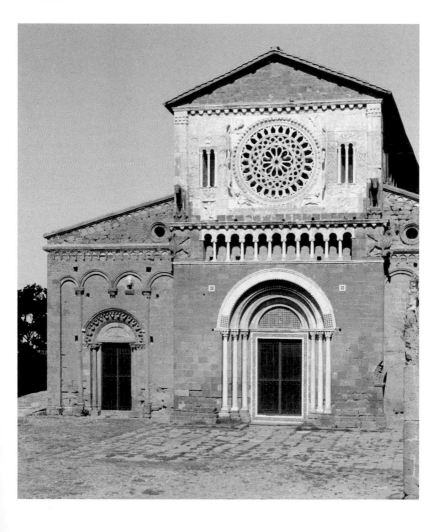

70
TARQUINIA

❖

THE 'noble house of Tarquin', as Lord Macaulay termed it, may never have ruled in Tarquinia. But there is no doubt as to the nobility of the necropolis of the former Etruscan city of Tarxuna, or Tarxna, that sprawled over a now bare hill set well back from the coast above the river Marta. The city fell to Rome in 308 BC. A millennium later, after a long period of decline, the site was abandoned, some of the inhabitants moving westwards to the northern tip of the ridge that had served as the necropolis, to found the city of Corneto. The associations of the former name had an irresistible appeal to Italian patriots, so the place was renamed Corneto Tarquinia in 1872 and Tarquinia, *tout court*, in 1922.

Although evidence of their activity is omnipresent in the swathe of central Italy they once controlled, the Etruscans are in some ways an oddly elusive people. This is partly because they chose the sites of their cities so well that their successors continued to occupy these. At Volterra the circuit of their walls impresses, and at Cerveteri their great necropolis haunts the imagination. In the archaeological museums of Florence and Volterra, of Chiusi and Rome, we can see something of the artistic vigour of their civilization. But it is perhaps most readily understood at Tarquinia, where the rich holdings of the Museo Nazionale Tar-

quiniese can be seen in conjunction with the lavish decoration of so many of the excavated tombs.

The museum is housed in the remarkable late Gothic Palazzo Vitelleschi on the north side of the Piazza Cavour. Cardinal Giovanni Vitelleschi, for whom it was begun, was a patron of considerable taste, as the frescoes in the studiolo on the first floor confirm. The building lends itself admirably to the display of the archaeological collection. The sculpture is for the most part of little sophistication. Sarcophagi with recumbent portraits pall, but in a small relief of the *Suicide of Ajax*, for example, evident energy is matched by a degree of refinement. Pride of place goes, on the second floor, to two fragmentary winged horses made in earthenware that flanked the approach to the main shrine in the Etruscan town. Nearby are murals salvaged from three of the tombs in the necropolis, notably the Tomb of the Olimpiads, datable to the late sixth century BC, and the early fifth-century Tomb of the Triclinium. The collection is rich in smaller items and in local ceramics. But it would be perverse not to admit that the latter are crude by comparison with the decorated black figure wares from Athens for which the Etruscan plutocracy had an understandable predilection. These are arranged by subject matter: war, sport and sex. And we are left in no doubt of both the visual preoccupations of the Athenian potters and the tastes of the Etruscan consumers who chose to be buried with such luxury goods.

The necropolis lies to the south-west of the town, an easy walk. Over 6,000

Museo Nazionale Tarquinese: Baccanti Tomb.

tombs have been found, some sixty with substantial decorative schemes. Only a dozen or so are open at any given time. Flights of steps lead down to the tomb chambers, which for conservation reasons are sealed with glass. The repertoire is varied: swarthy dark-haired men feast with, and less frequently make love to, fair-skinned women; they are seen wrestling and hunting; furniture and trees serve as props and animals abound. Intelligent labelling helps the visitor to make sense of the chronology of ancient painting, so much of the evidence for which is due to the very survival of the Tarquinia tombs.

Medieval Corneto should not be overlooked. On a spur at the north-western angle of the walls is the splendid and superbly sited church of Santa Maria di Castello, begun in 1121 and consecrated in 1208. The road to the left of the Palazzo Vitelleschi, Via Cavour, descends to the restrained front, which is flanked on the left by a handsome campanile. The interior has been responsibly restored and original fittings, including the font, the pulpit and a ciborium, are in place.

71

ROME

❧

NO OTHER European city can be compared with Rome. For none has enjoyed so long – or absolute – a pre-eminence. Founded, it is said, by Romulus and Remus in the eighth century BC, Rome gradually came to dominate its neighbours, a monarchy succeeded by the republic. Rome's territorial ambitions, in Gaul and elsewhere, were matched by the steady expansion of the great walled conurbation that sprawled over the seven hills between which the Tiber curves so majestically. Caesar's astute nephew Octavian became, as Augustus, an emperor who ruled the Mediterranean and beyond, and Rome was vastly enriched under him and his successors. The Emperor Constantine (AD 306–37), who recognized Christianity as the official religion of the empire, transferred his capital to Byzantium, but Rome remained the seat of what was to become the western empire, her importance reinforced by the spiritual primacy of the bishops of Rome, the popes.

The western empire was effectively destroyed when Rome was sacked by Alaric the Goth in 410. But Rome remained the seat of the papacy and a major place of pilgrimage. Roman monuments which had been adapted to Christian purposes, or – like the great girdle of the city walls – remained of use, survived while others mouldered. Major religious buildings continued to be constructed and adorned, their design and decoration echoing in varying ways that of classical Rome or Christian Byzantium. The medieval papacy was a great

power in western European political life, and from the fifteenth century a new age of construction began, driven largely by the aspirations of successive popes and their families, della Rovere and Borgia, Medici and Farnese in the Renaissance, Borghese and Pamphilj among others in the Seicento. Despite the more quiescent role of the papacy in the eighteenth century, Rome remained a major cultural centre where artists and archaeologists made vital contributions to the nascent neoclassical movement. The French invasion of 1798 was followed by a generation of Gallic bureaucracy, but in 1815 papal rule was reinstated. In 1871 Rome became the capital of the new kingdom of Italy, but it was only with the Concordat of 1929 that state and church were reconciled. Strict conservation rules have meant that the exponential growth of recent decades has largely spared the heart of the ancient city.

Rome, it is said, was not built in a day. The visitor with less than a month on his hands, as I had on my first visit in 1966, has to be selective. He would be advised to stay in the centre of the town, ideally near the Pantheon. And if you want to see the key sights, you must go off-season, in November perhaps or February. The Vatican in particular is not to be ventured at busy times. The layers of Rome are impacted, the ancient inextricably entwined with the modern – which in Roman terms means the post-imperial. Yet to some extent, it does make sense to take in the ancient and the modern cities separately, rather as the watercolourist Samuel Palmer did, surveying the first from the Capitol and the second from a point above the Piazza del Popolo where most visitors from the north traditionally arrived.

There is still no better way to get your

bearings than to enter through the Porta del Popolo and find yourself in the piazza that owes its present form to the great neoclassical architect Giuseppe Valadier, confronted by the great Flaminian obelisk, with the paired churches flanking the central Corso beyond. But pause to enter the church of Santa Maria del Popolo. At close quarters there are works by Pinturicchio, by Raphael, by the sculptor Sansovino and by three of the great spirits of post-Renaissance Italian painting, Annibale Carracci, Caravaggio and Maratta.

From the piazza, the Corso – where Dickens saw the carnival crowds being bombarded with sugar plums – runs straight, lined by the façades of churches and palaces. In a piazza on the right is the triumphal column of the Emperor Mar-

Trajan's Column in the Forum of Trajan (107–13).

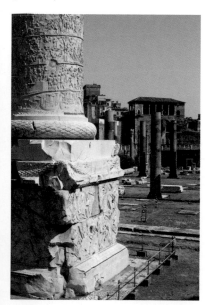

cus Aurelius, who died in AD 180, with the unfolding bas-relief of his campaigns in North Africa. The Corso debouches in the Piazza di Venezia, with the Renaissance Palazzo Venezia on the right, and, ahead, the Vittorio Emanuele Monument, the overblown pretension of which is shown up by the column below it commemorating the campaigns of a real conqueror, the Emperor Trajan. Leave this on the left and climb the great flight of steps to the Campidoglio. Ahead is the Palazzo Senatorio, with on either side the prodigious palaces that adhere more or less to Michelangelo's design and are now museums. In the centre is a cast of the celebrated bronze equestrian monument of Marcus Aurelius, preserved in the Christian era as it was thought to represent Constantine; the original has responsibly been moved to the Palazzo dei Conservatori on the right. The Capitoline Gallery in the same complex houses the outsize masterpiece of Guercino, the *Martyrdom of Saint Petronilla* completed in 1623, in which the young master from Cento proclaims himself one of the most brilliant artists of his century. The Palazzo Senatorio is more notable for its dramatic flight of steps. From the garden behind, look down on the Forum, the heart of ancient Rome, before returning to the Campidoglio itself to gaze over the centre of post-classical Rome, with its domes and roof terraces.

How you plan your Roman sightseeing must depend on opening hours – most churches close at 12 and only reopen after 4 – the availability of timed tickets to the Vatican museums and the Villa Borghese, for example, and of course the weather. There is a case for a chronological approach. Given a perfect morning, this might begin in the Forum, with the triumphal arches of Septimius Severus and Titus, and the Basilica of Maxentius which haunted Canaletto's imagination long after his only visit. To the west is the ruin-strewn Palatine Hill, still a wonderfully atmospheric place to walk. Emerging at the southern exit of the Forum, you reach the most sophisticated of the triumphal arches of Rome, that of Constantine. The narrative reliefs are of particular distinction. The arch is dominated by the vast bulk of the Colosseum behind, more beautiful in ruin that it can ever have been in its original state. Nearby is the Domus Aurea, the 'Golden House' of the Emperor Nero, which is the best preserved of the palaces of ancient Rome and has recently been reopened. Ten minutes south-west of the Colosseum is the greatest of Rome's thermal complexes, the brick Baths of Caracalla, prodigious in scale. One can walk back to the centre through the Circus of Maxentius, passing the splendid curved façade of the Theatre of Marcellus. If, at a later stage of your visit, you wish for a longer walk, make for Via Appia, the great Roman road south to Capua. From the Porta San Sebastiano a well-preserved section stretches southwards, shaded by pines. There are a number of Christian monuments, including the catacombs of Saints Calixtus and Sebastian, and numerous Roman tombs, some with portraits in high relief. The most celebrated is the Tomb of Caecilia Metella, which almost rivalled the vastly bigger Mausoleum of Hadrian, now the Castel Sant'Angelo, in popularity with landscape painters from the seventeenth century onwards.

The greatest single monument of classical Rome is the Pantheon, the wonderful porticoed domed rotunda built in 27 BC by Augustus's associate, Agrippa. A miracle of structural engineering, with

Via Appia Antica.

relieving arches that support a splendid coffered roof rising to the open central oculus, the Pantheon was appropriated by the Church and owes to this its remarkable state of preservation. Monuments to Raphael and to the kings of Italy, among others, sink into insignificance in the Pantheon's majestic space. It is marvellous on a sunny day when a great beam of sunlight bursts through the oculus. Yet the place is perhaps more atmospheric when rain falls through it.

The Pantheon remains a pagan place. Yet the debt of the early Church to classical civilization cannot be overemphasized. One sees this in the fourth-century mosaics at Santa Costanza on the Via Nomentana, and in the great circular arcaded church of San Stefano Rotondo on the Coelian Hill. Nearby is Santi Quattro Coronati, with its wonderfully preserved frescoes of 1246, murals that draw much of their artistic sustenance from the long tradition of mosaics inspired by Byzantium. This tradition was never forgotten in Rome. It can be experienced still in the narrative compartments of the frieze of the great basilica of Santa Maria Maggiore, and through the copies of the mosaics damaged in the tragic fire of 1823 in the second church of Rome, San Paolo fuori le Mura. It endured in the mosaic copies after the great masters of baroque Rome at St Peter's.

But before visiting that greatest of Catholic shrines itself, the visitor should come to terms with the strata of Christian Rome. The many catacombs that can be visited reveal not only the confidence of the early Christians in their faith but also the fact that increasingly they were individuals of influence or wealth. These are moving places. I prefer the smaller complexes, such as Sant'Agnese near Santa Costanza east of the Porta Pia, where there are fewer visitors. At San Clemente, beyond the Colosseum, you can descend to the original church mentioned by Saint Jerome that underlies the existing medieval church with the frescoes by Masolino that heralded the arrival of what we now think of as the Florentine Renaissance in Rome.

There is, of course, no better way to explore Rome than on foot. Start perhaps in Trastevere, with the mosaic-fronted church of Santa Maria in Trastevere, where the mid-twelfth-century apse mosaics are true to the taste of Byzantium, while Pietro Cavallini's narrative

scenes below announce the revolution that was wrought in the last years of the following century. Hardly five minutes away is the church of Santa Cecilia, from the adjacent monastery of which – at certain hours – is accessible the extraordinary, if fragmentary, fresco of the *Last Judgement* of 1292 by Cavallini. Cavallini's forms are true to the conventions he inherited, but have a largeness of scale and a humanity that paves the way for developments at Assisi and indeed parallels the art of Giotto. Beside Santa Maria in Trastevere a narrow street leads to the steps that mount to the church of San Pietro in Montorio on the hill above. To the right of the church is the small courtyard with Bramante's diminutive tempietto, an exquisite microcosm of the architectural revolution of the late Quattrocento. In the church, on the right, is the chapel with frescoes of the *Flagellation* and prophets by the Venetian Sebastiano del Piombo, for whom Michelangelo supplied drawings. These too are revolutionary, challenging the Peruginesque conventions of earlier murals in the church.

On Sundays the churches of Trastevere are crowded, not least San Francesco a Ripa, a few minutes from Santa Cecilia, *vaut le detour* for Gian Lorenzo Bernini's deeply moving statue of the *Beata Ludovica Albertoni*. Trastevere remains a working-class district. But it was not always so. A few minutes walk to the north is the Farnesina, the villa built by Agostino Chigi, a Sienese banker who employed a number of very distinguished artists in its decoration. Raphael's *Galatea* is in a class of its own, but the frescoes of Sodoma and Baldassare Peruzzi are also impressive.

Bernini was the universal genius of seventeenth-century Rome – sculptor,

Giovanni Lorenzo Bernini, Sant'Andrea al Quirinale, portico, 1658–71 (top) and
Michelangelo, Porta Pia, 1561–4 (above).

painter, architect, impresario – and Borromini his equal in imagination. Neither should be studied in pedantic isolation, and a short walk helps to set their contribution in context. Set out early for the Porta Pia, the admirably astringent eastern gate designed by Michelangelo and built in 1561–4, which will happily outlive Sir Basil Spence's nearby British Embassy, the travertine facings of which look like diseased concrete. Take the Via XX Settembre westwards towards the centre of Rome. After 600 metres, on the right, is Santa Susanna with, on the last altar to the left, Bernini's celebrated *Saint Teresa in Ecstasy*, which epitomizes the fervency of Seicento Rome. In the morning light the very marble seems alive.

Continue to the major crossing, the Quattro Fontane. As traffic roars nearby it is sobering to think that in the palace on the left, as recently as the 1920s, the daughter of the house, then Anna Maria Volpi, was regularly woken by the sound of sheep being driven along the cobbled street to market. On the far left corner is one of the architectural miracles of Rome, Borromini's San Carlo alle Quattro Fontane, begun in 1637. The ingenious façade does not prepare you for the subtle movement of the elliptical space within. Further on, as if conceived in direct competition, is Bernini's Sant'Andrea al Quirinale, built in 1658–61 for Cardinal Camillo Pamphilj. In the oval interior, marble and stucco are used to brilliant effect. On the first altar on the right is a moving late work (1676), the *Death of Saint Francis Xavier*, by the Genoese Giovanni Battista Gaulli, il Baciccio, who was the most dramatic painter of late baroque Rome. Heading on for the centre of the city, one route passes the Trevi Fountain, the baroque theatricality of which is evidently timeless in appeal.

The greatest of the fountains of Rome is Bernini's stupendous *Fontana dei Fiumi* of 1651 in the centre of the Piazza Navona, west of the Pantheon, the successor of the Stadium of Domitian. The piazza, crowded now except in the early morning, is one of the most satisfying urban spaces in Italy, with its three fountains and the concave façade added by Borromini to Rinaldi's Sant'Agnese in Agone on the west side.

The Piazza Navona is the ideal starting point for a circuit of churches which boast masterpieces that define the course of painting in Counter-Reformation Rome. Strike south for the Corso Vittorio Emanuele. Three hundred metres west, on the north side, is the Chiesa Nuova, the church of the Oratorians. The vast ceiling was frescoed by Pietro Berretini da Cortona, Bernini's only rival in the range of his gifts as both painter and architect. On the fourth altar to the left is the *Visitation* by Federico Barocci, a picture which profoundly moved the church's austere founder, Saint Filippo Neri. Beyond, in the left transept, is Barocci's incomparably lovely *Presentation of the Virgin* of 1594. On the high altar is a revered *Madonna* surrounded by cherubs and angels by Rubens, whose flanking groups of saints of 1606–8 express the artist's excitement at receiving a major Roman commission.

Rubens admired Barocci but, as it happened, took little if any notice of the most revolutionary painter of the previous years in Rome, Michelangelo Merisi, il Caravaggio. Two hundred metres apart, to the north-east of the Piazza Navona, are two of Caravaggio's most arresting works. Of these the later in date is the *Madonna dei Pellegrini* of 1605 at Sant' Agostino; the kneeling spectator looks up from the worn feet of the elderly peasants to the celestial purity of the Virgin. Caravaggio's three canvasses in the chapel of Saint Matthew at San Luigi dei Francesi were painted between 1597 and 1602. Seeing these by artificial light we do not appreciate immediately how intelligently Caravaggio allowed for the natural illumination of a north-facing space. His majestic tenebrous compositions found classical reposts diagonally across the church in Domenichino's frescoes of scenes from the life of Saint Cecilia, executed in 1616–17.

Why Domenichino's was to be the defining influence of early Seicento Rome is well demonstrated at Sant' Andrea della Valle, hardly 400 metres away. Follow the south side of San Luigi and turn left on the Corso del Rinascimento. On the left is the sixteenth-century Palazzo della Sapienza; across the majestic courtyard is Sant'Ivo, most idiosyncratic of Borromini's fantasies. There is little of fantasy in Rainaldi's imposing façade of Sant'Andrea across the Corso Vittorio Emanuele. Inside, we are impelled to advance to the domed crossing, with Domenichino's celebrated pendentives of the *Evangelists* (1621–8) and, above, Lanfranco's luminous *Paradise*, finished in 1625. The vault of the presbytery was decorated in 1624–8 with scenes from the life of Saint Andrea by Domenichino, dynamic in their classicism and impressive in their narrative legibility. By comparison the large murals below by the Neapolitan Mattia Preti seem overwrought.

On leaving Sant'Andrea, follow the street to the right of the church until it ends and then turn left: fifty metres away is San Carlo ai Catinari. Domenichino's *Christian Virtues* in the pendentives of the dome are of 1630; beautiful in colour, these are among the most satisfying cre-

ations of the Roman baroque. On leaving the church, turn left and left again to regain the Corso Vittorio Emanuele and make east for the Gesù, the main Roman church of the Jesuits, begun by Vignola and continued by Giacomo della Porta. The church might already have seemed somewhat old-fashioned when in 1672 Baciccio embarked on the decoration of the vault of the nave with the *Triumph of the Name of Jesus*, as well as the cupola and the tribune. The Genoese painter's innate sense of drama, a sense fortified by experience of contemporary sculpture, animates what was by any standard an ambitious scheme.

The palaces of baroque Rome are less accessible than her churches. No tourist should fail, however, to see the Galleria Doria-Pamphilj on the Corso, entered from the Piazza del Collegio Romano. The Galleria is in a section of the palace reconstructed by Gabriele Valvassori in 1731–5 and contains the remarkable family collection, with major works by Titian, Caravaggio and Claude, as well as Velasquez's arresting *Portrait of Pope Innocent X (Pamphilj)*, the uncompromising realism of which inspired Francis Bacon, and Bernini's more benign bust. For eighteenth-century visitors, the Galleria of the Palazzo Colonna, open less frequently, was a highlight of their Roman experience. And in its orchestration of pictures, notably landscapes, the Galleria still has no equal.

Rome boasts other remarkable collections of both sculptures and pictures. Pride of place must go to the Villa Borghese, built originally for Cardinal Scipione Borghese. It was redecorated for Marcantonio Borghese in the final decades of the Settecento by Antonio Asprucci. There was no pedantry in his neoclassicism, and the interiors he created constitute the perfect setting for a impressive dynastic collection. On the ground floor are the Roman marbles, outshone by a series of masterpieces by Bernini – of which the *Apollo and Daphne* is inevitably the most celebrated – and Canova's horizontal *Princess Pauline Borghese*, Italian counterpart of Goya's *Duchess of Alba*. Here too are the magnificent Caravaggios secured by the Borghese. Upstairs is the picture collection with two of the most significant milestones of the High Renaissance, Raphael's *Baglione Entombment*, appropriated from Perugia, and Titian's miraculous *Sacred and Profane Love*, both key early works of the artists.

Since 1929 the Vatican has theoretically been an independent state. Mussolini's decision to open the Via del Conciliazione means that St Peter's no longer takes the visitor by surprise. But the approach remains awe-inspiringly spectacular as the pilgrim or tourist advances into the vast piazza flanked by Bernini's prodigious colonnades. Ahead is Maderno's façade, finished in 1614, masking the church to which so many of his predecessors, including Bramante, Raphael and Sangallo, had contributed, crowned by the great dome begun by Michelangelo but completed by della Porta, who also built the two lower domes. Within, it is the baroque that dominates: Bernini's baldachin; the mosaics after Domenichino, Sacchi, Maratta, Cortona and others; the sequence of papal tombs – among which Bernini's to Popes Urban VIII and Alexander VII are of particular distinction. Canova's monument to the last Stuarts in the left aisle was, rather touchingly, paid for by their kinsman King George IV. The tour parties inevitably cluster round Michelangelo's peerless early *Pietà*.

The Vatican Museums are, even out of season, under siege. The new visitor centre is dire. But persevere. Most tourists head for the Sistine Chapel, where it is now virtually impossible to study, still less to enjoy, the frescoes by Perugino and his assistants, the epoch-making ceiling by Michelangelo or his great *Last Judgement* of the altar wall. It is easier to do justice to the equally cerebral frescoes in the Stanze di Raffaelo, commissioned like Michelangelo's ceiling by Pope Julius II; the *School of Athens* is perhaps Raphael's most extraordinary achievement. The force of numbers means, alas, that one can no longer enter the small chapel of Saint Nicholas decorated by Fra Angelico. This opens off the Sala dei Palafrenieri, from which is reached the Loggia di Raffaello, with the fifty-two biblical scenes devised by Raphael and his associates which exercised an immense influence on later iconography. The circuit of the palace continues with the Borgia Apartments, decorated at speed by Pinturicchio with the help of a troupe of assistants for Pope Alexander VI; here the sightseer has less competition.

The Vatican's holding of antiquities is extraordinary. No visitor should miss the Courtyard of the Belvedere, transformed in 1773, which houses what were for some centuries many of the most famous classical sculptures in the world, including the *Laocoön*, discovered in 1506, the *Apollo Belvedere* and the *Hermes*. But the Museo Pio-Clementino also deserves a *coup d'oeil*, for it is the most complete such museum installation of the eighteenth century to survive, its collections due to a very proper wish on successive pontiffs' part to preserve the archaeological inheritance of their state.

The Pinacoteca Vaticana, by contrast, celebrates the artistic tastes of the French.

When in 1815 Canova recovered the pictures Bonaparte's agents had appropriated from the Papal States for the Louvre, they were retained in Rome. In some instances – for example, the two predella panels taken from the otherwise complete Fra Angelico altarpiece at Perugia – the decision seems deplorable and should surely now be reversed. But it is nonetheless fascinating to see how systematically the towns of central Italy were raided. Raphael was high in the sights of the French, and is represented by three great altarpieces, the early *Oddi Coronation of the Virgin* from Perugia, the mature *Madonna di Foligno* with its breathtaking landscape and the late *Transfiguration*, so long regarded as one of the key masterpieces of western art. Almost equally revered was Domenichino's *Communion of Saint Jerome*. A modern audience may be more moved by Caravaggio's powerful *Deposition*. These pictures were all major public statements. Leonardo's *Saint Jerome* may, to judge from the unprecedented prominence of the lion, have had a more personal message. Unapologetically old-fashioned in its arrangement, the Pinacoteca remains an oasis of near calm which no one interested in Italian painting can miss. Appropriately, it also houses Lawrence's portrait of King George IV, who paid for the return of the works of art retrieved by Canova.

72
OSTIA

❖

EVIDENCE of the classical world is omnipresent in the hinterland of Rome. Ancient and modern coexist. But the tourist who arrives at the Aeroporto Leonardo da Vinci at Fiumicino, or has to kill time there, may not be aware that it is only a few miles away from the former port of Ostia, through which so much of Rome's human and commercial traffic passed. The site, by a bend of the Tiber, was well chosen. A fortress was constructed in about 338 BC, and the town grew steadily in importance, with no fewer than 100,000 inhabitants in its heyday. Silting of the Tiber led to the creation of a large artificial harbour under the Emperor Claudius, which was supplemented by a smaller one in the reign of Trajan. The centre of the city was substantially redeveloped under Domitian and in the second century AD. Decline set in during the following century, when much of Ostia's trade passed to Portus, on the right bank of the Tiber, and accelerated with the relative eclipse of Rome in the fourth century. That Saint Monica, mother of Saint Augustine, died there when the port was blockaded in 387 was a portent of what was to follow. The site was abandoned and the episcopal see transferred to Velletri; in 830 Pope Gregory IV founded his small town of Gregoriopoli half a kilometre to the east. Here, in 1483–6, the Florentine architect Baccio Pontelli built a state of the art fortress for Cardinal Giuliano della Rovere, the future Pope Julius II.

Portico of the Piazzale of the Corporations: a ship, mosaic.

Much of the town wall can still be traced. From the Porta Romana, the decumanus maximus runs to the southwest. This is flanked by the remains of the obligatory public buildings – no fewer than eighteen temples and sanctuaries, public baths, a palaestra and barracks – as well as numerous residential areas. The masonry is largely of brick, and it is the ensemble rather than the calibre of any individual building (with the exception of the Hadrianic Capitolium) that impresses. The shadows cast by the pines ensure that even in the heat of the summer it is a pleasure to walk and search out the grisaille mosaics that make the Roman world seem surprisingly close. One in the Baths of Neptune shows the winds of the provinces with which most trade was conducted: Sicily, Egypt represented by a crocodile, Africa with an elephant, and Spain. Others, in the portico surrounding the so-called Piazzale delle Corporazioni, illustrate aspects of Ostia's trade. Looking down on a mosaic of a ship under sail, we are left in no doubt of Ostia's vital importance to the economy of imperial Rome. It was through Ostia that the city received her tribute of oil from Africa and the grain of Sicily and Egypt on which her population depended. Where better to escape when stranded for a few hours at the airport?

73
TIVOLI

THE Roman campagna has, alas, been steadily encroached upon since the late nineteenth century. But the great aqueduct, so beloved by the young Corot, survives, and on a fresh morning or a cloudless evening one can still see the world as Claude did. The pope continues to retreat to Castel Gandolfo and numerous villas and gardens survive. But if the visitor to Rome has time only for a single excursion, Tivoli must win.

Villa Adriana: the north wall of the Stoa, 118–34.

The town hangs above the west bank of the river Aniene as it breaks through a barrier of rock to plunge into a deep gorge. The drama of the setting and the splendour of the views down over the campagna were clearly admired in ancient times, and from the seventeenth century few landscapes were painted more often.

Of the Roman town the outstanding survivor is the circular Temple of the Sibyl (or Vesta) that overhangs the falls of the Aniene. This owes its exceptional state of preservation for a monument in so exposed a place to its adaptation as a church in the medieval period. Within the town, several early churches survive. The finest is perhaps the Romanesque San Silvestro on the picturesque Via del Colle, to the south-west of the late Duomo, which contains a notable thirteenth-century carved group of the *Deposition*. Late Romanesque Santa Maria Maggiore adjoins the greatest monument of the town, the Villa d'Este.

Cardinal Ippolito d'Este was appointed governor of Tivoli in 1550, and proceeded to replace his official residence with a spectacular villa designed by the Neapolitan Pirro Ligorio, who was in so many ways the artistic heir of Giulio Romano. The architecture is magnificent and the villa retains much of its frescoed decoration. But the glory of the Villa d'Este is the garden laid out on the sloping ground below, with cascading terraces that offer, as it were, a formal counterpoint to the natural falls of the Aniene nearby. Ligorio himself was responsible for much of what survives, including the Fontana dell'Ovato and the Fontana dei Draghi, supposedly thrown up in a single night in honour of Pope Gregory XIII's visit in 1572. The garden was quickly recognized as the *ne plus ultra*

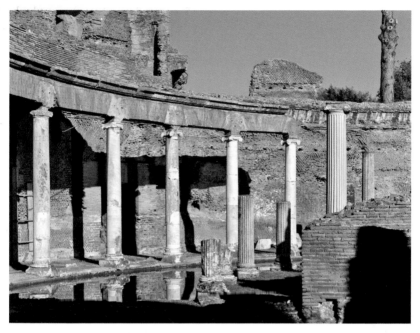

Villa Adriana: the villa of the island, 118–34.

of Renaissance design, and its echo can be sensed in many later schemes as far afield as Jacobean England.

The second of the great gardens of Tivoli is very different in character. The Villa Gregoriana is opposite the Temple of the Sibyl, entered from the Largo Sant'Angelo at the eastern end of the Ponte Gregoriano, built for Pope Gregory XVI (1831–46). The area had been built on in Roman times, but the garden, which has recently been restored, is a late creation of the Romantic movement. The circuit is punctuated by grottoes – that of Neptune was once a channel of the river – and the Belvedere, placed for the spectacular view of the Great Cascade.

At the foot of the valley into which the Aniene falls are the ruins of the vast complex of the Villa Adriana, built between AD 118 and 134 for the Emperor Hadrian. He travelled extensively for strategic reasons, and monuments in Alexandria and Greece were among those he sought to evoke in what Robin Lane-Fox has recently described as a theme park. The villa was first explored in the sixteenth century and received much attention from eighteenth-century excavators in pursuit of statues. The small site museum only houses those found since 1951. For the non-archaeologist, the charm of the site owes much to the juxtaposition of the ruins and the wooded hillside, the contours of which were intelligently exploited by the emperor's builders.

74
ANAGNI
❧

DESPITE the proximity of Rome, or perhaps because of this, the ancient cities of the southern Lazio are less well known than these deserve to be. Palestrina with its Roman past and Ferentino, still partly protected by its ancient walls, are both remarkable, but neither has quite the appeal of Anagni, which lies between them on a ridge. Anagni was taken by the Romans in 306 bc, but little survives of their ordered plan. The town even now has a medieval air. Long controlled by the Caetani, Anagni had its period of glory in the thirteenth century. Three members of a prominent family of the town, the

Segni, were elected to the papacy, the formidable Innocent III (1198–1216), Gregory IX (1227–41) and Alexander IV (1254–61), while Benedetto Caetani, Pope Boniface VIII (1294–1303), maintained a close association with the town.

Anagni lies at the centre of the prosperous Valle Latina, and I am glad I first saw it crowded on market day with vendors almost blocking the narrow streets. In the northern section of the town it is worth seeing a stretch of the early town wall and glancing briefly at the Casa Barnekow, a restored fourteenth-century house. Further on is the restrained, but also much restored, Palazzo Comunale of 1159–63, which has been attributed to Giacomo da Iseo. Higher up are a number of medieval palaces with later accretions. More remarkable is the palace of Boniface VIII, which was in fact built for

Cathedral, crypt: Virgin, fresco (detail of vault), after 1231.

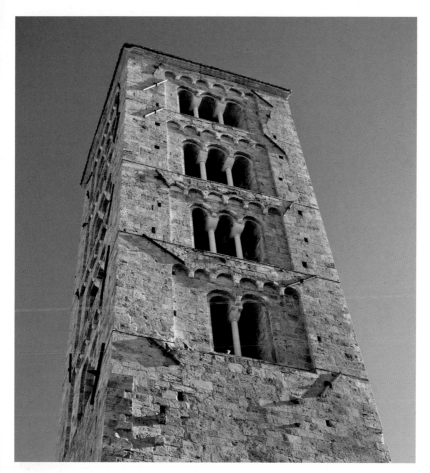

Cathedral Campanile.

Gregory IX, who was visited there by the Emperor Frederick II in 1230; it was here that Pope Boniface was seized by supporters of Philippe le Bel of France in 1303, only to be freed after two days by his local supporters. Two rooms retain sections of contemporary decoration, including the Sala degli Ocche (geese) with depictions of geese and other birds in lozenges arranged diagonally.

Nearby, at the south end of the town, is the Romanesque cathedral, largely built under Bishop Pietro between 1077 and 1104, but remodelled in the following century. It was here in 1160 that the intemperate Pope Alexander III formally excommunicated Frederick Barbarossa, a decisive moment in the long struggle between the Church and the Holy Roman Empire. The campanile is particularly satisfying, and the interior of the church is remarkable by any standard, with the pavement of before 1227 by Cosma di Jacopo, protagonist of the Cosmati family, a handsome ciborium, and an exceptional paschal candelabrum signed by Vassalletto, who also made the bishop's throne of 1263. Two flights of steps lead down to the crypt, the nave of which is screened by columns from the flanking aisles. The pavement of after 1231 is by Cosma and his sons, Luca and Jacopo. The frescoes of between 1231 and 1255 include scenes from the Old Testament and the Apocalypse, and are among the finest of their date in southern Italy, robust in colour and forceful in design. Off the crypt, with murals of the same period but of more routine calibre, is the chapel of Saint Thomas à Becket. Becket's cult was strongly encouraged by Innocent III and his successors, as he had so strenuously supported the pretensions of the papacy to control religious appointments in England. A contemporary Limoges reliquary of the saint is in the treasury of the cathedral. Equally remarkable are the vestments associated with Innocent III and a cope with New Testament scenes now thought to be from Cyprus, presented by Boniface VIII in 1295. At Anagni, perhaps more than anywhere else, one can still sense something of the frisson between the religious and secular in medieval Italy.

Palazzo of Pope Boniface VIII: Sala degli Ocche, fresco (detail).

76 Atri •

• L'Aquila 75

The Abruzzi

75

L'AQUILA

❖

FEW cities are so majestically placed as L'Aquila. It is backed to the north by the dramatic mass of the Gran Sasso and has long been the major town of the Abruzzi. On a roughly triangular site that falls steeply on two sides, the city was founded in 1254, apparently with the approval of the Emperor Frederick II, and reconstructed in 1265 by Charles of Anjou. Although challenged by rebellions and interrupted by invasions by, among others, Braccio Fortebraccio, not to mention the French occupation of 1798–1814, Neapolitan rule endured until the Risorgimento. In 2009 a severe earthquake shattered the ancient city; little is beyond recovery but it will take many years before all the monuments are fully in commission.

Cola dell'Amatrice, San Bernardino.

L'Aquila is rich in medieval churches: Romanesque Santa Maria di Paganica, with the vigorous reliefs of its portal; Gothic San Silvestro, for which Raphael's *Visitation* now in the Prado was painted; San Domenico founded by Charles II of Anjou in 1309; and a half-dozen more. All yield in ambition to the great Romanesque church of Santa Maria di Collemaggio south-east of the walls. This was founded in 1287 by Pietro da Morrone, who was crowned here as Pope Celestine V in 1294. The slightly later polychrome façade is striking, and there is an exceptional portal on the north front. In the chapel to the right of the choir is the Renaissance tomb of San Pietro Celestino by Girolamo da Vicenza (1507).

By the time this was commissioned, the church had been overtaken as a place of pilgrimage by the basilica of San Bernardino, to the east of the junction of Via Roma with the Corso Vittorio Emanuele in the heart of the town. Saint Bernard of Siena died at L'Aquila in 1444 and the church was begun ten years later. The confident classical façade, devised by Cola dell'Amatrice, was not built until 1524, and the interior was subsequently remodelled in the baroque taste. On the right is the chapel of San Bernardino, with the saint's mausoleum by the outstanding local sculptor Silvestro dell' Aquila, whose earlier monument of 1496 to Maria Pereira and her daughter on the left wall of the choir reflects both Florentine and Roman models.

The most assertive building of L'Aquila is the enormous castle at the north-eastern angle of the town, which seems to defy the Gran Sasso that serves as its backdrop. This was built after a rebellion of 1529 to the design of the military engineer Pier Luigi Scrivà, but only completed a century later. The plan is quadrangular, with formidable angle bastions. The castle now houses the Museo Nazionale d'Abruzzo, with comprehensive collections of both sculptures and pictures from the region. There are no outstanding masterpieces, but local artists such as the Master of Beffi and Andrea Delitio deserve to be more widely known.

The most idiosyncratic of the Abruzzesi of the Renaissance was the beautifully named Saturnino de'Gatti. The pictures by him in the Museo Nazionale do not prepare us for the enchantment of his frescoes of 1494 in the parish church at Tornimparte, eighteen kilometres south-west of L'Aquila – and best approached by the ordinary road rather than the autostrada. The choir is decorated with Passion scenes from the *Arrest of Christ* to the *Resurrection*, the vault with a vision of Paradise teeming with angel musicians. Saturnino is an artist of ingenuous charm – and I shall always be grateful to Everett Fahy for encouraging me to visit this 'Sistine Chapel of the Abruzzi'. The church was not affected by the 2009 earthquake.

Medieval prosperity means that there are many fine early churches in the hinterland of L'Aquila, some of which boast early murals. But the most atmospheric site in the area must be the medieval castle of Ocre, fifteen or so kilometres south-east. Begun in 1222, it is surrounded by a well-preserved wall. Within is a chaos of shattered buildings. From the eastern section of the walls one looks directly down on the township of Fossa some 290 metres below: it was over this precipice that San Massimo, the patron saint of L'Aquila, is said to have been hurled in AD 210.

The castle walls.

76

ATRI

❧

ATRI stands back from the Adriatic, surveying a wide swathe of the coastal plain. The ancient Roman town commanded the road to Pescara and the place continued to have a certain importance. With the disintegration of the empire of the Hohenstaufen, Atri was subsumed by the duchy of Spoleto and then taken by other local powers. But in 1395 the signoria passed to the Acquaviva family, who would retain it until 1775 when Atri was absorbed into the kingdom of Naples. It is to the Acquaviva dukes that Atri owes many of the monuments that make it one of the most interesting towns of its size in southern Italy.

The much remodelled palace of the Acquaviva now serves as the Municipio. The elaborate portal of the church of Sant'Agostino, attributed to Matteo da Napoli, reflects the late Gothic of that city. But the building that most completely expresses the ambition and taste of the ducal line is the cathedral of Santa Maria Assunta, which overlies a Roman cistern that can be reached through the Museo Diocesano. This austere structure of Istrian stone with an elegant west entrance and three differing Gothic doors on the south side was rebuilt from c.1280 onwards, and is overlooked by the splendid campanile constructed in 1502–3 by Antonio da Lodi, the Milanese architect who had completed the comparable campanile of the cathedral at nearby Teramo in 1493.

The remarkable cycle of frescoes in the choir represents the high point of

Cathedral: Andrea Delitio, Annunciation of the Death of the Virgin *(detail).*

Cathedral: Andrea Delitio, Annunciation of the Death of the Virgin *(detail).*

Abruzzese Quattrocento painting. Andrea Delitio is an elusive artist, recorded between 1450 and 1473. He clearly knew the work of that subtle Umbrian counterpart of Sassetta, Bartolomeo di Tommaso da Foligno; he had some knowledge of Uccello and other Florentines of the mid-century; and his delight in colour implies an awareness of the late Gothic painters of Venice, who had so many patrons on the Adriatic coast. Delitio was a narrator of genius, with an instinctive love of anecdote. An almost excessive enthusiasm for perspective characterizes the vault frescoes with saints and virtues – Saint Luke painting an emphatically Quattrocento half-length Madonna, Saint Ambrose seated at a disconcertingly insubstantial table.

It was when Delitio progressed to the narrative sequences of the walls that his full genius is expressed. These are treated in four tiers, commencing with the story of Joachim and Anna in the lunettes and continuing with the life of the Virgin and the childhood of Christ, concluding with the *Annunciation of the Death of the Virgin,* her *Dormition, Assumption* and *Coronation.* Federico Zeri fairly commented that the cycle is 'enlivened by a rich and appealing humour'. The viewer is transported to a world that Delitio's contemporaries would have recognized, with richly detailed architecture and a wealth of subordinate incident. Castles erupt from the hills behind the cavern that serves as stable in Delitio's *Nativity;* the train of the Magi moves through a rippling landscape of rounded hillocks; and the Holy Family sets out on the journey to Egypt from a ridge not unlike that on which Atri stands, followed by a heavily laden peasant woman who pays no attention to the eroded ridges that descend precipitously towards the fortress-protected roadstead, in which ships are ready for the voyage. The Virgin is born in a chamber with a chimneypiece of ducal scale and later embroiders under an arcade with a classical festoon. Most extraordinary of all is the fresco of the annunciation of her death, a concertinaed jumble of architectural components enriched with marble facings, in which Delitio distinguishes, for example, between the rendered front of the distant church and the rough-hewn wall adjoining it; the Virgin's attendants are caught in arrested motion and only the dog is unaware of the solemnity

of the occasion. In four fictive openings above the arches that flank the choir there are startlingly realistic portraits: the Acquaviva – if such they were – are unexpectedly animated. And it is not difficult to understand why they employed Delitio, whose own portrait looks across at theirs and whose frescoes are the enduring legacy of their long-lived signoria.

A few miles to the north of the city in the valley of the Vomano there is a cluster of three medieval churches, beautifully sited Santa Maria di Propezzano and San Clemente al Vomano, both Romanesque, and San Salvatore at Morro d'Oco, built in 1331.

78 Cuma • • Naples 77

• Pompeii 79
• Amalfi 80

• Paestum 81
82 Padula •

Campania

77

NAPLES

NEAPOLIS, the 'new city', was one of the major centres of the ancient world, and the tight grid of streets at the heart of the conurbation preserves that of the Greco-Roman town. Naples flourished as a major port, supported by the fertile volcanic soil of the hinterland over which Vesuvius broods so majestically to the east. In the sixth century the city became a Byzantine outpost, achieving independence as a duchy in 763. With the Norman conquest of 1139, her significance waned. Charles of Anjou, who seized the kingdom of Sicily in 1265, made Naples his capital. Under his successors, Anjevin and Aragonese, Spanish and Bourbon, the last supplanted by the French in 1798 and 1805–15, Naples retained this status until 1860, when the kingdom which had controlled the south of Italy from the river Garigliano in the west to the Abruzzi in the east was annexed to the new kingdom of Italy. Medieval Naples was already one of the larger cities of the Mediterranean, and by the mid-seventeenth century with a population of 450,000 the city was, in this respect, the biggest in Europe.

Despite the best efforts of the Savoys, Naples was in many ways a victim of the Risorgimento. But almost heroic work in recent decades by the state, the region and such private bodies as Napoli Novantanove has transformed the visitor's experience of the city. The demands of a large population on a restricted site has meant that the development of Naples was closely packed.

The patron saint of Naples is San Gennaro (Saint Januarius), whose great cathedral was built by Charles II of Anjou to the eastern section of the former Roman town. The building is now a palimpsest. What draws the pilgrim is the saint's chapel, the second on the right, a great domed space designed by the architect Francesco Grimaldi. The decoration of this was one of the major projects of Seicento Italy. Domenichino began work on his frescoes in 1631, and these constitute a glorious and cerebral climax to his career, astonishing still in their clarity of colour. He died in 1641, enervated by artistic rivalries, and two years later was followed by Lanfranco, whose Paradise in the cupola is of visionary conviction. The splendid altar, sculpture and furniture play their part in a consistently impressive programme. There is much else in the cathedral, but it is to the chapel that one inevitably returns.

Leaving the cathedral, turn left – south – and take the first street to the left. After a hundred metres on the right is the Monte della Misericordia, in the church of which is a seminal masterpiece of Caravaggio. Painted in 1607, *The Seven Acts of Mercy* still astonishes, a manifesto of Christian charity by one of the most deeply committed and visually persuasive of religious artists. A whole generation of Neapolitan painters, notably Giovanni Battista Caracciolo and Mattia Preti, were galvanized by Caravaggio's example.

Return to the Via del Duomo and continue, to turn right at the first significant

Opposite: Chiesa di Pia, Monte della Misericordia: Caravaggio, The Seven Acts of Mercy *(1607).*

intersection, the Via San Biagio – the 'Spaccanapoli', successor of the ancient decumanus, narrow and atmospheric. Palace follows palace, and side streets entice you to others. On the left is the small Sant'Angelo a Nilo, with the Brancaccio monument by Donatello and other Tuscan sculptors. Almost opposite is the Piazza San Domenico Maggiore, off which is the Cappella Sansevero, famed for its veiled statues by Antonio Corradini and Giuseppe Sammartino, virtuoso highpoints of the Neapolitan late baroque. Further on, the Spaccanapoli reaches the Piazza Monteoliveto, with its quintessentially southern *guglia* of the *Immaculate Conception* of 1747–50. To the south is the vast mass of one of the great monuments of Anjevin Naples, Santa Chiara, with its Gothic dynastic tombs. To the north, appropriating the diamond-studded façade of the earlier palace of the Sansevero, is the Gesù Nuovo of 1584–1601, with a constellation of baroque pictures and, on the entrance wall, Francesco Solimena's energetic *Expulsion of Heliodorus*. The Spaccanapoli continues, to intersect the main street of the old town, the Toledo, named after the Spanish viceroy who caused it to be constructed on the line of the former moat outside the Anjevin walls.

The heart of Naples with its teeming churches and spectacular palaces deserves to be explored in detail. Major works by such artists as Mattia Preti, Francesco Solimena and Sebastiano Conca are to be found in context. One is always aware of the proximity of the sea, and the importance of the port explains why Charles I of Anjou built his Castel Nuovo beside it. Most impressive from the outside, this was reconstructed by Alfonso I of Aragon. His entry to Naples in 1443 is celebrated in the reliefs of the triumphal arch above the main entrance. To the west is the ponderous Palazzo Reale, the façade of which is answered – in a particularly happy example of neo-classical urban design – by the basilica of San Francesco di Paola.

The perfect vantage point from which to survey Naples is the Certosa di San Martino, to which the energetic can walk from the Toledo. The visitor comes first to the church, completed by Cosimo Fanzago, which was adorned by some of the greatest masters of Seicento Naples. Above the entrance is Massimo Stanzione's noble *Deposition* of 1638; the vault frescoes are by Lanfranco, while the

Castel Nuovo.

Prophets between the side chapels are by the Spanish-born Jusepe de Ribera. Stanzione was also responsible for the second chapel on the left. In the presbytery is Reni's late unfinished *Nativity*, wonderful not least in its tonal restraint. To the left is the sacristy, through which one reaches the Chapel of the Treasury with Ribera's deeply felt *Deposition*, and on the ceiling Luca Giordano's enchanting and airy *Triumph of Judith*. Further rooms to the right of the presbytery lead to the Great Cloister that seems to overhang the city, which is literally laid out at the spectator's feet, the port to the right, the wide silhouette of the volcano beyond. There could be no more appropriate place to house the museum of the city of Naples.

Naples has long been famed for its museums. The Museo Archeologico Nazionale is on its eponymous piazza off the northern continuation of the Toledo. This houses two collections of major importance: the Roman marbles inherited by the Bourbons from the Farnese, including the *Bull* and the *Hercules*, which exercised so profound an influence on post-Renaissance masters; and the extraordinary haul of Roman finds yielded by the royal excavations at Pompeii and Herculaneum, finds that transformed the Enlightenment's understanding of classical art. The bronzes, the detached murals and, not least, the remarkable mosaic of the *Battle of Alexander* which was inspired by a Hellenistic prototype are of the finest quality, while the more intimate objects are of equal interest.

The royal palace of Capodimonte is, as its name implies, on a hill, to the north of the city, set in a splendid park, begun in 1735 and only completed a century later. It is built round three linked internal courtyards. On the first floor is the major sequence of staterooms, with portraits of the Bourbons and indigenous furniture. The collection of pictures falls conveniently into two sections. The Bourbons inherited the Parmese collection of the Farnese, including Correggio's *Zingarella* (the Gipsy Madonna) and an unrivalled group of Parmigianinos, as well as nine Titians, of which the disturbing portrait of Pope Paul III with his nephews is the most remarkable. The Farnese also owned Bellini's breathtaking *Transfiguration*. Capodimonte's holding of Neapolitan pictures and those painted in or for Neapolitan patrons is without rival, ranging from Simone Martini's *Saint Louis* to a constellation of Seicento masterpieces: Caravaggio's late *Flagellation*, Bernardino Cavallino's *Saint Cecilia* and remarkable holdings of both Preti and Giordano.

Capodimonte is a ponderous structure. So too is the great palace begun in 1752 for King Charles III by Luigi Vanvitelli at Caserta, magical as is its park. It is an earlier, if unfinished, palace that haunts the imagination, Fanzago's Palazzo di Donn'Anna, built about 1642 for Anna Carafa, wife of the viceroy Felipe Ramiro Guzman. Most Claudian of architectural conceptions, hanging above the sea, this is best viewed from the Via di Posillipo to the west of the city, begun in 1812 by the adventurer Joachim Murat, whom Napoleon had installed as King of Naples, but only completed after his expulsion.

78

CUMA

❧

THE modern visitor to Naples goes inevitably to Pompeii. For our eighteenth-century predecessors the Roman sights west of Pozzuoli held an equal priority. These used to be best explored on foot, as I discovered some years ago when it proved impossible to hire a car at short notice. A suburban train stops at Baia, near the so-called Temple of Diana, in reality part of the huge, partly excavated complex of an imperial palace. I headed west, across a low ridge, to descend to Lago Fusaro, which is separated by a narrow spit of land from the sea. Across the lake is Vanvitelli's Casino Reale, built in 1782 for King Ferdinand IV of Naples, floating as it seems on the surface of the water, and to the south looms the dramatic silhouette of Ischia.

Turn north for the road to Cuma. After about three kilometres you reach the amphitheatre which is cut into the hillside; an arcade, much eroded, presided over the terraces and fields of the nearby farm, but is now officiously fenced off. Further on is the site of the Roman town, and beyond this are the ruins of the sanctuary of the Cumaean Sibyl on the flank of the ancient acropolis above the coast. The metalled road goes directly to the official entrance, but it was more satisfying, 200 metres or so from the turn, to cross a field on the right to the insubstantial remains of a temple and then follow the Cripta Romana, the impressive tunnel which cuts through the hill from east to west. Of the Roman road tunnels in the area, this was the most readily accessible and few classical structures are

more suggestive. While I trust it may long be spared the restorer's attentions, and echo to the sounds not of tourists but of birds unaccustomed to unwanted disturbance, it is frustrating that access is now all but impossible.

The Sibyl was venerated by the Greek colonists who settled at Cuma, and it was they who in the sixth century BC embarked on the elaborate excavations of the rock which were extended some 200 years later. A gallery, over 130 metres long, was cut through the soft tufa. This is lit by windows on the west looking out to the sea. There are subsidiary arms to the gallery, and at the end is the rectangular room with three niches in which the Sibyl made her oracular pronouncements. To the north stretches the terraced acropolis, with the podium of tufa blocks of the Temple of Apollo and scattered vestiges of numerous other buildings; a road with Roman paving leads up to the husk of the Temple of

Approach to the Grotto of the Sibyl.

Apollo fringed by ilexes on the summit. The drama of the place inspired Salvator Rosa's *Landscape with the Cumaean Sibyl* of the Wallace Collection, and the views over the coast are astonishing, not least in the benign sunlight of a spring afternoon. But it is time to turn inland. Make for the Arco Felice, built under the Emperor Domitian (AD 81–96), a viaduct for the road from Rome to Pozzuoli. One is again reminded how ordered was the infrastructure of ancient Rome.

Alas, it is no longer possible to follow the Roman road to Pozzuoli by the Grotta di Cocceio – named after Cocceius, the architect who built it under Agrippa, the Emperor Augustus's associate – the tunnel a kilometre in length that cuts through the Monte Grillo to Lake Avernus. So the pedestrian must make a long detour by way of the smaller Lake Lucrinus. Lake Avernus is a perfect example of a volcanic crater, circled almost completely by steep wooded slopes. The place must always have exercised its spell upon the human imagination. Virgil regarded it as the entrance to the Underworld; Richard Wilson and other eighteenth-century painters responded to its magic. Few Roman remains are more beautifully placed than the so-called Temple of Apollo on the eastern flank of the lake, originally part of a bath complex, with a substantial circular chamber set in an octagonal structure. The reflections of the building stretch across the glassy surface of the water in the failing evening light.

79
POMPEII

❖

WHEN he described the catastrophic eruption of Mount Vesuvius on 24 August AD 79, the elder Pliny had no notion that this would actually preserve the fabric of so many of the buildings it overwhelmed. Pompeii, a significant town with a population of perhaps 20,000, was smothered by ashes: her smaller neighbour, Herculaneum, was entombed by the lava flow. The latter is the better preserved, but it is Pompeii, systematically excavated for the Bourbon kings, that captured the European imagination. It inspired the best known of Lord Lytton's novels, *The Last Days of Pompeii*, and the most dramatic canvas of the greatest Russian Romantic painter, Alexandre Brullov – before which Sir Walter Scott sat for an hour in silent admiration.

Right: Pompeii, road to the Porta Ercolano.

Stabian baths: stucco decoration.

The tourist is unlikely to find silence in the centre of Pompeii itself, even out of season. But then the town would not have been silent in its bustling heyday. Rather than follow a fixed route, it is best to wander, dodging the coach parties. While the public buildings deserve attention, what is exceptional about Pompeii is the number of private houses that survive. Guards will encourage you to visit those in their control, but after half a dozen interest can flag. It should, moreover, be remembered that many of the finer murals and the more significant finds are in the Museo Archeologico at Naples. The usual entrance is the Porta Marina to the south-west of the town, the gate nearest the forum, the centre of religious and civic life. Here are the impressive basilica, two temples and a covered market. Further east, off the Strada dell'Abbondanza, are the Stabian baths, with a striking section of stucco decoration and well-preserved interiors: nearby are the theatre and the smaller odeon. The very much larger amphitheatre is at the eastern angle of the walls. Built about 80 BC, this could sit 12,000: a mural now at Naples shows it in use. Beside the amphitheatre is the large palaestra, or gymnasium. Everywhere, one is conscious of the menacing cone of Vesuvius.

While one of the finest houses, that of Loreius Tiburtinus, notable for its garden, is opposite the palaestra, most are in the north-western section of the town, many off the Strada di Nola. Among the more interesting are the Casa del Poeta Tragica, described in Lytton's novel, and the Casa del Fauno, with two atriums and two peristyles; from a room between these comes the mosaic of the *Battle of Alexander* at Naples. A block to the north are the Casa dei Vettii, a prosperous merchant's ambitious residence, and the Casa degli

Amorini Dorati, both with excellent decoration. Yet more memorable are the murals of the large Villa dei Misteri, which lies outside the walls to the northwest. The Dionysiac scenes in the Sala del Grande Dipinto, which dates from about the turn of the Christian era, represent a high point of Roman painting.

Although Roman decorative murals had been known – and copied – since the Renaissance, the discovery of a large number of such schemes had an enormous influence on the direction of taste in the neoclassical era. Others have been discovered since. Particularly fine are those of the villa of Oplontis, in the immediate shadow of Vesuvius, not far from Herculaneum. No single complex perhaps gives a better notion of the sophistication of the most luxurious Roman villas or of the world of the Plinys, uncle and nephew, and their friends. After its discovery the villa was impeccably restored, but on my last visit it looked rather run down, its state paralleling the plight of the numerous ville vesuviane of the Bourbon era, classical in very different terms, that disintegrate nearby.

Below: characteristic street, with blocks to impede wheeled traffic.

80

AMALFI

❖

AMALFI is now so much a tourist town, with the hotels and shops this implies, that it takes some effort of the imagination to realize that in its heyday this was one of the major ports not just of Italy but of the Mediterranean. The area was recovered from the Goths by the Byzantines in 573, but distance from Byzantium meant that with time the Amalfitans gained de facto independence. The poverty of the local soil must have encouraged Amalfi's development as a naval and commercial power. In 812 her sailors achieved a significant victory over the Saracens, but the place was sacked in 838 by the Prince of Benevento, who controlled Salerno. A year later the Amalfitans returned. Their republic was ruled first by prefects who were selected annually and later by an elected doge. The Normans seized Amalfi in 1073, but it was briefly once again a free republic until 1101 and remained a significant maritime power. The Amalfitans' rivals, the Pisans, sacked the town in 1135 and 1137. Their town did not recover. In subsequent centuries it was to be controlled by the kings of Naples.

The Monti Lattari and the Sorrentine Peninsula rise steeply from the Gulf of Salerno. The coastal road as it winds above the shore westwards from Vietri is, even now, not for the faint-hearted. It passes Atrani, crowded within its narrow valley, and then twists down to Amalfi. The Piazza Gioia is on the waterfront; near this, from the Via Camera, you can look into the surviving portion of the Arsenale della Repubblica, an early

Cathedral, Campanile, after 1203.

medieval covered dockyard in two sections, recently restored as a museum. From the piazza walk north to the Piazza Duomo, overlooked by the Duomo to which a flight of steps ascends. The front is a reconstruction of after 1875, but the beautiful campanile on the left is original; begun in 1189, this was finished in 1276. The church is justly celebrated for its bronze doors, made in Byzantium before 1066 by Simone da Siria and presented by Pantaleone di Mauro, who in 1087 – the year in which he commanded the Amalfitan fleet in alliance with Pisa and Genoa against the ruler of Tunisia – gave a similar pair to the church of San Salvatore de'Bireto at Atrani. On the north of the Duomo is the small but singularly distinguished

Chiostro del Paradiso of 1266–8, intended as a cemetery. There is a strong Arab influence, with unexpectedly tall and narrow interlaced arches rising from the columns. The adjacent rooms house the museum.

The main street continues northwards from the piazza. A minor church apart, there is no building of particular interest, but the cumulative effect is compelling: every available piece of land on which it was practical to build was exploited.

High above Atrani is Ravello, which by the ninth century was subject to Amalfi, but in the eleventh sought to shake off its too powerful neighbour by supporting the Normans. With the eclipse of Amalfitan power, Ravello grew in both wealth and importance, and it is said to have had a population of 36,000 in the thirteenth century. The road from the coast writhes upwards, passing the Romanesque church of Santa Maria a Gradillo. Abandon your car as soon as possible, to walk up to the main piazza, which is overlooked by the Duomo; this was founded in 1086 when Ravello was made a bishopric. The austere façade has been restored. In 1179 Barisano da Trani supplied the bronze doors with compartments including scenes from the Passion and representations of saints. Equally remarkable are the ambone decorated with mosaic panels, commissioned in 1130 by the then bishop, and the pulpit of 1272 by Niccolò di Bartolomeo da Foggia.

Across the piazza is the Villa Rufolo, begun in the late thirteenth century for the prominent family of that name, a member of which is mentioned in Boccaccio's *Decameron*. The villa was purchased in 1851 and subsequently restored by a Scot, Francis Neville Reid; the most satisfying element is the courtyard with loggias on two levels. The terraced garden is reasonably well maintained. Higher up in the town is the church of San Giovanni del Toro, with a good twelfth-century pulpit by the obscure Alfano da Térmoli. The presence of works by artists not only from Byzantium but also from the Adriatic ports of Trani and Térmoli reminds us of Amalfi's former importance as a trading power.

Cathedral, Chiostro del Paradiso, 1266–8

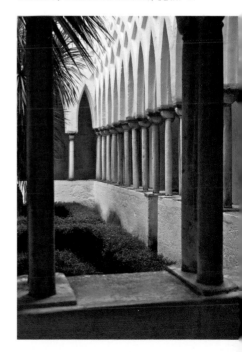

81

PAESTUM

❖

AS THE survival of so much at Pompeii is due to the eruption of Vesuvius, so that of the great temples at Paestum is owed to a more gradual scourge: malaria. Paestum, at the southern end of the once rich plain of Sale on the Gulf of Salerno, was colonized by Greeks in the seventh century bc. The original name, Poseidonia (city of Neptune), implies her importance as a port. In about 400 BC the city fell to the Lucanians, who were driven out by other Greeks in 332, only to return in 326. The Romans, who took the city in 273, renamed it Paestum. Their city flourished in its turn. In AD 370 no less a relic than the body of Saint Matthew was brought to Paestum, but in the centuries that followed malaria took hold and the site was gradually abandoned. The Norman king, Robert Guiscard, removed marble from the surviving edifices for use in his great cathedral of 1076–85 at Salerno. Shielded by woods, the temples were known to scholars, but it was only in the eighteenth century, when Antonio Joli and others depicted these, that Paestum came to wider notice.

However you approach, you come first to the walls, 4,750 metres in circuit, which enclose an area roughly oblong but cut diagonally across the north-western corner to follow a stream. The Greek line of the walls was restored by the Lucanians and the Romans. These are of large limestone blocks up to a height of up to seven metres, reinforced by a series of flanking towers. The circuit can be followed by road or on foot; there is less traffic on the north-western section.

It is, of course, the temples that draw the tourist. These lie in the centre of the town, west of the modern road that cuts across it from the Porta Aurea on the north. The entrance to the site is opposite the group of modern buildings and near the northernmost of the three extant Doric temples, the so-called Temple of Ceres. But before examining this it makes sense to walk to the southern end of the architectural area to examine the so-called Basilica, the oldest of the temples, built soon after 550 BC, and originally dedicated to Hera. The order is Doric, and all fifty of the original columns survive. A little to the north is the larger and yet more splendid Temple of Neptune. This was constructed in about 450 BC and is among the best preserved of all Doric temples, majestic in its discipline, both of proportion and detail. The honey-coloured travertine stone is of a particular beauty, responding to the natural light – in September when the sun sets almost directly to the west one can imagine that it is on fire.

Further north is the area of the Roman forum with the small Italic temple, built at the time of the Roman conquest and partly despoiled by the Normans. The other Roman buildings are for the most part poorly preserved, their charm due to the beauty of the place with its shading trees. The forum is crossed by the *decumanus maximus*. Continue north, following the Via Sacra, back to the Temple of Ceres, which was originally dedicated to Athena. This was built not long before 500 BC and in many respects adhered to the style of the Basilica. Its smaller scale may in part explain why the temple was converted into a church in late Roman times.

Across the road from the site is the excellent Museo di Paestum. Of particular importance are the metopes and the archaic frieze from the nearby sanctuary of Hera. The finds from Paestum itself are of considerable interest. And the extraordinary depiction of a boy diving on the lid of the so-called *Tomb of the Diver* is among the most vivid images to survive from antiquity.

Temple of Neptune and the Basilica, from the Roman road to the north-west.

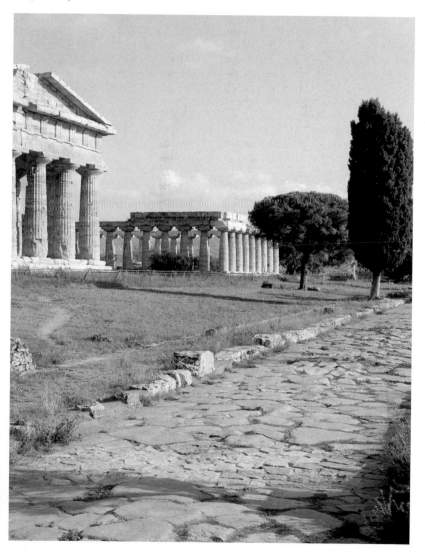

82

PADULA

❧

AMONG the most imposing monastic complexes in southern Italy is the Certosa di San Lorenzo at Padula. This was founded in 1306 by a loyal servant of the Anjevins, Tomaso Sanseverino, Count of Marsico, but was largely reconstructed in the baroque period, and offers a remarkable sense of the power and pretension of the Church at the time. The Carthusians were expelled by the French, who used the certosa as a barracks for 20,000 soldiers, but returned after 1815. The monastery was finally suppressed in 1866, and served as a prison in both world wars; Allied soldiers captured in North Africa were held there before being transported to northern Italy when the Germans retreated in 1944. Padula only came to more general notice after a major programme of restoration was underway in the 1980s. For two or three years almost every Italian seemed to have just been to or to be on his way to Padula, which is in easy reach of the autostrada and in a beautiful open setting.

The rectangular atrium precedes an elegant façade of 1718, the corridor beyond leading to the west side of the small Renaissance courtyard, from which the church is reached, and continuing past the main monastic rooms on the right to the west loggia of the spectacular Chiostro Grande with a double arcade projected in 1680. The corridor ends with the elliptical staircase built by the little-known Neapolitan Gaetano Barba

in 1761–3. Twin flights curl upwards to the top floor. One treads on air, so beautifully does the clear sunlight filter though the structure. Grand but not ponderous – as, say, the Bourbons' Caserta is – the staircase is in many ways akin to theatrical projects of the period.

The Soprintendènza of the Campania has done splendidly at Padula, and space has been found in the monastic buildings for the Museo Archeologico della Lucania Occidentale and also to display pictures from the area.

Certosa di San Lorenzo: the staircase.

• Monte Sant' Angelo 84

• Lucera 83

87 Castel del Monte • • Trani 85

• Bitonto 86

• Leccc 88

Apulia

83

LUCERA

FOGGIA has long been the dominant town of the Basilicata and has paid the price, not least during the last world war. Lucera to the south has been more fortunate. We think of Lucera, if we think of it at all, as the fortress town where the Emperor Frederick II settled his Saracens. But the potential of the site, on a rise above the plain, had long been recognized.

On my first visit, in 1985, I arrived in time for a late lunch, half dazed after leaving northern Umbria at dawn and pausing to survey Rieti and L'Aquila. As I walked towards the cathedral a distinguished old man in a dark grey suit handed me his card. I was still in driving mode and, besides, the gaunt Gothic church founded by Charles II of Anjou was predictably shut. But I still half regret not trying the services of the professore, who was one of the last *ciceroni* of his type.

I made off for the castle commandingly placed to the west of the town. This was constructed between 1269 and 1283 by Charles I of Anjou on the site of the fortress built for Frederick II two generations earlier; this too was closed. But it was not difficult to squeeze below the wooden door and enter the vast empty trapezoidal space within to see the base Frederick's palace. It is, however, from the outside that Lucera impresses, with its circuit of high curtain walls and well-preserved towers built of brick with stone dressings. The ambitious Anjevin king did not wish to leave his subjects in any doubt that he had expunged the power of the Hohenstaufen, crushing the descendants of the Saracens planted at Lucera by Frederick II after a six-month siege in 1269. But something of the taste he generated can be seen in finds from recent excavations in the castle, now in the Museo Civico, including a fine capital and ceramics of Islamic character.

When I returned to the town, the cathedral was open. The interior also is austere, a forceful reminder of the Francophile taste of the Anjevins. It says something as to the calibre of many Cinquecento pictures in the south that an altarpiece of 1535 by that modest Venetian Girolamo da Santacroce should stand out. The ruthless austerity of the cathedral itself, which is beautifully echoed in the nearby Franciscan church, seems more impressive every time I return. But it is with a sense of some relief that I speed on to Troia on its hill to the south, once settled by Greeks who it is not altogether fanciful to assume were ancestors of the wizened veterans gathered near the stupendous Romanesque cathedral, with its richly decorated front and bronze doors of 1119 by Oderisio da Benevento.

Museo Civico: fragment of thirteenth-century plate from the Castle.

Castle, with the lower wall of Frederick II's palace and the walls of Charles of Anjou in the distance.

84

MONTE SANT'ANGELO

✿

THE Gargano is a place apart. The promontory rises to the east of the plain between San Severo and Foggia, cutting like a spur into the Adriatic. The high point, the Monte Spigno, rises to 1,008 metres, and the land falls steeply to the coast. A local bishop experienced a vision of Saint Michael on the hill that now bears his name, 796 metres above sea level, and from the eighth century this became a major religious centre. The Norman conquerors of southern Italy first came as pilgrims, and, Assisi apart, there are few places where one feels closer to the pulse of medieval faith.

Lorenzo, the bishop who saw the archangel, held the see of Siponto. And unless you take the route that climbs from San Severo through the massif, the tourist-pilgrim would do well to pause at the two marvellous churches which survived when that town was destroyed by an earthquake of 1223. San Leonardo and Santa Maria Maggiore, the former cathedral, are Romanesque. Both have remarkable portals and are the more beautiful for their rural context. Siponto's successor was Manfredonia, founded in 1256 by the Emperor Frederick II's natural son, King Manfred. The grid street plan he imposed survives. Four miles beyond the town is the turn for Monte Sant'Angelo, which soon comes into sight high above. The road climbs steeply, with breathtaking views over the Gulf of Manfredonia towards Trani and the Castel del Monte.

The modern town cascades down the ridges that descend from the hill. The pil-grim would originally have walked up through the town, but now drives, or is driven, to a point nearer the shrine. The unremarkable entrance to this leads to a stairway of 1888, which must be very close in character to its thirteenth-century Angevin predecessor. The bronze doors to the basilica were ordered in Constantinople by Pantaleone of Amalfi in 1076. Their damascened decoration of silver and copper with coloured inlays is in twenty-four compartments: these include scenes from the Old Testament and a representation of the archangel's apparition. The Gothic basilica, incorporating the grotto where the vision took place, was built by the ruthlessly ambitious Charles of Anjou in 1273. In the grotto itself is a remarkable Romanesque episcopal throne, while further medieval treasures, including the Emperor Frederick II's gift of a filigree cross, are in the museum.

Pilgrims still flock to the sanctuary. But nearby the so-called Tomb of the Rotari is generally deserted. Originally perhaps a baptistery, this is crowned by a cupola reconstructed in 1109 for the alarmingly named Rodelgrimo and his brother-in-law, Pagano of Parma. The austerity of the structure is relieved by the energy of the sculptured reliefs. The building adjoins the elegant twelfth-century façade of the church of Santa Maria Maggiore.

Monte Sant'Angelo is particularly atmospheric in the late afternoon. The many stalls and restaurants make it easy to forget how remote the place must once have seemed to those who made the pilgrimage. The best way to sense this now is to leave at dusk and head inland, descending through what still seems an isolated valley. Pause and listen for the sheep bells.

Santa Maria Maggiore di Siponto: façade.

85

TRANI

TRANI has changed since I first knew it. I arrived at dusk on a festa and it took a good half-hour to get to the harbour. There I parked by a tiny restaurant, whose proprietor directed me to a hotel with the strictest injunction to remove everything that was visible and lock every door. Apulia is safer now. But it has often been a territory where interests clashed, and one still senses a frisson in its architecture.

Trani's early importance was due to the harbour. Much of her history can still be read from the paved waterfront, with the apse of the elegant Romanesque Templar church, the Ognissanti, hemmed in by lesser buildings. Behind is the core of the medieval town, whose successor spread to the south, its main arteries such as the Via Ognissanti notable for their

Cathedral: lion support of the west door.

later palaces. But despite the charm of these, with their rusticated and diamond-studded façades, or the larger buildings at the southern angle of the harbour – the Palazzo Quercia and the Quattrocento complex of the Palazzo Caccetta, not to mention the massive, and much remodelled, castle of Emperor Frederick II that guards the city on the north – it is the cathedral that draws one to Trani.

Medieval towns were competitive. The basilica of San Nicola at Bari was begun in 1087. A dozen years later, another Nicola, a pilgrim who had died at Trani, was canonized and work on his cathedral began. The site, above the shore, was that of an earlier church. By the time the structure was completed in the fourteenth century, the original Romanesque scheme had been substantially changed. Time and the restorer have claimed their due, but the first impression as you approach from the west, with the sea to the left, is of an unusually unified structure. The west front expresses the form of the interior, a tall nave flanked by aisles almost equally high raised above a crypt. If you are lucky, the lower door to the latter is open. Otherwise climb the steps to the upper level, where only the back arcade of the original portico survives,

Cathedral: Barisano da Trani, bronze doors (detail), after 1180.

Cathedral, from the Mole.

and the central door has lost the astonishing bronze doors supplied, perhaps in the 1280s, by Barisano da Trani, but now responsibly moved to the nave. The thirty-two panels of the doors are set in elaborate borders, classical in inspiration; in one, the patron San Nicola Pellegrino is seen with the diminutive artist in adoration at his feet. The vigorous sculpture round the door-case is reasonably well preserved. Above the door is the central arched window, with flanking columns supported on elephants; still higher is a fine rose window. To the right of the façade, improbably raised on a tall Gothic arch, is the great campanile, four-square, of five tiers, punctuated by openings each progressively wider, and crowned by a short octagonal steeple.

To appreciate the development of the building one should go down to the crypt beneath the nave, and then descend to the higher crypt below the choir. Admirable in its sense of space, this was the first element of the cathedral to be completed. The nave is an archetypal Apulian Romanesque structure of seven bays, supported by laterally paired columns below a triforium of triple arcades set within blind arches matching those below. The main capitals, alas, were destroyed to make way for Corinthian replacements of stucco. These in turn would be swept away when the post-Renaissance decoration was removed in the pre-war restoration. And it is to this restoration that the austerity of the church is owed. The impression is to some extent misleading. For while the bones of the structure were laid bare, its original texture and tonality were beyond recovery, for any counterparts to the admittedly provincial murals in the crypt have long since gone. Whatever has been lost, however, the soaring space remains impressive.

What I love about the cathedral is the exterior. This is magical in the early morning, seen from the mole to the east, as the sun defines the majestic curves of the apses. And as the light moves, so the sharp token buttresses of the lateral façades cast their lengthening or diminishing shadows. For the builders of Trani well knew the visual possibilities of shade in a land of bright sunlight.

Trani has a unique magic. But the city did not exist in isolation. To the south, beyond Bisceglie, is Molfetta where the cathedral by the shore owes much to Islamic architecture, while to the north is Barletta with a rival Romanesque cathedral. Inland at Canosa is an equally impressive cathedral, off the south transept of which is the mausoleum of Bohemund, conqueror and Prince of Antioch, where the bronze doors open to reveal an inscription of telling brevity: 'BOEMUNDUS'.

86

BITONTO

❖

THE relics of Saint Nicholas at Bari were stolen from Myra, and their arrival in 1087 heralded the great age of Apulian Romanesque architecture. This owed much to the prosperity assured by Norman rule. Robert Guiscard, already Duke of Apulia and Calabria, took Bari in 1071, and his successors ruled a strongly centralized kingdom that benefited both from the First Crusade and from trade with the East. The great basilica, defended by precinct walls, was not consecrated until 1197. Only a few hundred metres away, across the heart of what survives of the early city, is the cathedral. This was reconstructed in evident emulation of the basilica after Bari was sacked in 1156 by King William the Bad. Yet marvellous as the conjunction of the two buildings is, it is not Bari but its neighbour Bitonto, some seventeen kilometres inland to the west, that lingers in the imagination.

Unlike medieval Bari, the historic centre of Bitonto has not been swallowed by the modern town. Its plan survives, with twisting streets following the contours of the ground, punctuated by

Cathedral.

palaces with baroque portals or six-teenth-century loggias. Of these, the finest is in the Renaissance Palazzo Sylos Labini on the Via Planelli; it incorporates a Gothic doorway in the Catalan style that reflects the long Aragonese domination of the south heralded by the succession of Alfonso of Aragon to the kingdom of Naples in 1442. The palace is now a museum.

The cathedral of San Valentino, orientated to the south-east, flanks a narrow piazza at the very core of the town. It was built on the site of a much earlier church, the recently excavated remains of which, with fragmentary walls and sections of a mosaic, underlie the nave. Later alterations to the Romanesque structure were successfully reversed in the last century. Like the cathedral at Bari, that at Bitonto was inspired by the basilica there. The general disposition is the same, with a tall nave flanked by aisles only slightly lower, the soaring transepts, the three apses. But here the lateral façade facing the piazza, with the loggia of six recessed arches below elaborate clerestory windows and the blind arcading of the transept, surpasses its predecessor. The main façade is majestic, although the portico was never finished. The central door is richly decorated: the columns are supported on beasts and the architraves carved with scenes from the Christmas story and the Descent into Limbo. A rose window with more animals is set high in the central gable which is capped by a blind arcade.

The interior, like its counterparts at Bari, has been ruthlessly restored – English has no precise equivalent of the Italian *ripristinato* – but its scale has not been falsified, and the way the presbytery is raised above the level of the nave is both visually satisfying and functionally

Cathedral, crypt: capital.

appropriate. One significant original fitting survives, the elaborately decorated ambo of 1229, signed by 'Nicolaus sacerdos et magister'. The later tombs are of less interest.

Flights of steps lead down to the most thrilling of all Apulian crypts. Like the presbytery above, this has three apses. It is supported on thirty columns. The capitals are of exceptional quality, with bulls, pigs and other animals, humans in varying attitudes and vigorous foliage, as imaginative in design and sharp in detail as any of their date elsewhere in Italy or indeed in France. The sacristan knows not to rush the visitor.

As artists painted sequences of related pictures, so builders and craftsmen left clusters of closely interrelated monuments. Those who respond to the magic of Bitonto may wish to see two nearby cathedrals that also reflect the basilica of Bari: Ruvo, the steep triangular outline of which is explained by the narrow width of the central nave; and Bitetto, most memorable for the façade that was rebuilt in 1335, as a prominent inscription attests, by Lillo from Barletta.

87
CASTEL DEL MONTE

❖

NO OTHER medieval emperor was quite like Frederick II, and no medieval castle exercises so compelling a hold on the imagination as his Castel del Monte; the one extant document for its construction is of 1240. Castel del Monte on its hill is visible from afar. No traveller on the way to Bari or the south could have failed to see this, a gleam of white stone or, as the fall of light dictated, a dark silhouette brooding over the bare landscape. It still does.

Frederick II was the heir through his father to the imperial house of Hohenstaufen and through his mother of the Norman kingdom. He was crowned as Holy Roman Emperor in 1220. Ruthless and demanding, this *stupor mundi* – wonder of the world, as a contemporary chronicler described him – would have stood out in any age. His intellectual curiosity was matched by the sophistication of his taste. Castel del Monte was unlike any of its predecessors and indeed any of the numerous fortresses the emperor had willed into construction elsewhere. It is of octagonal plan with a central courtyard; at the angles are eight towers, false octagons in that their two inner faces do not exist.

The main entrance is on the east, a Gothic portal flanked by fluted pilasters with a pediment above, below a bipartite Gothic window. The sharp masonry is relieved by these enrichments, by the string-course that serves in visual terms to bind the towers to the central mass, by the postern of one façade and, on the others, a single window high on the ground floor, by the larger first-floor windows corresponding with that above the entrance, and by the numerous arrow slits.

The entrance leads to the first of eight soaring trapezoidal vaulted rooms on the ground floor. In the second of these is a door-case of deep-red breccia, the first evidence of what was evidently a lavish use of precious marbles in the castle. Before they were pillaged, the great rooms at Castel del Monte must have been among the richest secular apartments of the age. This second room leads into the courtyard, a noble space enriched by door-cases and window-frames, and not least by the blind arcade – in effect a trompe l'oeil loggia – of the upper storey. This is reached by stairways in three of the flanking towers. Here the rooms were yet more richly decorated. Acanthus abounds and ball leaf is found in two rooms; on the inner walls of three rooms were massive chimneypieces. Particularly memorable is the hexagonal vault above one of the stairways, which rests on brackets of crouching nudes.

In 1249, a year before Frederick II's death, his natural daughter, Violante, was married at Castel del Monte. Later this served as the prison of her brother Manfred's sons. The emperor clearly intended it for a very different purpose. Had he wanted to build a conventional fortress, he would have done so. The design of the entrance, and the use in some of the upper rooms of a technique akin to the Roman opus sectile, suggest that Frederick II – who was fully aware of the antiquity of his own title and also interested in classical texts – must have aspired to create a monument that would hold its own with those of ancient Rome. And in this, if not in his epic struggle with the papacy, he unquestionably succeeded.

Castel del Monte from the south-east.

88
LECCE

✤

THE Salento, the platform of the heel of Italy, has long known prosperity. After the collapse of the Roman world, this remained an outpost of the eastern empire until it was seized by the Normans in the mid-eleventh century. Thereafter it fell to the successive dynasties that ruled Naples. Otranto was the Byzantine capital, but under the Normans it was superseded by Lecce, which is more strategically placed. No work of art at Lecce is quite as memorable as the mosaic floor of the cathedral at Otranto, executed by a priest, Pantaleone, in 1163–6; and the city lacks the charm of Gallipoli, once a centre of the trade in olive oil with England, where on hot summer evenings the waving of fans drowns the voice of the celebrant in the cathedral. Yet the city has much to offer.

Although Lecce was an important Roman town, with a theatre and amphitheatre of which ruins survive, it is the post-Renaissance architecture that is of enduring interest. The so-called baroque of Lecce begins as an exuberant Mannerism. The local stone is easily worked when first quarried but hardens on exposure, and the builders of late sixteenth-century Lecce quickly learnt of its potential. Their taste for decorative detail made an indelible impression on such visitors as M. S. Briggs, author of the pioneering In the Heel of Italy (1910), and the Sitwells.

A good place to begin is the Porta Napoli with a rather theatrical triumphal arch of 1548 in honour of the Emperor Charles V, who had rebuilt the city walls and constructed the formidable fortress designed by Gian Giacomo dell'Acaja on the opposite side of the town. The straight Via Palmieri leads past several palazzi to the Piazza del Duomo at the heart of the city. This is dominated by the ambitious campanile of the great, if conservative, seventeenth-century architect of Lecce, Giuseppe Zimbalo. Zimbalo was also responsible for the comprehensive reconstruction between 1659 and 1670 of the cathedral, while the nearby Seminario, undeniably baroque with its striking channelled masonry and giant pilasters, was devised by Giuseppe Cino and opened in 1706.

The Piazza del Duomo is the great set piece of baroque Lecce. But almost every main artery has its quota of churches of the period, and there are literally dozens of distinguished palaces. The most spectacular among the churches is Santa

Cathedral: Giuseppe Zimbalo, Campanile, 1661–82.

Croce, just north of the Piazza Sant'Oronzo, reached from the cathedral by the Corso Vittorio Emanuele. Construction began in 1549 on relatively conventional lines. The upper part of the façade, finished almost a hundred years later, was designed by Zimbalo. Late Renaissance conventions are overwhelmed by encrusted caryatids and putti, and by a riot of ornament round a rose window that recalls so many Apulian Romanesque churches. Inexorably the craft of the stonemason establishes its own dynamic. The effect is not altogether elating.

The adjacent former convent of the Celestines, now the Palazzo del Governo, may also have been designed by Zimbalo, but was finished by Cino in a more measured baroque idiom. Some way south of the Piazza Sant'Oronzo, carefully calculated for its position at the junction of four streets, is the most appealing of the city's baroque churches, Achille Carducci's San Matteo, in which the art of Borromini is reinterpreted in the richly ornamented way Leccese patrons had evidently come to expect.

With the arguable exception of the Renaissance Palazzo Vernazza, the palaces of Lecce are not individually of particular interest. These testify to the agricultural wealth and commercial acumen of their owners. Many have excellent door-cases, some less restrained than others; many retain their iron balconies supported on brackets of varied form. Naturally, the richer families chose to build on the more prominent streets, and their competing yet in some ways complementary mansions contribute as much to Lecce's character as do its churches.

Giuseppe Zimbalo, Cathedral, 1659–70.

89 Matera •

Basilicata

89

MATERA

✤

MATERA is unique among Italian cities. The early medieval town was destroyed by the Saracens in 994, only to be re-occupied by the Byzantines. In 1064 Matera fell to the Normans and was incorporated in their kingdom. A period of sustained prosperity followed under Neapolitan rule. In 1663 the town became the capital of the province of Basilicata, a role it only lost in 1806 during the French occupation. Modern Matera is a bustling city, prosperous in a way that so many towns of the south are not. To the east is the extraordinary historic conurbation, built on and between two ridges, the Sasso Caveoso to the south and the Sasso Barisano to the north, and defended by the dramatic cliffs carved by the river Gravina.

The traveller from the north arrives in the Piazza Vittorio Veneto. To the left the Via San Biagio leads to San Giovanni Battista, an admirably austere Romanesque church of 1204, responsibly restored in 1926. The nave is unexpectedly high. Further on is the partly rock-cut San Pietro Barisano, another Norman foundation with a later façade. From the Sasso Barisano with its narrow streets there are tantalizing views over the town, its built façades masking houses largely excavated in the rock.

Return to the piazza and follow the central Via del Corso which leads to the Piazza San Francesco. In baroque San Francesco itself are panels from a polyptych by the Venetian master Bartolomeo Vivarini. Behind is the Via Duomo, which climbs past the substantial baroque Palazzo Bronzini-Padula to the splendid Duomo of 1268–70, raised on a terrace hanging over the heart of the town. The west front is admirably harmonious in its balance of pilasters, blind arcades and sculptural enrichments; and, unlike so many of its Apulian counterparts, the Duomo retains its subsequent decoration and additions, including the late Renaissance Cappella dell'Annunciazione.

After wandering in the narrow streets behind the Duomo, return to the Piazza San Francesco and turn south on the Via Ridola. On the right is a typical rococo extravagance of the south, the Chiesa del Purgatorio of 1747, its façade decorated with macabre motifs; the circular interior is happily intact. Beyond the church of the Carmine, turn left on the Strada Panoramica dei Sassi, which curls round to emerge in the Piazza San Pietro above the river. The road continues on the line of the cliffs, and the walk northwards to the Sasso Barisano is memorable.

Matera is visibly fragile. The eroded cliffs continue to erode, and rock-cut dwellings are not easily adapted to twenty-first-century domestic requirements. Much has been done to preserve a remarkable complex. And yet, more perhaps than in any other major artistic centre in Italy, you sense that Matera disintegrates before your eyes. Her protection is imperative.

Central area of the town from the west.

Calabria

Taverna 90

90

TAVERNA

ALTHOUGH Norman Douglas's *Old Calabria* (1915) must be the most entertaining book in English about any region in Italy, Calabria is not on most sightseers' agenda. Time and earthquakes have dealt harshly with the monuments of the area. And some of the greatest works of art to be seen are there, as it were, by accident. The two remarkable Greek bronzes of nudes at Reggio, among the greatest masterpieces of the age of Phidias, are only there because they were shipwrecked off Riace after being stolen in Roman times from the treasury of the Athenians at Delphi, while the elegant Gothic tomb of Isabella of Aragon, wife of King Philip III of France, is in the Duomo of Cosenza only because she was accidentally drowned in the river Savuto on her return from the East in 1271. However remote, Calabria was at times of strategic importance, and the first English victory over a French revolutionary army on land, at Maida in 1806, was quickly celebrated in the names of a new development in north London and of Walter Scott's favourite staghound. Like other parts of the former kingdom of Naples, Calabria did not benefit from the union of Italy.

No Calabrian city has been more abused in the last half century than Catanzaro, or so ruthlessly abandoned to the mercies of the road builder. But this is the obvious starting point from which to visit Taverna, the patria of the seven-

teenth-century painter Mattia Preti, il Cavaliere Calabrese, some twenty-six kilometres to the north. Once the seat of a bishopric, which was transferred to Catanzaro, Taverna is a sleepy rural town. The major church, San Domenico, was reconstructed in the 1670s. Preti, then based in Malta, was called on by his townsmen to supply a series of altarpieces between 1678 and 1687. Of the five canvasses on the right side of the church, only the fourth is not in its original position. The sequence begins with a key Dominican subject, the *Assassination of Saint Peter Martyr*. Preti himself presented the expressive *Martyrdom of Saint Sebastian* of 1677 on the third altar. The high altarpiece, the *Vision of Saint Dominic*, in which Christ appears like Jupiter with thunderbolts, is among the more dramatic of Preti's later works. There are four more altarpieces by him on the left wall, including the *Crucifixion* on the third altar and the appropriately eloquent *Preaching of the Baptist* on the first altar, in which the ageing Preti himself appears in his habit as a Knight of Malta.

Preti worked for other churches at Taverna, notably Santa Barbara, in the apse of which is a large canvas of 1688 showing the saint being received in heaven. Of Preti's four other altarpieces in the church, none isk in its original setting, and one, the charged and tenebrous *Baptism* on the right, was painted for the lesser church of San Giovanni Battista. The concentration of pictures by the artist at Taverna testifies to his patrons' pride in Preti's achievement and to the calm agricultural prosperity of the country on the southern flank of the Sila.

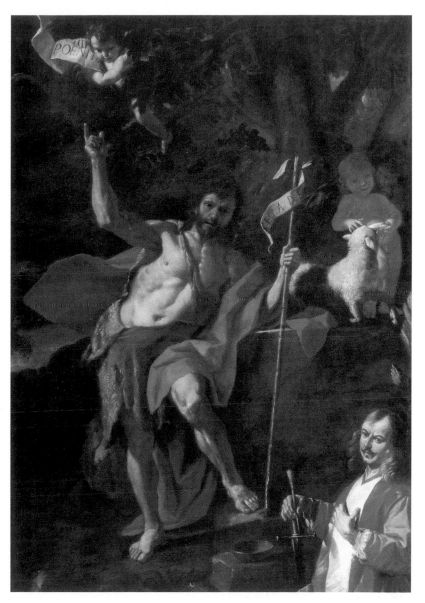

San Domenico: Mattia Preti, Saint John the Baptist with the Artist as Donor, c. 1687.

Sicily

Monreale 95
Palermo 96
Segesta 94

Pantalica 92
Siracusa 91
Ragusa Ibla 93

91
SYRACUSE

❖

SYRACUSE was one of the great cities of the Greek world. The wealth she owed to the excellence of her harbour inspired two of the great sieges of antiquity. In 416–413 BC the Syracusans defeated the vast Athenian war machine. A generation later the city was controlled by a tyrant, Dionysius I, the calibre of whose coinage has never been excelled. Rome was to be a more powerful enemy than Athens, and despite the ingenuity of Archimedes Syracuse fell after a protracted siege of 214–212 BC. There followed a long period of prosperity, broken only by the disintegration of the western empire in the fifth century. Belisarius won the city for Byzantium in 535, and it was controlled by the eastern empire until the Arab conquest of 879. With the Norman occupation of 1086, Syracuse was for the first time subordinated to Palermo, upon whose subsequent fortunes she was to depend.

The Corinthians settled on the former island of Ortigia in the eighth century BC, but Dionysius's city was altogether different in scale, defended by walls with a circuit of twenty-two kilometres. The

The Greek theatre.

expansion of modern Siracusa has affected the context of her most famous classical monuments, in the former suburb of Neapolis. Near the east entrance to the Parco Monumentale is what remains of the Roman amphitheatre. Three hundred metres or so north-west is the much more appealing Greek theatre, marvellously placed with wide views over the coast. Behind are the celebrated quarries, great gashes in the hillside where, as Thucydides relates, Athenian prisoners were put to work. The largest is the Latomia del Paradiso, forty-five metres deep in places, with the Ear of Dionysius – the cavernous excavation so named by Caravaggio in 1608. It is regrettable that public access is resticted to a small area, and that the atmospheric Latomia di Santa Venera to the east is now inaccessible.

At the northern extremity of Dionysius's city, some eight kilometres by road from Ortigia, is his Castello Eurialo. Built in 408–397 bc, this was one of the most sophisticated fortifications of the time, with an elaborate system of tunnels and sallyports. The fort withstood two years of the Roman siege. It is particularly atmospheric in the late afternoon. Other tourists depart, leaving you to the sound of the wind; a curious herdsman may pepper you with questions – 'How old are you?' 'Are you alone?' 'Are you married? 'Why not?' – as he pauses to gather his flock.

The archaeological museum east of the Parco Monumentale is uncompromisingly modern. It must be one of the most perfectly arranged institutions of the kind – a subtle orchestration of objects of every type with excellent photographs of the sites from which they came. Outstanding groups of Attic black figure vases and a handful of exceptional Greek

sculptures are shown to real advantage. Further east, above a complex of catacombs of the Roman era, is the much rebuilt church of Santa Lucia, the virgin who was martyred there in AD 303.

Modern Siracusa has little to commend it. But persevere, for Ortigia – a scant kilometre long – is remarkable. The main road crosses to the Piazza Pancali, behind which are the substantial ruins of the Greek Temple of Apollo. Take the Corso Matteotti, forking right on the narrower Via Cavour, which opens into the north end of the Piazza del Duomo, at the highest point of the island. This is fringed with excellent buildings: façades of private palaces (the most spirited is the Palazzo Beneventano del Bosco); the sober archiepiscopal palace, begun in a late Renaissance classical mode by the Spanish architect Andrea Vermexio in 1618; and, not least, the cathedral, the Christian successor of the Greek Temple of Athena, much of whose structure still survives. Shattered by the earthquake of 1693 which devastated so much of south-east Sicily, the cathedral was rebuilt from 1725 to the design of Andrea Palma from Trapani. At the south end of the piazza is the tall façade of Santa Lucia alla Badia, to which the *Burial of Saint Lucy*, the charged masterpiece supplied by Caravaggio in 1608 for the high altar of the eponymous church, has now been transferred. The setting is, most appropriately, an ancient quarry cast in shade: two muscular gravediggers flank the prostrate corpse; one of the mourners is dressed in red, but otherwise the palette ranges from flesh to umber. The church of Santa Lucia is orientated so the light falls from the right.

To the south of the piazza, in the former Palazzo Bellomo, is the Galleria Regionale. The building, begun in the

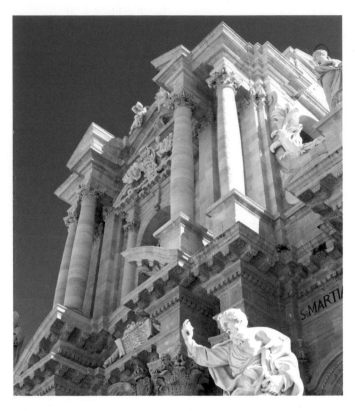

Cathedral: façade by Andrea Palma, 1725–53.

thirteenth century, has been ruthlessly restored. Among the pictures, pride of place goes to a masterpiece of Antonello da Messina, the Palazzolo Acrèidi *Annunciation* of 1474. Although a good deal of the surface is lost, this remarkable work shows how much Antonello had learnt from his experience of contemporary Netherlandish and southern French painting. Antonello absorbs, whether in the humanity of his types or the clarity of his detail. But he does not imitate. This in part explains why his impact on the Venice of Bellini was so immediate.

At the extremity of Ortigia is the Castello Maniace – named now after the Byzantine captain who took the body of Saint Lucy to Constantinople – built between 1232 and 1260 by the Emperor Frederick II, ruler in his mother's right of Sicily. The recent restoration means that the visitor can now see one of the most rigorously planned of all medieval fortresses, before walking back through the narrow streets and passages of Ortigia, past silent relics of the many phases of Siracusa's long urban evolution.

92
PANTALICA

❧

THERE is no more moving place in Sicily than Pantalica, a vast necropolis with a total of over 5,000 tombs carved into towering cliffs above the river Anapo and its tributary, the Torrente Cava Grande. Although accessible from both Sortino and Ferla, the gorge has not been compromised by development. So we are left to our thoughts as we follow ancient tracks or flights of steps and clamber up to the least inaccessible of the gaping doors framing dark shadows that are cut into the pale rock. The individual tombs are of little visual interest. It is the concentrations of these, grouped as the configuration of the cliffs dictated, that draw us on. Wind, the sounds of birds, and drifts of wild flowers play their part, and we can only wonder at the laconic account of Douglas Sladen in his *Sicily: The New Winter Resort* (1905): 'A gorge full of prehistoric tombs and with remains of a megalithic building and troglodytes' caves. Explored thoroughly by Prof. Orsi. Near Sortino, which has a mail vettura from Syracuse.'

The best approach is from Ferla with its quartet of fine churches. The road strikes eastwards. Pass the visitor centre and drive on to a point where the road crests the ridge between the two valleys. Just before a bend to the left the ground falls away steeply to the Anapo on the right. Just below the road, cut into successive strata of a natural amphitheatre, is the Filiporto Necropolis, with roughly a thousand tombs datable to the ninth and eighth centuries BC. Further on, to the left of the road, are the upper sections of the earlier (twelfth–eleventh centuries BC) North-west Necropolis, cut into outcrops hanging above the gorge of the Cava Grande; the majority of the tombs seem to have served for individual families. The road ends above the Anapo. A footpath cuts down to the left towards a partly rock-cut ancient road that curls down past scattered tombs to a ford across the Cava Grande; part of the original drain survives. There are more clusters of tombs, outliers of the North Necropolis, on the opposite bank, from which a well-preserved stairway cuts down to the Grotto dei Pipistrelli (Cave of the Bats) and implies the importance this had for the ancients. The path winds upwards towards Sortino. Return to the road and drive back for roughly a kilometre. A marked track to the left leads to the foundations of the so-called Anactoron on the crest of the plateau. From this a path above the gorge continues

Tombs in the Filiporto Necropolis.

North-west Necropolis.

Steps to the Cava degli Pipistrelli.

westwards, passing the troglodyte Byzantine settlement of San Micidiario to reach the road above the Filiporto Necropolis. A little below the Anactoron a steep path descends to the valley floor opposite the South Necropolis. The tombs of this, as of the South-west Necropolis and the Filiporto Necropolis across the gorge to the west, both most easily seen from the line of the former railway, are of the ninth and eighth centuries.

Protected as this was by the cliffs below, the high ground round the Anactoron lent itself to defence. It was apparently first settled by an indigenous people in the thirteenth century BC. The Anactoron itself has been compared with Mycenaean buildings. And it is hardly

surprising that the place has been associated with the early city of Hybla, the name of which would survive in that of the Megaran colony of Megara Hyblaea on the coast, which was founded in about 728 BC. Whatever its name, the city that must once have controlled a considerable territory suffered a gradual decline even before the arrival of the Megarans and the colonists from Corinth who settled at Syracuse a few years earlier. As the finds from the site now in the Museo Archeologico at Syracuse demonstrate, Pantalica was the centre of a sophisticated polity in the late Bronze Age. Looking up at the irregular tiers of the tombs, we can only speculate as to the causes of the city's decay.

93
RAGUSA IBLA

❧

THE GREAT earthquake of 1693 shattered most of the cities of south-eastern Sicily; it is to the spirited process of architectural renewal that the enduring interest of these is due. Catania is the grandest, her public buildings and palaces locked in an ambitious grid of streets. Noto is the most celebrated, ruthlessly moved towards the coast from its ancient site in the hills and laid out in a coherent plan that perfectly expressed the social patterns of the time and was realized by a succession of accomplished local architects, notably Rosario Gagliardi. Modica boasts the greatest of Gagliardi's churches and an impressive procession of palaces, while nearby Scicli

Rosario Gagliardi, San Giorgio, 1738 onwards.

is studded with baroque churches of inexhaustible charm. Yet none of these towns has quite the magic of Ragusa, where the old town and the new happily coexist.

The new town is to the west, an ordered plan with the substantial cathedral begun in 1706 but not finished until 1760, its façade oddly overbearing. The main road twists eastwards through the town down to the church of Santa Maria delle Scale, from where there is a splendid view over the promontory below, on which the earlier town, Ragusa Ibla, perches. Steps descend from the church steeply to the narrowest point, overlooked by the spectacularly placed church of the Purgatorio. The pretty pilastered façade, raised above a wide flight of steps, is, as it were, the frontispiece to the old town. Nearby are a number of palaces including that of the Cosentini family, with particularly ingenious corbels supporting the obligatory balconies.

The main road follows the northern flank of the hill, but you should try to lose your way in the maze of passageways and streets behind the Purgatorio. Eventually you will reach Gagliardi's extraordinary Duomo, dedicated to Saint George and designed in 1738, as drawings in the sacristy still attest. The soaring tiered façade of golden stone dominates the narrow central piazza. It is a wonderfully resilient statement of renewed faith in the destroyed town, although the more economical interior fails to live up to the dramatic promise of the entrance front.

At the further end of the piazza is a charming neoclassical survival, the Circolo della Conversazione, the façade with fluted Doric pilasters. It was here that the local gentry met, the inhabitants of the many palaces, mostly of modest scale, whose great-grandparents had been addicted to the corbelled balconies on which their masons lavished such inventive attention. To the east are two other buildings of particular interest. The nearer is the church of San Giuseppe: the façade, though smaller and less spectacularly placed than that of the Duomo, is in some respects more sophisticated, rising inexorably in serpentine tiers. The canopied window above the door is flanked by columns that bear the stepped-out broken triple-arched belfry.

The elliptical interior has a particular charm. Further east, the front of San Giorgio Vecchio is a Quattrocento Gothic survivor of the earthquake, Catalan in style, a precious reminder of Sicily's long adherence to the house of Aragon.

It is for these monuments that the visitor is drawn to Ragusa Ibla, but the whole town, renewed so lovingly on its sloping ridge, has a strange magic, not least when afternoon light lengthens the shadows and sharpens our perception of the way the site itself sits in what remains a relatively untrammelled landscape.

Attributed to Rosario Gagliardi, San Giuseppe.

94
SEGESTA

✤

MOVING westwards the visitor to Sicily is almost embarrassed for choice among the classical sites. Modern Gela is hideous, but the extant section of the Greek wall is substantial and the Attic black figure vases in the museum are remarkable. Inland, below Piazza Armerina, is the Roman Villa del Casale, with an unrivalled series of mosaics – but unless you go as once I did on a Christmas morning, finding myself alone for two precious hours, be prepared for crowds. Further west, at Agrigento, with its astonishing sequence of temples rising on a spine of rock, there is at least space for numbers to disperse. Beyond is Selinunte, the ancient Selinus. The vast earthquaked heap of columns from the enormous Doric temple was perhaps the most atmospheric sight in Sicily – until a brutal bank of earth and a new visitor centre cut this off from its views eastwards over the coastal plain; happily the ancient quarries some distance away have not been disturbed. In the far west is Motia, famed for the matchless mid-fifth-century BC Charioteer, dressed in a body-clinging pleated tunic that would have appealed to Fortuny. As the finest known statue from Magna Grecia this is much in demand for exhibitions, and was sent to the British Museum to coincide with the 2012 Olympic Games. So it might be wise to check that the statue is actually on the island before making the inconvenient pilgrimage.

Segesta by contrast never fails, despite the intrusion of the motorway and unfortunate 'landscaping' below the temple. We can still see it as Edward Lear did from Calatafimi in the mid-nineteenth century, rising among the hills. Motoring from Palermo, we see the temple perched high above the valley of the Gàggera, backed by mountains: as we draw nearer it disappears behind the Monte Barbaro on which the ancient city developed. Large enough to be the rival of Selinus by the early sixth century BC, it remained prosperous in Roman times and was only abandoned under the Vandals. Part of the city wall can still be traced. On the north-eastern bastion of the hill is the sympathetically restored theatre built in the third century BC. The marvellous views north across the valley would have been even more memorable before the incursion of the autostrada.

Motia: Charioteer as Olympic ambassador.

Edward Lear, Segesta from Calatafimi *(Private Collection; detail).*

Walking – or driving down – from the city, before climbing up to the platform on which it stands, one takes in the temple. This dates from the latter decades of the fifth century BC. The order is Doric and the building is hexastyle, the pedimented ends thus of six columns, the sides of fourteen. The massive columns stand open to the winds – nothing of the cella survives, as the regular blocks used for it have long since been recycled. The detail is austere.

No other extant Greek temple with the exception of that at Bassae in the Peloponnese is placed so dramatically. And we are awed, as the inhabitants of Segesta must also have been, by the contrast between so controlled an architectural statement and the wild hillside. But was the temple as originally built, and painted, so incomparably beautiful as it is now in venerable age, surrounded by the panoply of wild flowers of the Sicilian spring or drifts of black irises in December? One can only pray that those who wish to build a hotel below the temple will never be permitted to do so.

Opposite: Temple looking east, with the theatre in the distance.

95

MONREALE

MONREALE is only eight kilometres from Palermo. The modern road rises to the spur –310 metres above sea level – on which the town stands, skirting the processional route laid out in 1762. It was at Monreale that in 1174 King William II founded the great monastery of Santa Maria Nuova, which became in turn a royal palace and the archiepiscopal seat. The king's motive was to challenge the pretensions of the then Archbishop of Palermo – a neat solution by comparison with the murder of Saint Thomas à Becket by minions of the contemporary English monarch. And the riches of

Cathedral: apse mosaic, Pantocrator, late 12th century.

William II's realm were liberally lavished. By 1189 the building was effectively finished; it is the consummate achievement of the Normans in Sicily.

The façade is flanked by towers and partly masked by a late portico, which protects the wonderful portal with its bronze doors by Bonanno Pisano – the deviser of the Leaning Tower. The lateral (north-west) façade boasts equally fine bronze doors of 1179 by Barisano da Trani, and it is here that the tourist enters. The interior glows. Even on an overcast day, light is reflected from the glittering mosaics. A devastating fire of 1811 necessitated a long programme of restoration, but happily the apse mosaics were not significantly affected. The great Pantocrator dominates the long cycles of scenes from the Old and New Testaments. The scale of the project meant that, as for the doors, craftsmen had to be attracted from outside Sicily – from Venice and Byzantium. For uncouth adventurers as the Normans had so recently been, they had an instinctive respect for the artistic tastes of more established rulers.

The cloister, south of the cathedral, is one of the most beautiful complexes of its date in Europe. The ogival arches of the loggia rest on 228 double columns, variously decorated with mosaics and arabesques. The carved capitals of these are wonderfully inventive. On one, King William II himself is shown, offering his cathedral to the Virgin; there are biblical narratives and scenes of rural life, Norman knights and peasants, as well as a few animals and stylized plants. At the south-west corner is a fountain. This takes the form of the trunk of a palm and is enclosed within a square loggia, a wonderfully exotic touch that speaks perhaps of Cairo or Andalusia.

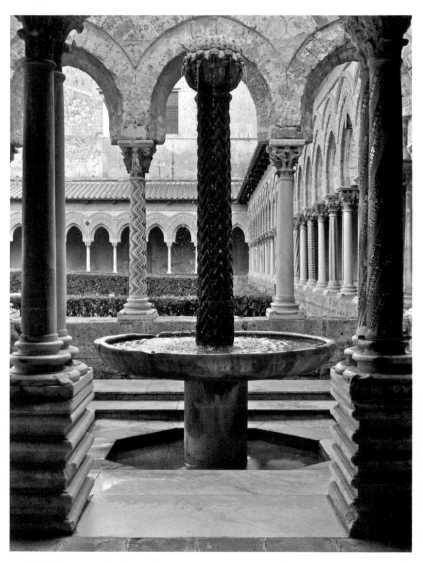

Cathedral: fountain in the cloister, late 12th century.

96

PALERMO

OF THE two great cities of the northern coast of Sicily, Cefalù is, alas, now only too firmly on the tourist trail. Palermo, in its inimitable way, is not, for it still has life as a capital, albeit merely of a region. The sightseer's time will not be wasted.

Few cities are more favoured by nature. Backed – and protected from its hinterland – by dramatic hills, the Conca d'Oro, and commanding a bay which has always boasted the best anchorage of the island, Palermo was inevitably settled in early times. The Phoenicians were followed by the Carthaginians and Rome. The Vandals were succeeded in turn by Odoacer and Theodoric, but in 535 Belisarius conquered the city for Byzantium. The Arabs prevailed in 831, to be defeated in their turn by the Normans in 1072. Palermo became their capital. The Norman kings built up one of the most efficient states of the time and their architectural contribution was immense. Their kingdom was inherited by Frederick II of Hohenstaufen, whose heirs were driven out in 1266 by Charles of Anjou. Sicily subsequently passed to the kings of Aragon, who first appointed a viceroy in 1415, and was a dependency of Spain until 1712. After a brief period of Savoyard rule, Sicily became the subsidiary kingdom of the Neapolitan Bourbons, Palermo serving as their capital while Naples itself was occupied by the French in 1798–9 and 1806–15. From 1815 the kingdom was styled 'of the two Sicilies'. As a result of Garibaldi's dramatic incursion, Palermo – and with it the whole island – passed to the kingdom of Italy in 1860. Areas of the city near the port were tragically affected by Allied bombing in 1943.

The old city is only a kilometre wide and a kilometre and a half deep, and the threads that link Palermo's past are so interwoven that at the risk of doubletracking it makes sense to explore the city stratum by stratum. Count Roger II was a determined builder. In 1130, the year of his coronation, he initiated work on the Cappella Palatina of the former Palazzo Reale (now the Palazzo dei Normanni), which was greatly extended during Spanish rule in the seventeenth century. The chapel shows how cosmopolitan the new king's taste was. Egyptian granite was reused and the ceiling of the nave is of Fatimid construction. But if Roger turned to the Arab world in this respect, for the mosaics of the upper walls and the nave he looked to Byzantium. A brief walk to the east is the austere church of San Giovanni degli Eremiti, also built for Roger II; this incorporated part of an earlier mosque. If time permits, this is the point at which to see two other royal buildings, both in walking distance of the Palazzo dei Normanni. The Zisa and the Cuba were in the Norman kings' huge park, the first begun by William I and completed by his eponymous successor (1165–7), the second undertaken by William II in 1180. As with the ceiling of the Cappella Palatina, Fatimid Cairo was the inspiration for these sophisticated summer retreats, which somehow still defy the encroachment of the modern town.

Roger II's admiral, Giorgio of Antioch, was also a notable builder. He built the Martorana, Santa Maria dell'Ammiraglio, in the Piazza Bellini at the heart of the early city. Much of the structure and the distinguished campanile survive; so do the glorious mosaics, which, like those commissioned for the king, are Byzantine in taste. Next to the church is San Cataldo, built about 1160 for another admiral, Majone di Bari. The greatest church of Norman Palermo was of course the cathedral, Santa Rosalia, roughly midway between the Piazza Bellini and the Palazzo dei Normanni. This was begun in 1184, but work continued over a long period, and the interior was remodelled in 1781–1801. The main entrance from the piazza, of 1429–30, is a masterpiece of the late Gothic style, while the royal tombs, now crammed into the chapels to the left of this, are unexpectedly moving.

The later medieval and Renaissance churches and palaces of Palermo are perhaps less memorable. The early sixteenth-century Santa Maria della Catena by the port mixes late Gothic Catalan forms with Renaissance motifs in a characteristically Sicilian way. More surprising is the Carrara marble fountain in the central Piazza Pretoria. Executed in 1554–5 by Francesco Camilliani for a Florentina villa, this was sold a generation later and installed at Palermo.

The Piazza Pretoria abuts on the Via Maqueda, cut through the ancient city by the viceroy of that name in 1600. A few paces to the west, where it intersects the former Via Toledo, are the Quattro Canti, with four matching façades, projected in 1608 and completed in 1620. Brave the traffic, for this is an early masterpiece of baroque town planning. It serves to remind us that Spain was one of the great powers of the period, and that Palermo derived some benefit from this.

In 1624 the young Anthony van Dyck – himself a Flemish subject of the King of Spain – arrived in Palermo to receive the commission for his wonderful Ma-

Oratorio del Rosario di San Domenico: Giovanni Serpotta, putto, plaster, c. 1701.

donna of the Rosary in the Oratorio del Rosario di San Domenico, behind the church of that saint off the Via Roma. In this sparkling canvas van Dyck came of age as a religious artist in much the same way he had recently done as a portraitist at Genoa. The oratory introduces the great genius of baroque Palermo, the stuccodore Giacomo Serpotta. His white plasterwork is of unequalled fluidity, with allegorical figures that vie with any sculptures of their date. The nearby Oratorio di Santa Cita was decorated with equal ingenuity between 1688 and 1718 by Serpotta. But his masterpiece is arguably the decoration of the Oratorio di San Lorenzo (1698–1710), from which Caravaggio's late *Nativity* was so selfishly stolen in 1969. Both here and at the Oratorio del Rosario one senses Serpotta's deep respect for the great altarpieces for which he supplied new settings.

Palermo was notably rich in baroque and rococo palaces. Many, alas, including that of the Lampedusa family, were damaged in the Second World War. Countless façades beckon, but few of the palaces that line the main arteries can be visited, although part of one, the romantically run-down Palazzo Filingieri di Cutò on the Via Maqueda, serves as a primitive hotel.

To understand something of the taste of secular Palermo it is necessary to go outside the city. To the north, off the Parco della Favorita, projected in 1799, is the earlier Villa Niscemi, while within the park is the stylish Palazzina Cinese, built by Venanzio Marvuglia in 1799 for King Ferdinand III, then in exile from Naples. Nelson and the Hamiltons were among his visitors. Many of the great Palermitan families had villas at Bagheria to the east of the city. The town has now grown, so some effort of the imagination is necessary to imagine its former charm. Walking is the best way to see something of the villas. The most accessible is the Villa Palagonia, built in 1715 for the prince of that name and long famous for the marble-encrusted saloon and the grotesque sculptures of the enclosing walls.

Finally, visit the museums. The Museo Archeologico is at the north end of the Via Roma. In contrast to the modern museum at Siracusa, this is a very traditional institution but none the worse for that. The high point is the room of sculptures from Selinunte, including metopes from two of the temples, as well as the fifth-century BC bronze Ephebe. In the room dedicated to bronzes are the *Ariel*, which was placed above the main entrance of Frederick II's Castello Mani-

Galleria Regionale della Sicilia: Antonello da Messina, Virgin Annunciate, 1476–7.

ace in Siracusa, and the *Hercules* from Torre del Greco, below Vesuvius, presented by King Francesco I. The Galleria Regionale is housed in the Palazzo Abatellis on the Via Alloro. The collection of Sicilian works has no rival. The star is inevitably Antonello's small *Virgin Annunciate*, his quintessential masterpiece and one of the most serene and human statements of the whole Renaissance. Very different in mood is the *Malvegna* triptych begun by Gerard David and completed by his younger contemporary, Jan Gossart, called Mabuse. Intimate in scale and exquisite in detail, this is eloquent of Gossart's interest in Italian art and, as a Palermitan commission, reminds us that the city remained a significant trading port.

• Ardara 100 • Olbia 101
• Toralba 99

• Abbasanta 99

• Oristano 98

• Cagliari 97

Sardinia

97

CAGLIARI

❖

CAGLIARI claims a precedence among the cities of Sardinia. The port of the Phoenicians and their Carthaginian heirs passed before 100 BC to Rome, and by AD 312 Cagliari was an episcopal see. With the Byzantine collapse in the West, the city – and indeed the rest of Sardinia – was subject to rival maritime powers. But in 1217 the Pisans established control, fortifying the ridge that remains the heart of the town. Cagliari fell to the Aragonese in 1326, and remained in Spanish control until 1720, when Sardinia was awarded to Vittorio Amadeo II of Savoy.

Although the tower of San Pancrazio of 1305 at the north-east angle survives, the Pisan walls have for the most part been replaced by successive Spanish and Piedmontese interventions, necessitated by the evolution of defensive warfare. At the higher, north, end of the ridge was the Citadel, and below this parallel streets were laid out. The Palazzo Reale, built for Carlo Emanuele III, and the cathedral dominate the central piazza that slopes steeply to the west. The Romanesque façade of the cathedral is a re-creation of 1933, but the side door to the right of this is an enchanting Gothic fantasy, as delicate as lace. The interior is memorable not least for its wealth of sculpture. At either side of the central door are two pulpits made up in the seventeenth century from that supplied by Guglielmo da Pisa in 1159–62 for the cathedral at Pisa, which was displaced by Giovanni Pisano's masterpiece and despatched in 1312 to Cagliari. Of the sixteen narrative reliefs, the most memorable is perhaps that of the soldiers – medieval knights in full armour – by the tomb. The church is rich in baroque altars and funerary monuments. Of these the most striking, in the

Cathedral: Guglielmo da Pisa, pulpit, 1159–62.

Cathedral: tomb of Bishop Bernardò dei Cariñeni.

last chapel on the left, is that to Archbishop Bernardò dei Cariñeni (d. 1722), whose effigy, framed by curtains that have been drawn apart, is beneath the altar.

Below the presbytery is the Santuario dei Martiri, three marble-faced chapels cut into the rock. The vault of the central Cappella della Madonna dei Martiri is enriched with 584 circular compartments, and the decoration of the sanctuary evidently reflects the taste of Archbishop Francesco d'Esquivel (d. 1624), whose monument dominates the vestibule. The smaller lateral chapels are dedicated to the martyrs of Cagliari, Saturninus and Luciferus. The marble facings incorporate fine Roman sarcophagi that had come to be associated with the saints. It is not difficult to understand why Prince Carlo Emanuele of Savoy, who died at Cagliari in 1799, was buried in one chapel and Queen Giuseppa Maria Luigia, who died in 1810, chose to be buried in the other.

Their restrained neoclassical monuments are respectively by Antonio Cano and the Sardinian Andrea Galassi, who had studied under Canova to some effect.

On the site of the Citadel a museum complex was built in the 1980s. This already seems outmoded. The Museo Archeologico houses the main collection of prehistoric material from the nuraghi and other sites for which Sardinia is justly celebrated. Apart from some small figurines and metal statuettes that anticipate Giacometti, most of the material is of specialized interest. The most ambitious of the Roman sculptures is a statue of the younger Drusus, efficient but uninspired. The Pinacoteca Nazionale is higher up. Sardinia was a backwater where painting was concerned, but the sequence of polyptychs from the church of San Francesco di Stampace is unexpectedly impressive, not least for that of San Bernardino of 1455 by two Catalan masters, Rafael Tomas and Juan Figuera. The selection of the saint's miracles includes one, of Bernardino floating across a river on his cloak, that Italian patrons seem to have considered too improbable to merit depiction.

There are other things to see at Cagliari, including the eroded and much restored Roman amphitheatre west of the ridge. But the tourist's time may best be used by making for some of the neighbouring sites: Dolianova to the north-east, with the marvellous and well-preserved church of San Pantaleo, begun in the twelfth century and completed by 1299; or, to the north-west, the smaller Romanesque Santa Maria at Uta, beautifully set among trees; and its more modest neighbour, San Platano of about 1144 at Villaspeciosa, in which the front is enriched with spoil from earlier monuments. These, and their numerous counterparts throughout the island, suggest the strength of the religious revival of their period.

The Nuraghe Su Nuraxi near Barumini, one of the three most celebrated monuments of the kind, is roughly an hour north of Cagliari. The Sardinian term, nuraghe, which may preserve its prehistoric form, meaning a pile of stones with an internal cavity, does less than justice to the sophistication of the prehistoric fortresses for which the island is justly famous. The tower at the centre, originally eighteen and a half metres high, is datable to 1500–1300 BC, while the four adjoining ones were added in about 1300–1100 BC; the fortifications were extended in the early Iron Age (after 1100 BC), when many of the circular structures in the village outside the walls were built. Further structures were added in the Iron Age (800–500 BC). Visitor numbers mean that guided tours are the rule; and the circuit of the tholos-crowned internal chambers and the narrow internal passages is not, perhaps, for those who suffer from claustrophobia, but tells us something of the cramped conditions in which the builders of nuraghi expected to protect themselves.

Two miles to the west is the parish church of San Pietro in the small town of Tuili. The retable of 1500 by the Master of Castelsardo is perhaps the masterpiece of Sardinian Renaissance painting, fascinating for what it tells of complementary strands of Italian, Spanish and northern influence. The anonymous painter's radiant colour is a wonderful contrast to the dark passages of the Nuraghe Su Nuraxi.

98

ORISTANO AND SANTA GIUSTA

❖

ORISTANO was the medieval successor of the Roman Tharros, the excavated ruins of which lie in the shadow of one of King Philip II of Spain's watchtowers on the peninsula across the gulf to the west. The heart of the town is rather well preserved. The apse of the much remodelled cathedral backs onto the main piazza. A little to the north is the tetrastyle portico of the circular church of San Francesco. This does little to prepare us for the masterpiece on the altar on the left, an intensely felt polychrome statue of Christ on the Cross by a Spanish sculptor of the late fifteenth century, which was clearly intended to be looked at from below. Beyond in the sacristy is the *Stigmatization of Saint Francis* by the only

competent Sardinian painter of the High Renaissance, Pietro Cavaro. Much of the rest of the retable is in the Antiquarium Alborense in the Piazza La Corrias, which holds a small collection of antiquities from local sites.

Some three kilometres south of Oristano is the smaller town of Santa Giusta. This was of some importance in early times, as the little Roman bridge beside the main road south hints. The great church on a rise to the north of the town was built in 1135–45 as the cathedral of the diocese of Santa Giusta, first mentioned in 1119, which was suppressed in 1503. The tall central section of the west front implies the structure of the interior, with a nave divided from narrower lower aisles by screens of columns. Taken from the town's predecessor, Othoca, and from Tharros, these are of differing colours and widths, one fluted, another spiral cut. The presbytery is raised above a wide crypt that rests on narrower columns. The arcaded apse is particularly successful,

San Leonardo de Siete Fuentes.

but the campanile beside it is largely reconstructed. The architect was no doubt Pisan, and elements of the building were echoed in other Romanesque churches on the island.

A number of such churches survive in or near villages to the north of Oristano. The small but elegant San Paolo by the cemetery at Milis, finished in the early thirteenth century, follows the model of Santa Giusta, the simple arcaded façade with bands of dark trachite stone alternating with the creamy pietra arenaria.

Five kilometres to the north is Bonàrcado. Built out from the hillside, Santa Maria, consecrated in 1146–7, was a dependency of the Camaldolese abbey of San Zenone at Pisa. Below the church is the small cruciform sanctuary of the Madonna di Bonacattu, an early foundation remodelled after 1242. Further on, across the Monte Ferra, built of dark volcanic stone and shadowed by trees, is San Leonardo de Siete Fuèntes, which also reflects elements of the design of Santa Giusta.

Nuraghe Oes.

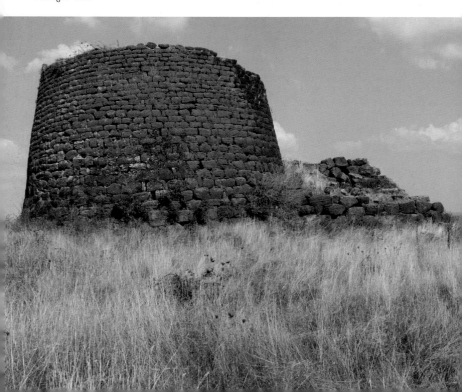

99

THE LOSA AND
SANTU ANTINE NURAGHI

❖

THE nuraghi of Sardinia are so numerous that the non-archaeologist will only
have the appetite for a selection. Of the
three most impressive, two, the Losa and
Santu Antine nuraghi, are some forty
kilometres apart and both in earshot of
the Strada Carlo Felice, the main road
from Cagliari to Sassari.

Despite the proximity of the road both
sites are more atmospheric than their
counterpart, the Nuraghe Su Nuraxi (see
no. 97). The great triangular basalt tower
of the Nuraghe Losa, near Abbasanta,
datable to the first half of the second millennium BC, now gilded with lichen,
rises above the splendid defensive wall of
the former town, which was reconstructed in the seventh century BC. The
carefully battered tower was protected by
three Late Bronze Age lower towers; that
to the south masked the main entrance.
Passages led to tholoi, in the flanking
angles, and to the central chamber, off
which there are three circular projec-
tions; just before this is entered, a flight
of steps, with sides like those of the other
passages tapering to the top, climbs to a
second tholos above the first, and then to
a third (of which only the lower part
survives). The external masonry is beautifully graded and eloquent of the engineering ability of the builders. The
nuraghe was a formidable place of
strength and refuge, and it is hardly surprising to learn that it continued to be
used until the early medieval period.

The Nuraghe Santu Antine near Torralba is similar in many ways. The central
tower, variously dated to the late ninth or
eighth century BC and still over seventeen metres high, is set within a lower
triangular outwork, with a projection at
the centre of one side, strengthening the
entrance passage to the courtyard within,
which has been variously thought to be
part of the original complex or an early
addition. At either end of the court are
openings to the tholoi in the angle towers, from which corridors lit by narrow
openings in the outer wall lead to the
tholos in the third angle, and subsidiary
passages behind the angle towers. In the
centre, the lower part of the wall of the
central tower is exposed. The entrance
leads to the impressive central tholos,
which is surrounded by a circular pas-

Nuraghe Losa.

sage except where stairs rise to a second, lower, tholos, and then to a third, of which only the lower courses survive. The masonry is of conspicuously fine calibre, with for the most part regular courses of carefully graded blocks, of which some thirty survive. And the detail, for instance the narrow outer faces of the window openings, is remarkably consistent. No wonder the place has come to be known as the 'Reggia nuragica'. Echoed to the south by the fine unrestored Nuraghe Oes hard by the railway line (take a torch!), the fortress dominates the so-called Valle dei Nuraghi, a natural amphitheatre that must long have known a gentle prosperity.

One wonders what was made of the nuraghi by the medieval bishops of Torres, whose beautiful church of San Pietro di Sorres on the ridge above Torralba was built between 1170 and 1190 under Pistoiese rather than Pisan influence. This boasts perhaps the most satisfying of all Sardinian Romanesque façades.

Few modern roads – even in a country with so consistent an interest in road construction as Italy – are so memorable as that from the Abbasanta turn near the Nuraghe Losa through the hills to Olbia.

A series of monuments that enrich our understanding of both prehistoric and medieval Sardinia are within easy reach: the solemn basalt church at Ottana, which retains a mid-fourteenth-century Pisan polyptych; a cluster of rock-cut tombs, Sas Còncas, half a kilometre from the turn for Oniferi; and, to the south of the turn for Lula and Dorgali, two exemplary monuments of the world of the nuraghi. Some four kilometres from the turn, on the left of the road as this rises, is the path to the Tomb of the Giant Sa Ena 'e Thòmes. The central monolith of this long barrow was carved to leave a raised border and central band; below is the small arched entrance to the tomb chamber. The tomb is better preserved than its counterparts at Arzachena and much more appealing as, lizards apart, it is likely to be deserted. Continue onwards towards Dorgali for a further four kilometres for the entrance to Serra Orrios, the best-preserved nuragic village, with groups of round structures and two shrines of the Late Bronze Age. Alas, we know nothing of the religion practised here, but the charm of the site, shaded by olive trees, is not in doubt.

100
ARDARA AND SANT'
ANTIOCO DI BISARCIO

✤

EVERY visitor will have his own favourites among the Romanesque churches of northern Sardinia. The largest is San Gavino of Porto Torres, with apses at either end; more charming are the black and cream striped San Pietro di

Simbános on an isolated ridge inland from Castelsardo and its pink neighbour at Terqu. But to sense the resilience of the twelfth-century church we can do no better than visit the sequence of five churches of the period on a forty-kilometre stretch of the main road from Sassari to Olbia.

The best known is the controversially restored abbey of La Trinità di Saccargia, founded in 1116, with an assertive striped church and a soaring campanile. The apse was frescoed in the thirteenth-

La Trinità di Saccargia.

century, with Christ in Majesty above the Virgin and the apostles and, below, Passion scenes above fictive hangings, the only such scheme to survive on the island. A couple of kilometres east, abandoned on a rise between the modern road and a power station, is San Michele di Salvènero, also radically restored. This was built in 1110–30 for the Vallombrosan Order – which of course had strong Tuscan connections – and altered a century later. The apse is particularly successful, and there are numerous parallels in design with the church's larger neighbour.

Some ten kilometres further on is Ardara. The black church of Santa Maria del Regno lies on a terrace east of the town. External detail is pared down to the point of severity. But the interior is remarkable. The entire altar wall of the wide nave is filled by a glowing retable with scenes from the life of the Virgin by a later Quattrocento master, possibly Martin Torner from Majorca. The predella, however, is from a different world. The central panel, Christ set against a landscape, bears a cartellino with the date 1515 and signature of Giovanni Moru, who must have known northern Italian pictures of the previous generation. On the left wall is a damaged dossal of the Passion by a Pisan of the late Trecento.

Sant'Antioco di Bisarcio is some six kilometres east, easily visible from the road: a great church with a campanile and the remains of associated buildings on a platform above the valley floor. Bisarcio was the seat of a bishopric until 1503. The original church, of before 1090, was destroyed by fire and reconstructed after 1150 by builders aware of developments at Santa Giusta (see no. 98). A generation later, after 1170, an extension on two floors was set against the entrance front; part of this was lost when the north-west corner collapsed in the fifteenth century, but the elaborate decoration of what survives implies an understanding of French work. There are worn carvings of animals and, above the left door, of prophets; much of the detail is classical and acanthus plentiful. The entrance opens to a narthex, above which were three rooms reached by a narrow stair and, originally, by a passage from the episcopal palace. The first, with a bench and a chimney, was the chapter house, and beside this was the bishop's chapel, its altar below the central window of the original façade. The church itself is admirably coherent, the uniform columns with capitals of Corinthian derivation, with heads or stylized flowers between the volutes. The exterior of the apse, splendidly placed above a low cliff, is beautifully handled. So is the campanile, with generous angle shafts and narrower central ones that are linked by pairs of twin arcades.

Sant'Antioco is so perfect in its way that it may seem pointless to go on to the less ambitious Nostra Signora di Castro on an isolated rise east of Oschiri. But this too has a rare charm, not least on a morning when the buildings emerge from swirling mist and you rouse the resident cats. The controlled façade, with plain pilasters and blind arcades defining the roof line, might stand as a microcosm of the Sardinian Romanesque.

Sant'Antioco di Bisarcio.

101

OLBIA

OLBIA, on the north-east coast of Sardinia, was a major Greek and Roman port, and survived as a more modest provincial town, Terranova, under Spanish rule. The place is not particularly eloquent of its past. Eroded arches of the Roman aqueduct stretch to the northwest, and on the site of an early necropolis there is the fine early twelfth-century church of San Simpliciano. Now entered from the east, this may have been planned with apses at either end, as at Porto Torres; classical spoil was put to use and the initial stone structure was heightened, so that a second blind arcade, largely of brick, rises above the original. Fine as it is, the church is outshone by perhaps two dozen others on the island. Olbia's claims on the tourist are owed to the discovery, when a road

Pozzo Sa Testa.

was tunnelled through the site of the former harbour, of a remarkable number of ancient boats.

Some of these are housed in the impressive new museum on the waterfront, which was built to display a sequence of local finds ranging from the Bronze Age of the early nuraghi to the time of the Phoenicians and their successors. Fortunately, the building was ambitious enough in size to accommodate such of the vessels as have thus far been prepared for public view. There are no fewer than four great oaken masts of boats of the time of Nero, rare survivals. Shown with these in the first room are two Vandal ships of the sixth century, compelling evidence of the new power that had seized the North African underbelly of imperial Rome and wrought havoc throughout the western Mediterranean. The outer timbers are of oak, the joists, attached to them by both copper and wooden nails, of pine. The larger of the vessels was found in two sections, broken to the right of the keel, which itself had already had to be repaired. The Roman ships await attention, but a small medieval boat is already shown, its dimensions implying the level of silt that had choked the harbour and thus preserved the hulks of the earlier vessels.

The modern ferry port of Olbia is matched by the industrial zone that has crept round the bay, almost engulfing the beautiful nuragic well, Sa Testa, the path to which is behind a supermarket, Centrocash. The small enclosure leading to the steps down to the water seems a miraculous survival. So in a different way is the Nuraghe Cabu Abbas on an outlier of the range of hills to the north, the early inhabitants of which must have been able to monitor movements on the roadstead.

GLOSSARY

Ambo, ambone Pulpit
Ambulatory Area round a choir or presbytery
Arca Tomb

Baldachin A columned structure above an altar
Balze Eroded hillsides (especially in Tuscany)
Barrel vault Arched roof
Broletto Communal palace

Ca' Venetian for palace
Campanile Bell-tower of a church
Campo Venetian equivalent of a piazza
Camposanto Cemetery
Cantoria/e Balcony for a choir
Cartellino Label, often inscribed
Cella Central chamber of a classical temple
Certosa Charterhouse (Carthusian monastery)
Chasuble Ecclesiastical vestment
Ciborium/ia Canopy above a high altar
Cimasa Cresting or upper section
Cinquecento Sixteenth century
Collegiata Collegiate church
Condottiero Mercenary commander

Decumanus maximus Principal cross-street of a Roman town
Dugento Thirteenth century
Duomo Cathedral

Enceinte Line of walls of a castle
Exarchate Byzantine province, governed by an exarch

Foresteria Guesthouse
Forum Roman marketplace

Ghibelline Adherent of the Holy Roman Empire
Grisaille Decoration in shades of grey
Grotteschi Type of classical decoration with exotic detail
Guelf Adherent of the papacy
Guglia Free-standing conical monument

Intarsia/e Inlaid woodwork

Lungarno/i Road beside the river Arno (e.g. in Florence and Pisa)

Metope Section of Doric frieze
Mole Pier of harbour

Narthex Vestibule at west end of a church
Necropolis Cemetery
Nuraghe/i Sardinian fortified structure(s)

Oculus Circular opening in roof
Opus anglicanum Medieval English embroidery
Opus sectile Type of Roman construction with small pieces of stone arranged diagonally

Pala Altarpiece
Palaestra Roman gymnasium
Paliotto Small altarpiece
Patria Home town

Pentatych Altarpiece with five main lateral panels

Piano nobile Principal floor

Pietra arenaria Sandstone

Pietra serena Grey stone, easily carved

Pilaster Engaged column

Polyptych Altarpiece of many panels

Podestà Mayor

Portico in antis Portico recessed from a façade

Predella Row of small panels at the foot of an altarpiece

Presbytery Area of chancel reserved for priests, usually raised

Profil perdu Lost profile, turned away

Reliquary Container for a religious relic

Quattrocento Fifteenth century

Salita/e Street on a slope (especially in Genoa)

Scuola Venetian confraternity

Seicento Seventeenth century

Settecento Eighteenth century

Sgraffito Incised decoration

Signoria Lordship

Stela Upright stone memorial

Stucco/stucchi Plaster

Studiolo Study

Tempietto Small temple

Tholos/oi Round room rising to an internal dome

Tondo/i Circular picture or sculpture

Trecento Fourteenth century

Tufa Volcanic stone, tufo

Tympanum Recessed face of a pediment, often carved

279

INDEX